Did You ▱ S0-ARY-440
This Dream?

You face a difficult decision, announce you're going to "sleep on it," and then the answer comes to you in a dream . . .

You find yourself living in the historical past, and you wonder whether somehow you could really have been there . . .

You float out of your body and fly to a place you've never been before, or to a place where you "see" friends or relatives . . .

If your answer to any of these questions is "yes," then you've experienced the phenomenon known as psychic dreaming. Many people are working with their dreams right now: programming themselves to recall their dreams, using their dreams to improve their lives, and linking themselves with other minds and with the larger world around them. They've discovered that once they understand their dreams, anything is possible. You're about to make that same discovery.

PSYCHIC DREAMING

PSYCHIC DREAMING

A Parapsychologist's Handbook

LOYD AUERBACH

WARNER BOOKS

A Time Warner Company

WARNER BOOKS EDITION

Copyright © 1991 Loyd Auerbach
All rights reserved.

Cover photo by Will Crocker
Cover design by Anne Twomey

Warner Books, Inc.
666 Fifth Avenue
New York, N.Y. 10103

 A Time Warner Company

Printed in the United States of America

First Printing: August, 1991

10 9 8 7 6 5 4 3 2 1

To the memories of D. Scott Rogo and Alex Tanous.

As a writer, parapsychologist and friend, Scott had an enormous influence on my professional life, my attitudes towards parapyschology, and my desire to present information to the general public.

As a psychic practitioner and as a research participant at the ASPR, Alex, too, had an impact on my professional base. More, though, he somehow led me to experience what people call "psychic."

You will both be missed.

ACKNOWLEDGMENTS

In writing my first book, I thanked everybody who had a hand in "making" me personally involved in the field of parapsychology. You are all thanked, again.

As for this volume, I'd like to especially thank my interviewees Keith Harary, Beth Hedva, Montague Ullman, Joanne Mied, and Pat Kampmeier for giving me time and putting up with my questions.

Thanks to Kathy Dalton, Doug Day, and Brian McRae for moral support, and to Rachel Seaborn for helping Kathy and Doug go through a lot of letters.

A special nod of the head to my agent, Linda Mead, to Brian Thomsen who came up with the idea for this book, and to Beth Lieberman, for being a great editor to work with.

Thanks again to the great people I've been working with at Mead Data Central in San Francisco. It's great being there, and without the LEXIS/NEXIS information services I'd have had a much tougher time writing the proposal (let alone the book).

Thanks, Marcello Truzzi, for keeping me abreast of a lot of happenings in and around parapsychology (and for all the jokes).

Lots of love to my parents, Barbara and Dick Auerbach, and to my brothers, Ron and David, for their continued support.

Finally, a loving thank you to Cathy Mock for her support while writing this book, and for her help.

May the Force Be with You All
Loyd Auerbach
February, 1991

CONTENTS

PSYCHIC
DREAMING

INTRODUCTION

Why This Book?

One of the more frequent questions a parapsychologist (and certainly a psychologist) gets asked outside of their regular working situations is "I had this dream, can you tell me what it means?" Of course, the psychic twist to all this is the second question of "Will it come true?"

Many people are fascinated by experiences we call psychic, but more people, including skeptics of the psychic, are even more infatuated with the surreal (though often frighteningly real) world of our dreams. We want to know why we dream certain things, what they mean, how we can control them, and will they come true (or have they already happened). There are dozens of books available on dreams, everything from interpretation books to workbooks to books with particular scientific emphases, from psychology to neuropsychiatry. There are many books on the paranormal that touch on dreams, even a few which deal specifically with dreams and their connection to a particular psychic ability, such as telepathy. But there's really no other book out there which examines the potential range of psychic components of our dreams, with the idea of offering suggestions on how to use that information.

In this book, I will explore both sides of the ESP/dream connection. To understand how psychic information can appear in dreams, in what form, and through what sort of interpretations, we need to look at dreams and the dreaming process in the brain. To understand the forms of psychic abilities and information and how such can be used by those of us who have such experiences through our dreams, we need to look specifically at the different forms of experiences, at least in the ways they are categorized by parapsychologists today. In order to understand how to work with such information that may come through our dreams, we need to look at the connection between those experiences and the form and process of dreams.

I'll be starting out with dreaming, looking at some basics of that area, including how some other cultures deal with dreams, then a break for a review of the range of psychic experiences. From there you'll find more on the forms of dreams and their connections to the mind/body organism we call a human being, then on to the psychic abilities that manifest themselves most often in dreams. After that, we'll look at theories of both dreaming and psychic experience, and we'll talk with a few people who help others work with their dreams. You may get answers to some of your questions about psychic dreaming, but you will also undoubtedly end up with more questions as you proceed. Such questions are good, because they spark the human thirst for more knowledge, which leads to searching for (and hopefully finding) answers.

We really don't know just what dreams are. There are many, many ideas, hypotheses, theories, and suppositions, and some appear to work when placed into practical application, or as part of experimentation. There are, however, many missing pieces to the puzzling existence of the dream world and how we tie into it. We don't even have complete information on how the brain works, let alone what this thing we call mind or consciousness is.

I'm not of course speaking of an objective dream world (at least, not until you begin to discuss dealing with beliefs of other cultures, or include discussion of some dreamscapes and a few nightmares on Elm Street). I'm speaking of our own world of dreams, the one within each of us, and how it relates to our daily lives, and perhaps to objective reality.

It is, assumed our daily lives and stresses influence our dreams. But do our dreams influence our waking lives? If so, how? And what about all the "extras" that often appear in dreams? How can two people have the same dream at the same time? How can what one person experiences influence the dreams of another person at the same time? How is it possible for someone to dream of an event which hasn't happened yet, only to see the event happen? And what of dreams of places never visited before in which dreamed information appears to be true? Are there answers to these questions? That's what we'll explore here.

Experiences people have with dreaming do occasionally involve information in those dreams of past, present, and future events which appear outside of the knowledge base of the dreamer. These experiences seem to draw a connection between people and their environment, where there is an information flow without the use of the "normal" senses or through logical inference.

Such dreams are an example of what J.B. Rhine called ExtraSensory Perception (ESP), and places them in the realm of parapsychology. Parapsychology is the science which looks at those and other connections between the human mind and its environment, connections currently unexplained by our mainstream scientific base of information. This book, while dealing somewhat with the current theories of dreams and dreaming from the perspective of a variety of sciences, will mainly deal with paranormal dreaming experience.

In my previous book, *ESP, HAUNTINGS AND POLTERGEISTS: A PARAPSYCHOLOGIST'S HANDBOOK* (Warner, 1986), I wrote mainly about what I called the "big three" of spontaneously occurring psychic experiences: apparitions, hauntings, and poltergeists. That book included (as does this one) a survey for readers to return dealing with psychic experience. At this time, I'd like to thank the hundreds of people who returned the surveys. We are looking at them now and will eventually be releasing the results. (Unfortunately, time and person-power are very limited, which is why it's taking so long to do anything with the surveys.) I especially want to thank those of you who took some time to write about your experiences and send them along. Some of you may even recognize your experiences here in this book (but not to worry, the names have been deleted to protect those of you who don't want your friends to think you are psychic . . . or weird . . . or crazy, as skeptics would wrongly suggest).

The surveys are very interesting, and continue to come in. From the number of them, from the wide age and occupational range of the people returning them, it is very obvious that psychic experiences don't just happen to "psychics," they happen to ordinary folks more frequently than many would like to believe (or accept). And psychic-seeming dreams appear to be a good part of those experiences. Keep them coming.

As to why many of you haven't received a response to your survey, I've tried to keep up on the mail that included a self-addressed stamped envelope. Parapsychological funding being what it is (basically nonexistent), there's a lack of help for folks like me (paid help, to respond to and analyze the surveys). Hopefully, things will change, and to this end I have, together with paranormal investigator (and magician) Christopher Chacon, established The Office of Paranormal Investigations. Check the appendices at the end of this book for further information on that venture.

As mentioned earlier, there are myriad books that deal with dreams and the process of dreaming. There is an excellent book by Stanley Krippner, Montague Ullman, and Alan Vaughan called *Dream Telepathy*, now in its second edition, dealing with the work conducted at the Maimonides Hospital during the sixties and early seventies. Dr. Krippner has continued with this work in a recent paper published in *The Journal of the American Society For Psychical Research* (which will be discussed later). This book is intended to survey what we know about dreams and the purpose of dreaming in our lives, specifically with respect to how psychic experience might relate. I'll be looking at some of the latest dream research, theories, and new studies in parapsychology that tie in. I'll take you through some experiences people have reported and show you how a parapsychologist might look at those experiences, as well as how an informed skeptic who doesn't believe in psychic ability might deal with them. This will hopefully give you a balanced picture of how you can look for the degree of "psychicness" of your dreams.

To this end, it's important to also look at how non-western cultures deal with dreams, and with psychic functioning in general. As in my previous book, I'll also be covering, though to a lesser extent, how psychic experiences are viewed in western culture, through discussion of a few popular media (film and tv) examples that connect to dreams. If you don't recognize the movies mentioned, check your video store. Finally, there are a few lessons that can hopefully be learned with respect to what to do when you believe you have had a psychic dream, especially one of the future. Can you or should you tell someone? Can you change the future?

We'll see.

Some of you reading this book after my first one may seem a bit surprised that it is dealing with dreams. After all, from my previous book and media exposure, you have come to believe that Loyd Auerbach is a simple "ghostbuster," and nothing more.

As someone involved in parapsychology, even someone who may specialize in the investigation of apparitions, hauntings, and poltergeists, things are never "simple." Parapsychology is so much more than the "ghostly" phenomena of investigations (and films). It is *mainly* research, both in the laboratory and in the field, dealing with ESP and psychokinesis (mind over matter), rather than the third area of survival (of bodily death). As someone often in the media eye with regards to expertise on the paranormal, the everyday psychic experiences of people come to my attention much more frequently than any poltergeist reports ever will (simply because such experiences are so much more frequent than poltergeist situations or apparitional sightings).

I've been called by that "ghostbuster" sobriquet so often that people often forget I'm basically a generalist where parapsychology and the paranormal are concerned. I'd like to believe that my strength (as pointed out to me by a few of my colleagues and some skeptics) is in explaining parapsychological research, investigation, and theory to members of the general public. While I do plan on following up on the investigations aspect of parapsychology in a future book, I did want to move on to other areas of parapsychological study that ought to be brought to the reading public.

A book on dreams and their psychic component was actually not an idea I had first. The idea for this book came straight from the editor of my first book. And when it was suggested to me, I got excited about it (why hadn't I dreamt of it?). Hopefully you will, in the future, see other volumes from me on different areas of psychic experience and research (write to me, care of Warner Books or The Office of Paranormal Investigations, and let me know what topics you're most interested in).

So, thanks to Brian Thomsen, (many thanks), editor of my first book, I get to move on from "ghostbusting" and discuss with you another area of major interest where being psychic is concerned. And thanks to Beth Lieberman, my current editor, this book hangs together.

You will find that this book relies on much more than my own paranormal expertise. There are several people in a number of fields whom I have interviewed and consulted to make sure that you get the fullest possible picture of the connection between dreams and psychic experience. Of course, it is important to remember that the field of parapsychology, as well as other fields of science, is always in a state of flux. By definition, parapsychologists study phenomena whose explanations are time-dependent. In other words, just because something is unexplained by scientific "laws" today does not mean it will not be explained by tomorrow or next week or next year. Not having an explanation does not mean it doesn't happen. So what you read here about psychic functioning as well as about dreams is based on current knowledge of the two, as well as on current knowledge of how the brain operates (limited though that certainly is).

In an address to the Parapsychological Association at the

32nd Annual Convention held in San Diego in August, 1989, Michael Crichton, M.D., author of such books as *The Andromeda Strain*, *Sphere*, and *Travels*, made the point that there are a lot of things for which we don't have answers. Medical science knows that anesthesia works, but not so much why it works or how it affects the human brain. Of course, part of that problem is the lack of knowledge of how and why the human brain works. Similarly, we don't know the exact story behind dreams, and certainly not how psychic ability works (or even what it is and what it says about our minds).

In addition, there's an important point I'd like to get across here, since we're just beginning. Many people who dismiss psychic experience as unreal or as wishful thinking of people who don't want to deal with the real world have missed this point. There appears to be either a misunderstanding or block of an implicit concept in parapsychology, one not voiced loudly enough. Parapsychologists, in their own way, have been saying that with these "abilities" called psychic, ESP (information flow into the mind from the environment or other minds) and psychokinesis (mind interacting directly with the physical world around us), the human mind has more of a direct connection with the environment and with other human minds than I think most people would really like to recognize and accept. With such an acknowledgement of that connection would come an understanding that we may have even more of a responsibility for our own actions (and thoughts) than what we're looking at right now, in looking at new emphases on health and the environment. People are taking more responsibility in that way, in "outer" ways, and perhaps what is needed next is for all of us to start coming around to looking at our own internally generated connections with the outer world and the human race.

Psychic experience as it occurs within dreaming is one place to start looking for such connections, so let's proceed to see what we do know about psychic dreams.

This book will hopefully do for psychic dreams what my previous book does for the "ghostly" side of the paranormal: de-mystify. While people are outright frightened by apparitions and poltergeist experiences (with real reason to be), those who have psychic dreams tend to keep them to themselves, to forget them until much later, to ignore them, to be frustrated by their seeming lack of complete information, and sometimes to be frightened by them. Let's see if we can't go along those lines here and help you better understand, at least from today's knowledge base, how psychic information passes in to and out of dreams, and what we can do with and about them, and how to use that information.

Dream along with me . . . .

CHAPTER 1

In Your Dreams

"The black and white ones are the reruns."
Dr. Keith Harary, when asked about whether
people dream in color or black and white

I woke up this morning, groggy as usual, partially remembering something or other. I knew I had dreamed something, but I couldn't quite get it. My alarm had gone off when I was in the wrong stage of sleep, for me anyway, at a point where my brain just couldn't quite even pull together anything more than just a suggestion of what the dream had been about.

So what good are dreams if we can't remember them? When we can train ourselves to remember them, as many people have, are they worth anything to our conscious minds and daily lives? Those dream analysis books tell us lots of things about the value of dreams and what just about each and every item or object or event means, even if the books differ from author to author.

Are dreams always merely symbolic, pieces of experience that we must analyze to get anything out of them, or can they simply give us the plain truth from time to time, taken at face value?

Dreams seem to be mostly extensions of our own experience, though as I hope to show you in this book, there is a possibility that they're more than that. Dreams may be a perfect vehicle for information to flow from both our creative sides and from the outside world through psychic ability, although admittedly it is a vehicle that changes color from time to time. There is much we do and do not know about dreams, just as there is much we do and do not know about the human brain.

What do we know about dreams?

Manifest dreams are what we remember, the "normal" dreams or nightmares that impinge on our conscious mind. Of course, people have been able to train themselves to make more of their dreams manifest in their memories, to remember more of them. *Latent* dreams are those that address our unconscious thoughts and wishes. *Lucid* dreams are those in which the dreamer "awakens" in the dreamscape, aware that he or she is dreaming and capable, if he or she so desires, of shaping that dreamworld.

There are a number of influences that shape our dreams. First of all, sensory input from the environment around us can affect our dreams. When one is asleep, there is still some sensory "scanning" of the environment happening. Even though our eyes are shut, our hearing, smelling and sense of touch are still operating (as is our sense of taste, but that would usually only pick up the taste of the inside of our own mouths . . . as awful as that might be after a few hours sleep). An alarm clock that didn't wake us up might become a telephone in a dream, an elbow in the back from the person in bed with you transforms in a dream into a knife, a whiff of cologne or perfume becomes a field of flowers. Any "odd" noises, such as the house settling, the water heater or heat coming on and shutting off, the cat or dog sneaking around (and making noise while doing it) can become a stimulus for some specific event in a dream. However, this is likely to be a very small influence on our dream content, given the rich material available to our brains through memory.

Of course, daily conflicts or stress-inducing events can be translated into the dream, during which we're looking for some kind of conflict resolution. A problem at work can be played out to conclusion in a dream or hidden as part of a kind of mental fable with its own moral.

Movies, TV, and literature can affect what we dream. How many times in your life have you heard (from parents, friends, spouses, etc.) that the scary movie you're watching will give you nightmares—and it does? Anything that stimulates our emotions and thought processes while conscious to the degree a really good horror—or comedy, romance, or science fiction—film, show, or book can is almost certainly the kind of stimulus that will affect our dreams, as it may even affect the content of our daydreams (if you're prone to daydreaming, that is).

Another form of outside stimulus is information brought into your mind through psychic abilities. If we are truly capable of receiving information from the minds of others and from the environment as many believe (telepathy and clairvoyance, respectively), then it follows that this information is just as likely to influence our dreams. Since parapsychologists have found that our conscious belief and disbelief in psychic functioning can have an affect on how psychic we are (disbelievers tending to block out psychic information), and since during the dreaming process our "guards" are dropped, there is a good opportunity for psychic information to be pulled into dreams and incorporated into them. This added information provides more raw material for whatever the mechanism is in us that creates dreams and their content. With all that information stored in our long-term memories, we can tap quite well into things we know but didn't remember we know.

Of course our own past experience, that which is locked in our memories, can bring forth an enormous source of raw content for dreams. There is quite a lot we experience in our conscious exploits that we are unaware of. Our senses continuously scan the environment, while our minds focus on particular things to which we pay attention. We truly are unaware of all the memory of all that our ears hear and our eyes see, yet this is accessible in our dreams and by our intuition.

There seems to be a relaxing of the ingrained "censorship" of our conscious thought processes during sleep, thus allowing impulses and information from the subconscious to slip through into the dream. According to some experts, many instinctual impulses that may be infantile in nature can come through, as well as impulses that may be ancestral or simply ingrained into the human "animal."

During the sleep process, we tend to dream a certain amount. The ratio of time spent dreaming to that of "straight" sleep changes from the time we are born through adulthood. Newborns may dream as much as 80 percent of the time they are asleep, though generally closer to 50 percent. Children may dream between 30 percent and 40 percent and adults a mere 20 percent to 30 percent. It would seem that as we grow, as our minds get filled with other information, the need for dreaming, for creative but internally suggested information, decreases to less than 20 percent of the time we spend sleeping. How much we *think* we dream may be a function more of how much we can remember dreams rather than how much we actually dream. We do dream every night that we enter REM (Rapid Eye Movement) sleep. Can we do without it altogether?

We do know dreaming is absolutely necessary to our own sanity. Sleep deprivation studies have shown that people may begin to hallucinate, to dream while awake, if deprived of sleep and the dream process for too long. There are mixed results from studies where people still may sleep, but are deprived of the dreaming stage of REM sleep.

Dreams are often essential to the creative mind as well. Many people, from scientists to artists to writers to businessmen, have found themselves in the position of having a dream offer them the bit of information that allows them to say "Eureka! I've got it!" after having worked on a problem consciously for too long with no result. Even the saying "I'll sleep on it" indicates this. There are examples of this throughout history, from Robert Louis Stevenson taking *The Strange Case of Dr. Jekyll and Mr. Hyde* from a dream, to Friedrich Kekule coming up with the structure of the benzene ring due to dream imagery; we might not have the sewing machine from Elias Howe if not for dreams.

Sigmund Freud saw dreams as wish fulfillment. In latent dreams, our repressed feelings or unconscious desires and conflicts may show through strongly. Freud, like many since, felt that desires and feelings are often so threatening to our conscious minds that they need to be represented in disguised form so as to not directly arouse a person's conscience. Symbolism is heavily at play in Freud's dreamworld; things are not what they seem. A single character or object can represent many, and the most important emotions or messages of a dream may be reintegrated in a "safe" or seemingly unimportant image. Freud's analysis of dreams dealt with sexual images, as did much of his psychoanalytic imagery-process, and often symbols were the same for all dreamers.

On the other hand, Carl Jung felt that there are no fixed symbolic meanings for all people with the exception of a few very basic archetypes. One must take each person separately, studying that person's dreams over a period of time, to get a handle on that particular person's system of symbols, he thought. This is how many dream-work groups operate today.

One basic problem with the process of working with dreams is that of secondary or conscious elaboration. We have a tendency to reorganize and elaborate on a dream while remembering it, to make it more logical and add to it so that it makes sense to our conscious minds.

This is a problem we have in dealing with our own psychic experiences. As a psychic image or information piece comes into our minds we immediately want to categorize what it is we are "seeing" or "hearing" with our psychic sense. If our mind gets a sudden picture of something, rather than taking it at face value, we seem to have to identify it with something we already know, as though we need to make that image symbolic of something already in our experience. What is unfortunate here is that often the psychic information is about something new to our experience, and there is little to be used if we fit the new information into an old category.

There is a lot of discussion as to the role of both dreams

and the REM stage of sleep in our lives. Sleep and dream research have yielded rich information, yet there is often much discussion as to how to interpret that information.

It is known that we, as human beings, go through three or four stages of sleep where the brain and body are fairly inactive. Dr. Stephen LaBerge of Stanford University considers this (all three to four stages) as the "quiet" state of sleep. Then, we come out of these inactive stages and into one where there are several characteristics. The main characteristic is that of Rapid Eye Movement (REM) under the eyelids. The eyeballs move from side to side and sometimes up and down, indicating activity in the brain. In addition, there is paralysis of the limbs and irregularity in the heartbeat and respiration. It is in this state, what LaBerge calls "active" sleep, that we dream. The brain may be more active during this "active" sleep state than at some times when we are awake.

Mammals, with rare exception, experience REM sleep. Whether that means they are dreaming is difficult to determine absolutely, since getting your pet dog or cat to tell you about their dreams or whether they even had them seems to be out of the question. According to experts, humans begin dreaming in the womb, as early as the twenty-third week of fetal development.

During REM sleep, the nerve connections that allow and control movement of the body essentially shut down for our own protection. This temporary paralysis prevents us from moving to act out what we experience in our dreams (to keep us from hurting ourselves). We come out of this state of non-movement fairly quickly, though there are times when the paralysis may take a bit of time to wear off (ever wake up feeling as though you can't move—or even feel—an arm or leg?). Therefore, those who sleepwalk tend to do it in the non-REM stages of sleep, rather than while dreaming, as one might expect.

We enter REM sleep anywhere from an hour to ninety minutes after falling asleep, and move in and out of that stage and non-REM stages throughout the sleep period. The amount of dreaming—the length of the REM sleep stage—tends to increase with each successive REM stage, the longest period of dreaming occurring in the last cycle before we wake up. That may mean that the more (the longer) you sleep, the more you dream, and the more dreams you have.

While there has been discussion as to how long an individual dream lasts, evidence indicates that the length of "dream-time" approximates the actual "waking-time" or clock-time of the non-dreaming, outside world. Of course, many of us apparently remember dreams that seem to cover weeks or months or even years of time, leading to what is apparently a false conclusion (if experimental evidence is correct) that dreams compress time, so that minutes or hours of subjective dreaming pass by in a matter of seconds of real time while dreaming. LaBerge and others have suggested that such dreams use similar imagery and "plot devices" as films and television programs use to show that time passes (hopefully minus commercials), such as perhaps fading to black then fading back to a morning image immediately to indicate that a night has passed, or even (and I remember this from a dream of my own) the flipping of calendar pages to indicate many days, weeks, or months passing.

How have experiments indicated this? Apparently, in the REM state, the eyes often move back and forth in the same pattern they do in a dream. A recollected dream of the observation of a tennis match will generally yield the same back and forth pattern as what is remembered from the dream. LaBerge conducted experiments with communicating from the lucid dream state in which he was to move his eyes in that dream in a particular pattern at a certain time after beginning to dream. Others have reported using a code with regards to eye movements in the dream state to actually send messages to the waking world. Eye movements can indicate the start and finish of a count of time (say ten seconds) and can be compared by an observer with clock time.

Dreams tend to reflect current issues in our lives, and may be excellent mood reflectors as well. Our mood right before sleep may directly affect the content and quality of our dreams, and our dreams during the night may affect how we wake up and in what mood we're in (something about waking up on the "right" side of the bed). Other stimuli such as movies or TV, fantasizing, or neighborhood or household noise occurring before we head for sleep might also affect dream content, specifically the emotional "feel" of the dream.

Our perceptions of the "real" world while awake during the day also appear to affect our dreams directly. Experiments with people wearing colored glasses or goggles often yield dreams with those colors showing predominantly. Looking at the world through rose-colored glasses may result in dreams of rose-colored imagery.

We usually talk of dreams in terms of imagery, of visual information, but blind people also dream, though generally with the auditory being the overwhelming mode of "imagery." People not born blind but who later lose their sight stick with the visual, though there is evidence that indicates that this peters out down the line in favor of the sense now most relied on (hearing). Dreams are typically composed of the visual and the auditory, though some people do report other senses sometimes having their say in the dreams. In this we see that dreams are tied most closely to the waking senses we rely on. This may depend on which neurons are firing during the dreaming (those related to the visual system of the brain, the auditory, or otherwise).

It's interesting to note that psychic experience is very similar, with visual-form information predominant in the experiences, over simulations of other senses. Most people experience psychic information as visual imagery through the "mind's eye," though some may lean toward the information being presented as sound-simulation (the mind's ear?) or through feeling and touch or even smell.

As an example, if a group of people likely to have psychic experiences enters a "haunted" house, a place where there is much history, some people might report "seeing" a ghost that the others don't "see." A couple might experience a cold chill, or the sense that someone has touched them on the shoulder or arm when there's no one there. Some others might "hear" the sound of footsteps "walking" down an empty hallway, and still others might "smell" perfume or cologne or something not so nice. If there were attempts to record what was "seen" or "heard," nothing is typically what you'd get. The stimulus of the psychic information appears to cause the mind/brain to respond with appropriate "images," more or less as hallucinations with outside causes.

So, we tend to "perceive" things in dreams or in psychic experience with much the same hierarchy of senses as we do with our waking perceptions. Since sight is the sense most relied on by the majority of us, that is the "sense" we use most in dreams. Most people do dream in color, but we sometimes forget the color schemes, and the dream might then be incorrectly remembered as having been in black and white. This does not preclude us from having dreams in black and white. In fact, I can remember a couple of my own dreams where I was watching a film or TV show that was in black and white (although everything but the film/show was in color). I have also heard from friends and acquaintances that they have occasionally dreamed they were part of an old movie scenario, and that it appeared to have been a black and white dream (it obviously hadn't been colorized yet). Or maybe Keith Harary is right, and the dreams we remember as being black and white are the reruns.

Dreams appear to range from the incredibly exciting and utterly fantastic to images that approximate or appear to be real events (but are not, in fact, true events that have happened to you) to replays of real, daily events which may be very, very boring. In fact, it's possible that some of the experiences we have that we call déjà vu, where we could almost swear we've been through a situation or to a place before, are actually situations where the real event triggers a half-remembered reality-approximating dream. You may even have a dream coming close to reality that you forget was a dream, one you integrate as a "real" memory.

There are many ideas about the functions and forms of dreams, and many of these are often at great odds with the ideas of Sigmund Freud, the name people (who haven't read anything about dreaming) would most often associate with psychiatric/psychotherapeutic analyses of dreams (Jung most likely being the second name). Why dream? This is still a controversial question.

As mentioned earlier, Freud dealt quite a bit with wish fulfillment and latent dreams, and often saw dreams as disguising deep-seated feelings and unresolved issues. The disguises may be thinly veiled, ones we can see through right away or maybe even totally nonexistent. Dreams also had much to say in the way of the individual's subconscious with regards to sexual impulses. Freud's ideas often related to regressive, infantile, sexual desires. Of course, when people (the general public) discuss Freudian analysis of anything, discussion of Freud's views on sexual imagery always seems to pop up.

Jung disagreed with Freud on the sexual issue. He saw dreams less as the vehicle for sexual repression or impulses and more as a forum for voices of the collective unconscious, a "place" for us to tap into the archetypal images of the human psyche, images from a shared pool of common symbols and experience.

Are dreams a channel to understanding your self? Some researchers and theorists do see dreams as that channel to understanding. Gayle Delaney, director of the Delaney & Flowers Professional Dream and Consultation Center in San Francisco, for example, sees dreams as being like poetry, with metaphors created by the brain/mind representing real information and emotions. Others see dreams as some kind of mechanism of the brain for rest and recreation, as well as potentially for repair of brain circuitry.

Dreams can help resolve problems and integrate change into our lives, or they can be unhealthy, keeping us dwelling on past problems without a chance of resolution. The content of dreams tends to vary according to issues in your own life, as well as issues in the world around you. Dreams may be dramatizations of hidden feelings. They may show us these feelings that we refuse to consciously acknowledge, and they may provide detail as to the reasons behind these feelings. What most tend to agree on today is that the symbols in dreams are not absolutes, unlike what many of those dream analysis books would have you believe. They are not the same for all people, although there may be themes that are common to many. Recurring dreams may simply be recurring because they reveal issues you are avoiding or not addressing while awake.

According to LaBerge, dreams help us work through ways of interacting with the world and our expectations of it. In our dreams we can address how to get what we want and avoid what we don't want, although the messages/answers provided may be symbolic or metaphorical, or they may be plain as writing on the wall.

Dreams may simply occur to entertain us. They don't necessarily have to be windows into the unconscious or filled with exceedingly important messages. They could simply replay a film you just saw or dramatize a book or short story you just read (how many of you have had *Star Trek* dreams? Or am I the only one?).

From the mechanistic perspective, dreams may simply occur to keep circuits of the brain "ready and able" for the intellectual challenges of the next day. Neuroscientists often have very straightforward ways of looking at REM sleep and dreaming. Neuroscientist Robert Vertes sees REM sleep as helping to keep us alive, acting as the brain's "pilot light" during sleep. Jonathan Winson of Rockefeller University discussed in 1987 the idea that dreaming helps with information processing of stuff we can't get through while awake. Consider it off-line processing of information through the brain's computer center, with the on-line processing being conducted during waking hours.

In the early 1980s, Francis Crick (the unraveler of DNA) and Graeme Mitchison of Cambridge University brought in the theory that dreams are not necessarily worth remembering, that such recalling may be hazardous to our (mental) health. They see dreams as the way the brain/mind fine-tunes itself, flushing out the extraneous garbage we pick up while awake. In dreaming, the mind detects and "unlearns" or tries to forget this unwanted, unneeded information. The brain is working in REM as a sorting mechanism, deciding what to save to the hard disk of your mind (long-term memory) and what is junk to toss out (short-term memory, soon forgotten). By this notion, it's easy to see that remembering such "stuff" could be detrimental to our normal functioning.

However, not many dreamworkers go along with this, as the overwhelming majority do see the recalling and working through of dreams as a valuable process.

Another mechanistic view of dreams is that of Dr. J. Allan Hobson of Harvard University. REM sleep (and dreaming) is a survival mechanism to keep the circuits of the brain viable and ready for the non-sleep periods of our life. The brain is randomly firing neurons during REM sleep that may approximate the firing of neurons during the waking stages, and then creates a story in which to place the actions that would normally result from the firing of those same neurons.

Since your body is effectively paralyzed during REM sleep, the firing of the same neurons that would not cause you to get up and walk but could otherwise result in your walking or picking something up, would create signals that can be the basis of the same or similar action in a dream. The dream, then, is truly a representation or metaphor or acting out, but it is one of the impulses of the nervous system, rather than solely based on what is in your conscious or unconscious. Most of the outside sensory input is tuned out, but that which gets by might be incorporated with the dream. Finally, the story created might be added to by extraneous information the brain can pull from memory (otherwise we might simply have a pretty dull story). Effectively, the brain takes what might otherwise (in your state of REM paralysis) be meaningless, mental static and uses it as the building blocks of a dream.

We'll get a bit further into the connections between the mind (the dreams) and the body (the brain) a bit later, but as you can see by this little peek at some of the ideas surrounding dreams, there are a number of ideas, though many of them seem to be able to work together to form a larger picture of brain/mind functioning.

Assuming for a moment that there is something useful in dreams, that Crick and Mitchison are a bit off the mark, how can we use dreams if we can't remember them? The answer is that you can learn to remember your dreams, and can, as many suggest, even learn to program them to deal with certain issues and problems (or for entertainment value) or to become lucid dreams in which anything goes and you're really in control. According to many who have learned to work with their own dreams (and learned to remember them first), something as simple as the interest level in your dreams and the intent to remember them can help that recall process. In fact, from the time I started writing this book, I began spontaneously to remember my own dreams more than I think I ever have since college.

LaBerge and others say that you can program yourself to remember your dreams. The issue of belief, in believing you *can* remember them, is very important here. If you doubt you can remember, you very well may never learn to do that. Of course, belief versus doubt is of essence in many areas of human endeavor, from performance in sports to having psychic experiences. Intention, interest, and willingness to believe you can will affect the recall of dreams. I'll deal a bit more with this later on.

Once we've begun to recall and sift through our dreams, we can begin to make use of them. We can make suggestions to ourselves before going to bed that may actually affect what we dream, so that we can dream to deal with our everyday problems, to relieve stress, to confront our fears and overcome our nightmares, to entertain ourselves, to enhance our own creativity, to help with decision-making, and to get to know ourselves better.

We may also be able to use dreams for healing our bodies through appropriate imagery that might help speed up our own body's healing processes, and for healing our minds through dealing with the underlying issues that may cause us to be psychologically distraught or unstable or stressed out.

And of course, we may use our dreams as vehicles for psychic connections with those around us and with our own environment, scanning both our past experiences and perhaps other points in time and space with psychic ability for the information needed to complete a dream scenario.

Throughout the rest of this book we will look further at that last possibility, that we are not only dealing with our own experiences. You and I will look a bit more into other connections we make with the world outside our minds, awake and dreaming.

CHAPTER 2

Other Lands, Other Times, Other Dreams

Most of us think of dreams in the context of our own experience, in terms of not only the kinds of dreams we have, but also ways of picking apart and analyzing them. We discuss our dreams every once in a while (when we remember them at all) with friends and relatives, along the order of "I had this really weird dream last night . . ." or "Hey, you were in this dream I had the other night . . ." We consider the dreams of children to be of different content and context than those of adults. Those of us with pets often throw out offhand comments on the order of "Isn't she/he cute . . . she/he's having a dream" when the animal is sleeping yet making sounds or movements that might lead us to that assumption. And when it comes right down to it, we generally think of analyzing and working with dreams to be a fairly recent activity in human history, maybe only as recent as Freud's dream theories.

But the working with dreams, the analysis and application of them, the programming of them, the fascination (or fear) with dreams, has been with humanity since the beginning. In fact, the observance of dreams and what they tell us may be the most prevalent form of divination, of obtaining "advice" from other sources with regards to past, present, and most importantly future.

One of the oldest ideas about sleep and dreaming confuses sleep as some form of state related to death. The reduction of bodily function, the inability to move (especially during REM sleep), and the occasional dream remembrances of the sleeper all pointed to the concept that the spirit—the soul—of the sleeper actually left the body, as it does in death, though unlike death, the soul is called back to the body, returning life as the sleeper wakes. As in true death of the body, the "life" of the spirit continues after the body "dies" in sleep. Unlike death, sleep is only a temporary state, a respite for the soul so that it may wander the earth and other "places" unencumbered by the constraints of the flesh.

Along with this concept, some people see the dream-state as one in which humanity can be in touch with divine entities, with the gods themselves, with other wise beings (such as the spirits of our ancestors, or with some inspired part of our inner selves). The myths of people all over the world have connections to dreams, and dreams may reflect the mythology of the people, and therefore important societal, cultural, and very human issues, problems, and solutions.

According to mythologist Joseph Campbell in his book *The Hero With a Thousand Faces* (Princeton University Press, 1968): "Dream is the personalized myth, myth the depersonalized dream; both myth and dream are symbolic in the same general way of the dynamics of the psyche. But in the dream the forms are quirked by the peculiar troubles of the dreamer, whereas in myth the problems and solutions shown are directly valid for all mankind" (p.19). He further goes on to say that "In our dreams, the ageless perils, gargoyles, trials, secret helpers, and instructive figures are nightly still encountered; and in their forms we may see reflected not only the whole picture of our present case, but also the clue to what we must do to be saved" (p.101). Myths and dreams both are carriers of cultural metaphors.

Our ancestors all over the world made much of the content of dreams, whether one considers their impact on forming a view of the world and its creation, or looking at those dreams as contacts with the supernatural, with the afterlife, and with the divine, or as omens of the future.

As far back as the time of the ancient Mesopotamian civilizations and that of ancient Egypt, we can find records of people working with dream information and its application to the workings of society. The study and analysis of dreams was an established cultural practice in ancient Mesopotamia, and dream analysis "books" have been found and decoded. However, dreams normally would be considered nothing more than omens, unless interpreted by experts, who might prescribe rituals to carry out or prevent what the dream was to have predicted. There were several types of dreams considered by the dream interpreters, including dreams of a prophetic nature, those carrying messages from the gods to kings or other important societal persons, and those which relate specifically to the dreamer (whether relating to health or personal future of the person having the dream). The Babylonians, often concerned with their future, used dreams as omens for the path of their waking lives.

The dream connections between royalty and the gods was also evident in the culture of the Egyptian pharaohs. The gods often appeared to the royalty with messages and advice to consider and carry out, or so they were interpreted. Because others besides royalty had dreams, and those dreams could not be messages from divine sources (who only spoke to royalty), a form of dream interpretation and divination came about. The belief developed that one could ask for dreams that might provide answers or advice for the dreamer. At the same time, the ancient Hebrews saw dreams as connections between God and selected individuals charged with delivering God's word.

The ancient Greeks had a long tradition of working with dreams, although the ideas surrounding what caused dreams, how they could be used, and where the information in dreams came from changed over time. Dreams began as signs and messages from the gods, providing useful information to guide their lives, or providing special "peeks" at the lives of the gods themselves. Later, health issues became the central points of the analysis and decoding of dreams, with people often obtaining the information through dream incubation practices. Plato was interested in the ways dreams affected people's lives, though it was Aristotle who pushed the idea that dreams came from within the dreamer's experience, not from outside divine or other supernatural sources.

In looking at the content of dreams over all, there is a wide range of imagery that might be presented. Many interpreters of dreams dealt with specific kinds of dreams, applying the special information to anything from divination to healing. Hippocrates was one such healer who, when dealing with dreams at all, dealt only with those that had to do with the state of the body, with which he was specifically concerned.

The most comprehensive written work from the Greeks comes from Artemidorus, in the second century A.D., who wrote a volume called the *Oneirokritika*, considered by some the most comprehensive work before Freud. This book laid out a systematic way of dealing with dreams as an extension of daily life. He placed dreams in two major categories, those that were related to some event that was fairly immediate in time to the dreamer's experience, and those that were more symbolic or metaphorical and may have required more time to relate to the waking experience of the dreamer, with special regard to the individual characteristics of the dreamer.

Early Christians saw dreams as a time when the body and spirit were vulnerable to influences from the outside. Nightmares, of course, were those dreams in which demons and monsters, often sexually related demons (incubi and succubi), invaded or affected the body and soul of the dreamer in some way. Practices to deal with demons evolved in the religious context, as with other cultures. In examining other cultures with similar views of evil spirits attacking in the night, one often finds shamans or priests or medicine men or others with rituals that help ward off outside supernatural influences. In such a view of dreams, it would be unlikely for people to want to open themselves to dreaming. The practice of asking for something through dreams has always been very prevalent, since dreaming is a time, many consider, when we are open to outside influences (such as from the gods or ancestor spirits or even demons). In some cultures, dreams may not only present direct messages, but might be signals of power being achieved by the dreamer. Dream content may have in it "lucky" or "unlucky" omens, totems, and symbols, and purposefully dreaming of certain things may speak of the dreamer's own power, as with the Washo American Indian tribe of central California and Nevada. Asking for divine guidance or even achieving it with no direct request is part of many cultures. Much of the Koran was dictated to Muhammed in dreams, and there are other similar stories of important religious literature or lore passed on through dreams from apparently divine sources.

The practice of dream incubation for the programming of dreams can be connected with ancient cultures, from the Egyptians, Babylonians, and Phoenicians to ancient Hebrews and Greeks. In addition, it is a practice that was common among tribes of American Indians, by peoples in the Himalayas, in China, in Japan, and in other places around the world. In this practice, dreams are asked for and obtained by having the dreamer sleep at a particular "sacred" or "magical" site, such as a temple or natural landmark associated with some divine power. There may be a ritual associated with the visit to the shrine, in asking for the powers-that-be to answer a problem with a visit of information (or the gods themselves) in the dream. The typical dream incubations began (more or less as cultural practice) as requests for prophecy, for spiritual insight, but became in Egyptian and Greek cultures, for example, requests for information with regards to personal health and well-being. The dreamers visited, possibly participated in a special ritual, and slept in (or near) the sacred place or object; in return they would have (and hopefully remember) a dream or dreams in which their questions and problems were addressed.

Another way to receive such information and advice comes in the form of dreams that are deliberately induced. Many peoples around the world have had some form of dream inducement included in rites of passage or in prayer for divine guidance. Such rituals may include the use of fasting, prayer, magical rituals, dancing, and even drugs, or some combination of these. American Indians, in particular, made use of (and still make use of) various methods of dream inducement in order to receive guidance or to become adults. The

Ojibwa, for example, used fasting as a means for adolescent males to gain power, good fortune, and knowledge, revealed to them in dreams. The adult Plains Indians sought the knowledge the soul could gather through their "vision quests," which involved not only fasting, but sometimes self-torture or mutilation. Whether such visions occurred during sleep or not is difficult to say (except perhaps on a case-by-case basis), but the importance of the dream/visions was evident in their cultures.

Drug-induced dreams and dream ceremonies occur in cultures all over the world, whether through the ingesting of "sacred mushrooms" or some other fungus, or through the taking into the body of other natural substances such as hallucinogens that create other bodily reactions. The difficulty in looking at such practices, however, is in dealing with when the "dream" happens. Such substances may place the individual in an altered state of consciousness while still awake, or may influence the dreams of that individual once he or she has gone to sleep.

Other forms of programming dreams also occur, including the idea of working with requests in lucid dreaming, or simply focusing on a request or subject matter before going to sleep with the hopes (often justified) that our own minds will address such things in dreams.

The importance of dreams in other cultures is part of the historical and anthropological record. Other American Indian tribes such as the Winnebago and Algonquin had their adolescents search out dream-visions as part of their rites of passage. The Mohave Indians see dreams as a source of knowledge about workings of their societies and religion, though often presented in mythic form, and therefore needing interpretation (by shamans) to be accepted as true. The Navajo medicine men spend their first waking moments in the morning contemplating and interpreting their dreams, and often deciding whether there are events in the dreams that need to be dealt with in the waking world, either symbolically or ritualistically.

The Iroquois nations dealt with dreams extensively. In reports from missionaries during the seventeenth century, it was seen that the Seneca and Huron nations of the Iroquois had their own ways of dealing with their dreams (which were heavily invested with power), ways that could be called psychoanalytic by today's standards. They saw dreams as manifesting secret wishes of the soul and portraying them through dreams, and as vehicles for supernatural beings to relay messages and wishes for the dreamer or for the entire community.

The Iroquois recognized the importance of dream symbology and what it had to say to the individual and the community as a whole. They recognized that the interpretation could sometimes be the opposite of what the dream "said," and they therefore often needed interpretation by someone other than the dreamer. In order to relieve any stress indicated by the symbology of the dreams, dreamers acted out the situations in their dreams, though often in a symbolic way. In doing so, by effectively carrying out the dream scenarios in some symbolic, ritualistic, or real way, they were essentially dealing with the frustrated desires presented by the dreams. The sharing of dreams was essential to this process.

On the other side of the coin are the Maricopa of Colorado. As with other peoples, they believe that while dreaming, the spirit or soul leaves the body during sleep. The spirit seeks out another spirit or supernatural being who will eventually lead them down the path of knowledge, through success in a spiritual journey (which would lead to success in life). This was a long process for them, and speaking of such dreams depended on how far along one was on that journey. Speaking of the dreams too soon could cause the other spirit, the guardian of the dream journey, to abandon the dreamer.

More cultures seem to be of the Iroquois mind on the issue of discussing dreams. The Chippewa Indians actively cultivated dreaming as a means for receiving knowledge about themselves and the world around them. Children were encouraged to try to remember their dreams, and the male rite of passage also included a fasting ritual in order to receive the important dream-vision.

Probably the most frequently mentioned culture that deals directly with dreams is the Senoi of Malaysia. The late Kilton Stewart was the first to write about the "dreaming people" as they are often called, having visited them and studied their culture back in the mid-1930s. The Senoi are a particularly cooperative and peaceful people, with little or no crime or conflict, and very few mental health problems. Whether the lack of violence and the presence of such a cooperative spirit actually is a result of their daily dream work (as postulated by Stewart and others) is unproven. However, their unique views on resolving conflict through one's dreams has been adopted by many therapists and dream workers.

The Senoi believe that each person has his own internal universe and forces to deal with that connect with the outside world, and that they should learn to master these internal forces from childhood. Patricia Garfield, Ph.D., in her book *Creative Dreaming* (Ballantine Books, 1974), relates three steps the Senoi take toward that mastery of conflict presented in dreams or present in their waking lives. Dreamers are to "confront and conquer dream danger," "advance toward dream pleasure," and "achieve a positive outcome." To do this, they learned to program their dreams, to shape them by suggestion, and often to work in a lucid dreaming state.

Their activities in the social context often center around the sharing of dreams, starting with sharing and discussion of dreams at breakfast with one's family. Later in the day, individuals might continue this process with friends or colleagues.

Dealing with any conflict presented in the dreams might come through direct play within the dreams, acting out and working through problems in the dreams, or through acting out (in the waking world) what was presented in the dream, whether realistically, symbolically, or ritualistically. Programming or working with the dream is the most common method of working through situations. They might recreate a situation from their daily lives in a dream in order to deal with that problem, or they may confront a problem presented first in a dream (unrecognized or even non-existent in "real" life). Dreamers must confront ideas and characters present in their dreams, calling on friends or other helpers necessary to deal with the dream situation. Dream characters are only harmful, bad, as long as the dreamer is afraid and retreats from them. Facing them and winning a battle or conflict in a dream often results in the "bad" character becoming "good." Altering your own actions within the dream also helps. For example, purposefully causing the flying dream to continue, though changing the falling into flying under your own (dream) power empowers you, the dreamer.

This is not unlike dealing with ones' nightmares according to methods of western dream workers, which will be discussed in Chapter Four. The writings on the Senoi, and the applications of what has been interpreted as their dream methodology, seem applicable even to Western societies and culture.

I should mention that there has been some recent discussion of the Senoi dream theory that attempts to undo the theory, that there may be problems with Stewart's descriptions of the Senoi and their dreamwork, possibly due to exaggerations of their lucid dreaming abilities due to poor translation or other problems of misinterpretation by Stewart. Since it is impossible to go back in time to do a reassessment of the Senoi and their dream culture as it was when Stewart investigated it (at least, impossible by 1991 standards), we can really only look at what was written about them with an eye toward the question of "But does it work?"

Since it appears that the methodology of the Senoi, real or imagined, appears to work well for many people who wish to work with their own dreams, or work in a group setting, since there are many therapists and other individuals who have applied what has been described as the Senoi dreamwork method and come up with very positive reactions and results, it may not matter to most of us if Stewart misinterpreted the Senoi or not (unless you are basing some academic thesis, research, or dissertation on Stewart's work, of course). The methods do appear to work for many. If Stewart happened upon such a methodology through misinterpretation, then he, not the Senoi, deserves any credit (or, some would add, blame) for the dreamwork methodology he attributed to this culture.

Other cultures tell us that working with dreams can help us in our spiritual journeys through life as well as in dealing with reality. The question of reality and what is real is an important one, especially in connection to dreaming. Do we know, at any given point, that we are not dreaming, that we are really awake? Pinching yourself may not help, as you could dream of pinching yourself and feeling pain. Ever had a dream of waking up and turning off the alarm clock, only to have that turn out to be a dream (and you know this only because you wake up and turn off the alarm a *second* time)?

Stephen LaBerge suggests trying something that shouldn't work in real life, such as flying or floating under your own power. I suggest a simple levitation or flight around the room, not a leap off (or over) a tall building (which, I'm sure, is not something Dr. LaBerge would suggest either). If you fly, you're probably dreaming (or you ought to be wearing a costume and cape).

This question of reality and dreaming is an important one to some cultures. There are people around the world who believe (as a culture) that what happens in a dream is real. Some believe that the soul or spirit actually does leave the body and can travel around this world (or other dimensions) and even observe real situations, bringing back information. This kind of dream belief would be considered by many to be indicative of "out of body experiences" (read on for more information on such experiences).

Others, such as the Ashanti in Africa and the Kai in New Guinea, believe that what happens in a dream *is* reality. If you dreamed of traveling to Japan, you really did, according to such a belief system. And there is the belief of other peoples that what occurs in a dream is reality, but not necessarily the reality we live in.

For the Australian Aborigines, there is the Dreaming (with a capital "D"), also called the Dream Time. The Dreaming is Time everlasting, an eternal Now from which everything else has sprung. The world we live in sprang from the Dreaming ages ago, on the say-so of various deities that live in that reality, which is more "real" than our own. While the reference to the time of the Dreaming typically refers to a creative era, to that time long ago when our world came out of it, Aborigines use the term to refer also to the present and future, as that past from which we sprung continues to be relevant to our world and all things (and people) living on it.

Looking to the Dreaming, to the Dream Time for information, for inspiration, and for action is part of the Aborigine culture, and reinforces their cultural belief in the connections of humans and the natural world. The Dreaming yields information that we might consider psychic, and there have been reports of Aborigines using their connection to the Dreaming to enable them to do things we might consider unusual, if not paranormal. Many of the rituals conducted by the Aboriginal "clever men" are aimed at regenerating the connection between physical reality and the Dreaming if the physical world is to continue to be.

Dreams (with a small "d") do play a role in connecting with the Dreaming, though dreams are by no means more than one small way to connect with this other reality. According to Ronald Rose in his study of the psychic "life" of Aborigines (*Living Magic*, Rand McNally & Co., 1956, p. 141):

> It does not seem unlikely that the dream state— that fringe of consciousness that is a condition of quiescent receptivity—is well suited to psychic impact. If we are indeed capable of experiencing telepathy, this is likely a favorable state.
>
> To the Aborigines, whose psychic nether world they gave the name Dream Time, this is indeed so. And, as with us, clear-cut, vivid dreams, dreams that are easily remembered, comparatively free from distortion, rich in detail, are those to which Aborigines attach considerable importance.
>
> In their dreams, items of tribal, totemic, or family significance have their place.

There is an Aboriginal belief that holds man as a reincarnation of a being from the Dreaming. Before the birth of a child, a "totem" creature from the Dreaming makes itself known to one or both parents or to other close relatives in a dream. That dream of such a spiritual being connects the baby to the Dreaming, to the baby's pre-existent form in the Dreaming. With that link, a bit of the totem's power is passed. The dream seems to be a necessary medium in establishing that link to the Dreaming. In essence, one might look at dreams in such a context as establishing the "reality" of the newborn, since the physical reality in which we're born into is an extension of the reality of the Dream Time.

The issue of reality and what it is, in and out of dreams, is a question being approached by many fields, from philosophy to quantum physics. Dreams present an interesting paradox, in that we rely on our subjective experiences to tell if we are dreaming or not. Over 1,500 years ago, the Chinese philosopher Chuang-tzu explained the paradox of subjective experience and dreams: "One night, I dreamed I was a butterfly, fluttering here and there, content with my lot. Suddenly I awoke and I was Chuang-tzu again. Who am I in reality? A butterfly dreaming that I am Chuang-tzu, or Chuang-tzu dreaming he was a butterfly?"

Another way I've heard that expressed is as a question: "Are we real or are we characters in the dream of God or some other being? And what happens if he (or she) wakes up?"

We'll have to assume we are real, at least until you finish reading this book. The question of "What is reality?" is a subject for other books and discussions, since it seems to be a lot easier to tell if we are dreaming, as suggested by Stephen LaBerge, than deciding what reality is.

Believing that messages from dreams hold information from beyond ourselves leaves us with possible spiritual connections, to psychic realms beyond our own. It is on the psychic level that we connect, that we become more like one another.

The content and form of dreams of people from other cultures may vary as much as the cultural and mythic images of that group varies from those of other cultures. The themes, the way we deal with them, are often the same. It's the same story, but the story is retold with different "dressing," with appropriate cultural artifacts and "labels," or from differing viewpoints. Dreams have always held information for us and have shaped our development, regardless of cultural background and beliefs. The themes are often the same or extremely similar, and say many of the same things no matter what the culture, and this is extremely interesting. It simply points out that we are alike not only in our waking lives, but in our dreams as well. No matter the diversity of the groups or individual differences, we all dream pretty much the same way.

CHAPTER 3

Psychic Means What?

The title of this book is *Psychic Dreaming*. What does that mean? What does it mean to be psychic, to have psychic experiences? Let's explore that and the range of experiences and abilities attributed to "being psychic."

In order to look at the idea of psychic dreams, we need to first look at just what that really means. What does "psychic" mean, and what kind of psychic abilities spill over into our dreams? Parapsychology is the science that looks at those questions.

Parapsychology is the scientific study of psychic, or psi (pronounced "sigh") phenomena. These are exchanges of information between living things (mainly people, of course) or between the minds of living things and the environment (without the use of what we call our "normal" senses), or are direct influences of the minds of living things on the environment (without the use of physical bodies or technology). Of course, these interactions do not seem to be currently explainable by the "known" physical laws of nature. Throughout the remainder of this book, I will be using the term "psi" interchangeably with "psychic." Psi, by the way, is the term chosen by parapsychologists to refer to these experiences because it is a fairly clean term, being the twenty-third letter of the Greek alphabet and denoting simply an "unknown."

To say you are "psychic" may simply mean that you have

some other way besides logical deduction or inference to come up with information to solve problems. Whatever it is you're using to gain "extra" insight, whether we use jargon terms like "psi" or ESP or not, is something worth paying attention to; our minds are telling us "There's a bit of information that needs considering . . . so consider it already!"

People who call themselves "psychic" can run a wide range, since everyone has some degree of psychic ability, according to the tenets of parapsychology. However, there are those who call themselves psychic with a capital "P." "I am a psychic" is a different phrase than "I am psychic." So, the people claiming to be "a psychic" are people who have, by their own statements, a better grasp of their own abilities, and therefore some degree of control of those abilities. Such a job title (psychic or psychic reader or psychic practitioner) often doesn't mean that person really has any degree of actual control of their abilities, only that they recognize all the "extra" information coming into their minds, and that they can utilize or apply that information in different situations. And of course, there are many phonies out there, people who not only are not terribly psychic (not any more than anyone who visits them as clients), they are also aware of their un-psychicness and fraudulently put themselves out there as "ones who know."

Are some people more psychic than others? Good question, though for the answer we have to again define terms. Someone who is "psychic" is someone who has psychic abilities and experiences. Since the majority of human beings have experienced something "psychic" in their lives, and since the experiments in parapsychology indicate that psi is evenly distributed across the population, as are the reports of psychic experiences, it would appear that everyone is psychic to some degree. Whether one person is more psychic than another is a valid question, but one difficult to assess in a given case.

The analogy used to relate psi to something in science fiction is that psi is like musical "talent." Everyone has it to some degree, whether that means you can tap your foot to a beat or can play a concerto on a piano. Recognition of musical talent is a key to developing it. Some people are child prodigies, able to jump right into the music with little or no training, and others, try as they might throughout their lives, can never get any better than playing "Chopsticks."

Psi is similar, though certainly not as trainable. Being psychic may mean recognizing the difference between information received or perceived by your "normal" senses and anything "extra" that comes through. It may be that those people who call themselves "psychics" are able to separate that noise they get through their senses and pick up fainter signals from the background. Whether you can train yourself to do this remains to be seen.

Who believes in psychic interactions and experiences? Well, if you really speak with people around you, as I do, you'd find that most people are at least open to such experiences occurring, although interpretations vary. In a poll conducted in the latter part of the eighties by George Gallup, Jr. and Jim Castelli, and reported in the *Los Angeles Times* ("If There's a Ghost of a Chance, Americans Will Believe It," by Dick Roraback, October 31, 1988), 46 percent of all Americans believe in extrasensory perception, 24 percent believe in the ability to receive information from the future (precognition), and 15 percent believe in ghosts.

In a similar poll conducted by the University of Chicago's National Opinion Research Center and reported by priest/novelist Andrew Greeley, 42 percent of Americans report contact with someone who died, and 67 percent believe in ESP. Surveys and polls of groups around the country have reported similar numbers. So a hefty percentage of people believe in psychic experiences, and have reported them. With such high numbers of experients, the image often projected by opponents to parapsychology and by many psychic practitioners that these experiences are "not normal" is false. Psychic experiences, or those experiences we call psychic, are in actuality part of the normal range of human experience.

About those interactions: ESP is the interaction involving information flowing into someone's mind. The physical interactions, the idea of mind over matter, are often called telekinesis, but parapsychologists find that term limiting, since it usually conjures up images of a person levitating objects. The mind can apparently do so much more, from psychic healing to affecting computer chips to movement of objects, and so the term Psychokinesis, or PK, was coined.

Parapsychologists study these phenomena both in the laboratory and in the field, as these things happen spontaneously in people's lives. Parapsychologists apply the scientific method to study psychic experiences, and this involves much more than just collecting "stories" from people. In addition, the idea that the human personality, spirit, soul, or mind can survive the death of the body has also involved parapsychologists from the very start.

There are many opinions as to whether parapsychology as a field of study is truly a science, given the problems parapsychologists have in examining psychic ability both in and outside the laboratory. However, accepting that it is a science there are still confusions as to what sort of science parapsychology is. There are basically two groups of sciences: physical (i.e. chemistry, physics, biology) and social (anthropology, psychology, sociology). While parapsychologists do indeed bring in notions and theoretical models of physicists (and the physicists themselves in many cases), we primarily work as a social science, utilizing methodologies similar to those used by experimental psychologists. We study the human mind, behavior, and experience, as well as the mind's connections with the physical world.

Whether a particular phenomenon exists or not does not necessarily invalidate a science. Parapsychology is the search for and study of a particular group of phenomena that at least exist as far as human experience is concerned. That, in my opinion and the opinion of others, validates the continued existence of the field. Millions of people have reported experiences they have classified as "psychic" or "paranormal." Parapsychologists study those experiences and try to isolate what we think may be causing them, in this case psi. Yes, we are also looking for the physical explanations for how psi might work, how people might gain information from the future or the past or from thousands of miles away, or how we might possibly be able to affect that computer across the room. But we primarily study the experiences of people, looking for explanations.

Parapsychology as a field of study may some day invalidate itself. We may learn that our critics have been right all along, that there are perfectly "normal" explanations for these experiences. What I find interesting, though, is that the only group of researchers really trying to explain these experiences, one way or another, is the group called parapsychologists. With the exception of an isolated researcher here and there in another field of study, we're effectively the only ones addressing the question of what it really means to have a psychic experience. Others, often those calling themselves "skeptics" (many of whom are actually disbelievers, rather than doubters, and therefore not truly skeptical), hold that because there "must be other explanations" that the experiences can just be dismissed or ignored.

Parapsychologists study subjective paranormal experiences, or SPE. This phrase, coined by neuro-psychiatrist and parapsychological researcher Dr. Vernon Neppe describes very well what happens to people. The SPE relates to any experience one has that seems or feels paranormal or psychic. We call it "subjective" because it is that personal interpretation that the experience is out of the normal range of experience and can be called "psychic." This does not mean the SPE doesn't relate to objective, real happenings, just that the objective, real evidence might not be available.

Let's take a look at the classifications we've made with regard to these experiences. ESP is basically receptive in nature, as our minds receive information from other sources. When the information apparently has its start or origin in the mind of another person (or even an animal) we call it telepathy, mind-to-mind communication. Unlike what you see on television, this really doesn't mean that someone can "read" another person's mind. It's more the idea that images, sensations, and information can somehow be shared between two or more minds directly. As far as dreams are concerned, we are looking at the idea that in our dreams, information that originates in the minds or experience of others somehow finds its way into our dreams.

Clairvoyance is an idea that goes way back in human history. This is the ability to "see" objects, people, or events happening at the same moment as the receiver's "vision" but outside the range of our "ordinary" senses or inference. Most people have "visions" or "see" the information in their "mind's eye" apparently because sight is the sense we rely on the most. When the psychic information comes into our heads, our brains translate it into imagery as the first form of perception. Clairvoyance means "clear seeing," but people also relate "hearing" psychic information (clairaudience . . . "clear hearing" with the "mind's ear"?). In addition, we often "feel" or "sense" things happening elsewhere (clairsentience) and there are reports of "smelling" things at a distance (clairolfaction).

While we're not quite sure just what determines whether someone will receive psychic information in a "vision" or through something that causes us to hear or feel or smell something in our minds, it may actually relate to what kind of person you are. Are you primarily visual, auditory, or kinesthetic (feeling with your body)? This may affect just what form psychic information takes in your perception, and of course, in your dreams.

Another term used for such real-time psychic perceptions is remote viewing, or more properly, remote perception. These phrases, well-used since the early seventies, more correctly identify the ability we're looking at—we perceive things, people, or events from a remote location. Experiments in remote perception have provided a good base of information supporting the existence of psi of this type.

Of course, we do have problems separating telepathy and clairvoyance in many situations. For example, let's say our experiment involves you going to a distant place, and at that time I am to describe that location. Let's say I am able to give a rather good description of that place. The question is, am I describing the location by psychically tuning in on *it*, or am I tuning in on *your mind*, relating what you are observing, what you are looking at.

In a psychic dream, we have the same problem. If the dream I have relates to something happening to you at that moment, am I receiving the information from your mind, or am I somehow describing the situation, the place, the events by psychically observing it directly? *Does it really matter which?* Probably not. It is still happening somehow. We call that "somehow" psi.

As you might imagine by the above examples, it's difficult to create a true telepathy experiment, since if someone observes the "target" the information could come from either the mind of the observer or from the target itself. In either case, psi is operating, and that's what's most important, at least for the time being.

It's easier to create a clairvoyance experiment, since all we need do is have the target, whether a photo, drawing, card, symbol, coordinates of a distant location, or other information source sealed up in an envelope or maybe flashed on a video monitor in a sealed room with no one there to see it. To be a decent experiment, the target must be randomly selected from many other sealed targets (or maybe randomly selected by a computer programmed with a number of locations), so that no one could possibly know what the target is. With no one observing the target, the possibility of telepathy has been ruled out (more on this later).

But while telepathy and clairvoyance relate to things happening at the same moment as when the person receives the information, most of us think of "psychic visions" as relating to the future (or, at least that's what the tabloids and the skeptics would have us believe).

The apparent ability to receive information from future events is called precognition. Clairvoyance crosses space to grab information, while precognition crosses both space and time. In other words, one doesn't only seem to get information about your own location in the future, but also about events and locations far away from where you are now or even will be in the future.

We constantly hear of people making predictions of future happenings (just look at the tabloids at the beginning of each year . . . "Top Ten Psychics Predict . . ."), and, as the skeptics have pointed out, we hardly ever hear of the outcome of those predictions if they've failed. Psychics often state after the event has occurred that "I predicted it months ago." Rarely can they produce evidence that supports that claim.

Psychics also often relate general predictions to events as they occur, such as "a major world leader will die next year" or "a disaster will occur sometime in the next few months claiming many lives." I can predict, especially right now, writing this particular chapter in October of 1990, a year after the San Francisco-Area earthquake of 1989, that there will be several earthquakes of 3.0 and above before the end of 1991 (or 1992, etc.) in northern California. Those of us living in the aftermath of the 7.1 quake in northern California have already experienced many aftershocks of that quake measuring 3.0 and greater. And, unfortunately, there are bound to be more.

But there are hundreds of reports of specific incidents predicted and coming true, not months in advance, but often hours, or minutes. Such premonitions are not generally about earth-shattering (or quaking) events. Rather they are more personal. These may be sensations that you may be in danger if you do something tomorrow (like get on a particular ship or plane which turns out to be at the center of an accident) or maybe that you will run into a friend you haven't seen in years this afternoon (and you do) or perhaps that a relative or friend may die suddenly (not of a lingering illness . . . that could be guesswork) or that a friend or relative is offered a new job . . . or wins the lottery.

Most predicted events that come true (or don't come true) involve human decision-making (should I take that flight or not . . . should I bet on that horse or not?). In studies of precognitive experiences, it's been related that the overwhelming number of experiences involve predictions whose outcomes would be different if a different decision was made.

In dreams, precognized events seem to be more easily remembered, but can also be confused with other dream imagery. How do you know it's a precognition of the future or simply our wishful thinking in our dreams? You can't always, until the event happens. And sometimes, you can't even remember that you had the dream until the events start occurring.

For example, have you ever been in a situation where you suddenly feel as though you'd experienced it (the situation) before? That sensation is called déjà vu, the feeling that you've "seen this before." Vernon Neppe has identified more than forty possible explanations for the déjà vu experience, where but a few are psychic explanations (others range from associating incorrect memories of a similar situation to actually having been in that place before).

One of those psychic explanations is that the sense of familiarity results from your having had a precognitive dream of the situation, a dream you possibly forgot. As you get into the situation, the memory of the dream comes flooding back into your mind, giving that déjà vu sensation, and with it sometimes the full memory of the dream which tells you what's going to happen next. Sound familiar? I've had a number of those experiences, and have spoken with many people who have had them as well.

Of course, that's all to say that there is a way to actually receive information from the future, that the future even exists for us to gain information from. This in itself is a problem, since we have theories and models of how time works, but we really don't know for sure. I'll discuss this more as we get to the chapter on precognitive dreams.

If we do acknowledge that it's somehow possible to gain information from the future (which may or may not yet exist), then it follows, perhaps more easily, that we can somehow gain information from the past (which has already happened). We call this ability, when information comes psychically from past events, retrocognition (in other words, information comes from some past object, event, or person without the use of normal senses or logical inference, or through looking up the records). Such "peering into the past" does seem to occur in the dream state and may even be related to reincarnation. As I'll discuss later, there may be some spillover to clairvoyant experience.

When one draws a connection between dreaming and psychic experience, there are two types of such experiences that immediately come to mind. One is the precognitive dream. The other is out of body experiences (OBEs). If that language doesn't sound familiar, how about the occultists' term "astral projection?" The idea of the OBE is not strictly psychic in nature as defined by parapsychologists or psychologists, it is simply the experience or feeling or sensation that you are somehow outside of your own body. The concept of astral projection is that somehow the spirit or soul (or "astral body") leaves the physical shell of the body for a time. Since there is little evidence available that there is an astral form which can truly leave the body behind, let's stick with the OBE definition.

An OBE is a psychological one, not necessarily psychic. Have you ever had the experience or dream that you were floating outside your body and possibly were even able to look down on it? That could be dream imagery or just the mind giving you some imagery that fits what you're feeling at that time. Have you ever felt that, while out of your body, you traveled someplace else? If that happened while you were dreaming, maybe it was just that: a dream that you left your body behind and flew away. If it happened while awake, though relaxed (which is the state that the OBE most often occurs), again it could have been something analagous to a daydream. Psychological, but not necessarily psychic.

But let's say in your "travels" you overheard a conversation in another part of your house or apartment building. Or maybe you observed something happening in another country, where you "traveled" while out of body. And let's say that the observations checked out, that the conversation really occurred or the event in that other country did happen. That perception of events outside the range available to your physical body just made your psychological OBE a psychic one.

Doesn't that sound similar to a remote viewing, the only difference being that you somehow "traveled" to the distant location rather than simply "picking up" information? Yes, it is similar, and the reason may be that they are the same experience. Whether it's clairvoyant, rather than the idea of part of your consciousness (or all of it) will be discussed later.

As mentioned earlier, parapsychologists also study psychokinesis. Very few dreams seem to be connected to psychokinetic experience, although having some understanding of dreams and their imagery can help us look at and decipher the meaning of psychokinetic experiences as they occur in everyday life. In parapsychology, we view a wide range of occurrences and experiences under the heading of psychokinesis, the mind affecting the material world around us, most of which have nothing to do with the dream state.

Psychic healing may be PK by a healer on sick person's body, or may be the sick person speeding up their own healing processes (as perhaps in spontaneous remission of cancer). We do know a little bit about how our minds affect our own health, certainly more than how another person can affect us. One thing has come out of research and reported experiences, and that is that to be healed, it would appear that a person must be open to getting better. On the flipside, in looking at the idea that someone can psychically attack another, we find that unless one is open to being hurt or taking ill, we can't be harmed by others in this way.

Psychokinesis is also being looked at in the context of human/machine interactions. What kind of effect does our mind have on the technology around us? Quite a bit, it would seem from recent research. Parapsychologists are quite interested in looking at how our moods, our likes and dislikes towards computers and other machines seem to be played out in how well or how poorly that computer works for us.

When most people think of psychokinesis, of mind over matter, they think of films or books like *Carrie* or *The Fury*, where the mind of someone is capable of destruction of property and of other people. Well, nothing so dramatic happens in real life, although there are reports of physical movement of objects, especially in what are known as poltergeist cases. Unlike the film, poltergeists have nothing to do with beasts from other dimensions.

Poltergeists are situations, not entities. According to the main model subscribed to by most in parapsychology, a model put together by William G. Roll, this is a situation in which someone living in the household or office setting is undergoing some kind of tension or stress. This stress is released by the subconscious mind through the ability we all have called psychokinesis, and is called recurrent spontaneous psychokinesis (RSPK). In other words, the movement of objects or other physical effects in the home or office setting that occurs in these situations is caused by psychokinesis, it occurs spontaneously (without conscious control) and it is recurrent (happens again and again).

The effects that occur in such poltergeist situations are not as dramatic as in the horror films, but are certainly dramatic in the context of "normal," day-to-day experience. Movements of objects reported in these cases have ranged from "small" movements of ashtrays or books or papers or knick-knacks, to pictures and shelves falling off the wall, to small objects flying through the air to furniture being moved (though, in the case of furniture, the movements are not great . . . maybe a chair is tipped over by itself or a couch moves slightly). Other physical effects have included miniature flames (which appear to damage furniture slightly, but are not dangerous) and bursts of water appearing out of nowhere.

The model of RSPK, or poltergeists, relates directly to a living person or to a group dynamic between people in the setting. It would appear that the subconscious mind of the poltergeist "agent" acts out frustration or tension or relieves stress through the inherent psychokinetic ability that we have. The situations may be a single occurrence or last as long as (in some instances) a year or so. Typically, however, they average between a week or so and a couple of months.

How does this connect to dreams? In looking at understanding dreams, we typically try to connect dream imagery with something going on in the dreamer's life. In the same way, in the investigation of poltergeist cases, we try to first identify who the "agent" might be, and then to see how the effects, the objects being moved, the type of movements, or the other physical effects, may connect with or represent an issue in that "agent's" life.

For example, in one case investigated by parapsychologist Julian Isaacs, mini-fires represented anger and resentment on the part of the poltergeist agent. In another of Dr. Isaac's cases, water drenching the people in the case represented grief not realized and tears not shed on the part of the poltergeist agent who had not yet dealt with the death of relatives.

In a water-poltergeist case of my own, there were bursts of water appearing just below the ceiling (witnessed by several people). After eliminating physical possibilities (like leaky pipes), the phenomena was related to one of the children in the household. In a discussion with him during which I tried to find something that may have related to water, I learned that he was being pushed by his parents to join the swim team, that he didn't want to compete at swimming but didn't know how to tell his parents that, and that the water-bursts started shortly after this pressure to join the team started. Once this was all out in the open and the boy no longer had to worry about joining the team (he hated competition of any kind, he told me), the water-bursts stopped (except for the one time that coincided with his bringing home his report card . . . he didn't do all that well).

So, in looking at the phenomena in a given poltergeist case, we have the analogy to dream work. We look for what the specific effects may represent or relate to in the experience/life of the "agent" (or dreamer, if we were working with a dream). Working through the issue resolves the problem/frustration/stress that brings up the RSPK to begin with. The recurrence of the PK halts, as a recurrent dream might stop after identifying and working through the issue at the root of that repeating dream.

Large scale PK has been connected with dreams in a couple of ways. In the book (and film) *The Lathe of Heaven* (book by Ursula K. LeGuin), a man has the ultimate PK ability attached to his dreams. Any changes he dreams of in the world have come true when he wakes up. Unfortunately, so complete are the changes that all people (except himself) have had their memories altered, so no one except the dreamer even remembers the world as it was before the change.

In the film *Dreamscape*, there is an attempt to kill people by invading their dreams, killing them in the dreamworld, and having that translate to an actual death. This is successful in the film, but relies on the idea that one can actually penetrate into the dream state of another's mind and manipulate the reality found there. The victim dies a fairly quiet death, with no indication that a dream or something paranormal was responsible.

In the film series *A Nightmare on Elm Street*, Freddy Krueger is alive only in the shared dreamworld of humanity, and appears capable of selecting the dreams of particular victims, pulling often more than one person into a shared dream, then manipulating that world with dire effects for the person being attacked in the dream. In that series, the person killed in a dream doesn't merely die quietly (as in *Dreamscape*), but rather there seems to be a psychokinetic effect on the victim's body, with people slashed in a dream slashed in reality, and so forth.

Well, if any of that was going on, we may never really know. There doesn't appear to be any way, outside of literary license, to invade the dreams of another. And while there is a good deal of folklore around about the effects of dreaming something bad having a correlation in real life, the facts don't really fit. One such tale I often hear is "If you are falling in a dream and don't wake up before you hit the ground, you'll die." That doesn't fit, especially since people do have dreams of falling and do sometimes dream of hitting the ground. (In their dreams, they can usually get up, brush themselves off, and continue with the dream, kind of like Wile E. Coyote.) It certainly doesn't fit with the number of dreams reported where the dreamer finds him or herself in the midst of an accident or disaster, seeing themselves die, or getting otherwise hurt. No real effect, other than perhaps a psychological one. Unfortunately, if people do die this way, we'd probably not know it at all, as evidenced in the film *Dreamscape*, that is, unless the person hung around as an apparition.

Is there really proof of ESP and PK? How do these abilities work? Are some people more psychic than others? Are children more psychic than adults? Aren't people who have psychic experiences just plain crazy? What about that magician who goes around debunking this stuff? These are a few of the questions commonly asked of me and my colleagues by members of the media and the general public.

Parapsychology was admittedly in a "proof" phase of research during the days of J.B. Rhine and parapsychology at Duke University. The lab was disassociated with the university in the mid-sixties when Rhine retired from Duke, yet continues as an autonomous entity, the Institute for Parapsychology at the Foundation for Research on the Nature of Man in Durham, North Carolina. Experiments were designed to gain statistically significant results that would "prove" psi was real.

Being that we are dealing with a phenomenon, experience, ability, or whatever you want to call it that is tied to human psychology, there seem to be a lot of stumbling blocks in providing the "proof" that would satisfy most of the scientific community. In fact, most parapsychologists and many scientists in other fields are satisfied that we are studying a real "anomaly" in human experience (whether it's psi or not, there's something here that needs an explanation). Others are not so accepting, since they appear to want the sort of experiment a physicist could provide, one who's outcome is consistent. In dealing with human psychology, which is not a physical science, this just doesn't happen. Perception by a human, whether through the "normal" senses or "paranormal" channel, is dependent on the individual (ask any good magician).

Research moved from "proof" to "process," to experiments looking at how psi might work with a given type of individual or in a given task or situation. Process experiments take different psychological variables into account, such as state of awareness (relaxed, asleep, etc.), personality (introvert vs. extrovert, thinking-type vs. feeling-type of person, etc.), and even belief and performance issues.

Experimental results are often consistent in that they frequently provide that the same variable results in the same sort of scoring, significant or not. For example, the well known "Sheep/Goat Effect" that Dr. Gertrude Schmeidler first looked at has been repeated over and over again. In this "effect" people who believe in the existence of psi tend to score above chance, while disbelievers tend to score below chance. As with athletes and their sports or with students taking tests, belief in their own skill or in success is important. It would appear that human beings must, in general, have some belief that they can complete a task, that the task is possible, for any success at all. Doubt in our ability is often our undoing in everyday tasks, and that seems to be so where psi is concerned as well.

What's interesting to me is that this repeatable effect is often pushed aside by skeptics. If there really is a consistent effect, whereby there is a difference in the scoring rates of believers and disbelievers in psi, shouldn't that effect be of interest to psychologists and others *even if psi doesn't exist*? So why isn't anyone looking at these effects, trying to explain them in some model where psi is unnecessary to account for it? Maybe there's fear that what's found may not be liked (in other words, that the disbelieving "skeptic" may find that the only explanation is psi). More likely, it's a fear that such research even from a purely psychological stance would be connected with psi research and is therefore "taboo" in the minds of most scientists.

There are two lines of research that have yielded excellent results under well-controlled conditions. One of them is the experiments in psychokinesis utilizing a random event generator (REG). This device usually utilizes a tiny radioactive source (which sends off particles at a natural random rate as it decays). The subject tries to affect the display of the REG which relates to the rate of particles given off by the source. Experiments with REGs have indicated that there is some sort of effect by the human mind on either the radioactive source or on the device itself. This is being followed up by experiments where people attempt to affect a computer display in a particular way. It may be possible to do experiments with psychokinesis in dreams by using an REG and placing it close to a dreamer to see if the dreamer has any affect on the REG output during any stage of sleep, but specifically during REM sleep.

The other line of research relates more to our topic of dreams. The state where we are dreaming is an altered state of consciousness. Work with such altered states has involved everything from hypnosis to biofeedback (and dreams, of course). The ganzfeld experiments primarily conducted by the Psychophysical Research laboratories in Princeton, New Jersey (The PRL, by the way, has, at the time of this writing, been closed due to lack of funding) have yielded extremely good results.

The ganzfeld, or "whole field," setting involves a person designated as "receiver" in the experiment who is placed in a mild sensory deprivation. The person reclines on a comfortable couch and has sight cut off through the use of halved ping pong balls placed on the eyes and hearing cut off through headphones that play only "white noise," or static. In another room, the "sender," usually a friend or relative, is looking at a video monitor. Once the experimenter starts things up, it's all run by computer, the experimenter knowing nothing of the target selection until after the experiment has run its course.

The computer randomly selects a video-clip from hundreds on a tape in a VCR, then causes the VCR to scan for the correct clip. That clip is presented on the monitor for the "sender" several times, while the "receiver" says anything that comes to mind of what is being "received." This is recorded by the experimenter over a microphone system. When the video runs its course, the experimenter reads back what the "receiver" described. Then the "receiver" is asked to remove the headphones and blinders. The "receiver" is shown, on a monitor, four video clips chosen by the computer, one of which is the actual target. He/she tries to rate each one, giving (hopefully) the highest ranking to the actual target.

Finally, the actual target is revealed by the computer to both "receiver" and experimenter. The experimenter checks both the ranking and the descriptions against the actual targets.

Scoring in the ganzfeld setting has been as high as 50 percent, though more consistently in a range of 38 percent, much higher than chance. In an examination and subsequent debate on the ganzfeld experiments by experimenter Charles Honorton and critic Ray Hyman, there was some agreement. There was, as both concluded, "something" happening out of the ordinary, a communications anomaly worthy of further study, but while Honorton suggested psi as responsible for that "something," Hyman couldn't agree to that interpretation.

In any event, while experiments in parapsychology continue, and we learn ever so slowly, there is evidence that these experiences can teach us more about the way we function as human beings. Ignoring the experiences teaches us nothing and is hardly science.

One other question that comes up often has to do with children. I'm often asked if children are more psychic than adults, if we lose our abilities as we grow up. It would seem that children appear to be more psychic only through a twist of fate, that being education. Children don't question or categorize their experiences in the same way adults do, they haven't always learned that things like "knowing what's in Uncle Harry's mind" or "making that ashtray move by itself" are impossible. We seem to be educated out of being psychic as we grow up, learning to question and even disregard experiences that don't fit the "norm." This is quite evident when you look at cultures whose belief systems incorporate psychic happenings, and when you look at the previously mentioned "Sheep/Goat Effect." Bring in doubt and disbelief and you drop scoring and ignore the experiences.

Of course, we also can't rule out the power of a child's imagination in a given situation. It is not responsible to view every report from a child as psychic just because it fits under that category. In looking at any psychic experience after the fact, whether ours or someone else's, it is necessary to look at all possible explanations, to discard the "normal" possibilities first before assuming something is paranormal.

As to whether the people who have the experiences are "crazy" or "insane" or "psychopathic" or "deranged," yes, it is possible that some people have psychic episodes as part of their psychological problems, but the sheer numbers of people around the world (whole cultures, in fact) would indicate that these are part of normal, human experience. People will typically not think you are crazy if you have psychic experiences. In fact, you'd probably find that as long as you speak rationally about those experiences, people will tell you similar experiences they've had. In other words, as long as you keep your feet otherwise planted in reality as defined by our "normal" senses, or grounded as some people like to say, you'll have little problem even talking with skeptics (they might feel you're wrong, but not crazy).

There are those debunkers of psychic experience who claim all sorts of things about the people who have these experiences. The main claims are that you're either crazy or lying (possibly to yourself as well as to others) when you describe a psychic experience. Let's set the record straight. Most people who have psychic experiences are not crazy or disturbed. They are, in fact, part of the "norm" of western society. Most people who describe these experiences are not lying (even the ones who report ghosts and poltergeists). They may be mistaken; there may be human error or suggestion involved in a given situation that makes one "think" you've had a psychic experience, but very, very few people make this stuff up.

And those magicians who run around saying people are crazy or lying? Well, maybe they should look again at their so-called "open minds." It's much more likely that someone is mistaking a coincidence or has a slight memory lapse or misunderstands something he or she perceives as being psychic, than the idea that the experience is purposefully made up or that the person or persons is/are crazy. Magicians, who deal in playing with people's perceptions should, above all others, understand the role of human error in any human experience. I should know something about this area, since I'm a performing magician myself.

To those who subscribe to the same ideas as those debunkers, keep in mind that magicians are themselves fooled by other magicians (that's how a new trick becomes enticing to a magician . . . because it fools him or her), and keep in mind that magicians' claims to knowing scientific methods in studying these experiences are often false. Just because you know sleight of hand, doesn't mean you know science or truly understand human behavior.

What about explanations for how psi works? That is problematic in itself, as we may be trying to explain something without the words or physics to do it justice. Discovering electricity is a far cry from understanding what it is and how it works. There are many theories and models of psychic functioning, how it is possible to relay data without the use of the normal senses, or how it is possible to affect matter directly with our minds. As we proceed with the study of dreams and connection with psychic functioning I'll try to address some of those theories.

What can parapychologists do with dreams? As you move through this book, you will discover the answer to that question. For example, there has been much research in the area of telepathy in dreams, and recent discussion of how the earth's magnetic field affects the incidence of telepathy, clairvoyance, and precognition in dreams (and in the waking state). As we work with our own dreams, we may learn not only to control the content of the dream, but also to ask for specific information to come into that dream, information that may be beyond our own memory and experience and senses (and therefore psychic). Parapsychologists looking for experiences to research or explain and study can use dreams as source material for psychic experience. Since we all dream every night, and since it would appear that many people (if not everyone) can learn to recall and even affect the content of their dreams, such a form of human experience may be a fertile ground in which to plant the suggestion to have a psychic experience.

So who or what is a psychic and how can we judge our own experiences as psychic if there is so much room for human error? Do we even need to *know* that the extra information we're getting is really psychic? Is there something special about psychic experiences in dreams that makes them different from waking psychic experiences? Good questions, which I'll be addressing as you read on.

Are you psychic? If our research, both in and outside of the laboratory is any indication, yes, you've probably had at least one experience that could be classified as "psychic," one which you may have a name or label for now that you've learned the kinds of experiences and abilities parapsychologists deal with. But remember, words can be deceiving. The words I've used to describe psychic abilities, even the word psychic itself may be inadequate to describe what's really going on here, or may be inaccurately describing something else entirely.

And where dreams are concerned, it seems that anything's possible. . . .

CHAPTER 4

Dreams On The Dark Side
Nightmares and Daymares

The president of the United States is concerned about the escalating possibility of nuclear war. His sleep is fitful and most of his dreams center around one theme: He is alive in the desolate, burning wasteland that is left of the country after the nuclear holocaust. The dream, a nightmare, is recurrent, causing him to lose more and more sleep, and bringing questions to the mind of those around him as to whether he is still capable of using good judgment to make decisions as president. And still, the nightmares persist. . . .

You may recognize the above scenario from the film *Dreamscape*. The real possibility of nuclear war has given more than a few people nightmares. In fact, there have been reports of children having such bad dreams. These nightmares seem to be caused by real-life anxieties and fears. Nightmares in general have often been described as dreams in which our waking fears have gone wild.

But is that all they are? Do nightmares only have to do with the real, overt fears we face in our waking lives? Let's explore the "dark side" of the dream for a bit.

The origins of the word "nightmare" betray ideas of what people thought these extremely vivid, but terrifying, dreams were, "night demons" or "night goblins" or "night spirits" depending on who you talk to. All relate to the idea that the nightmare was thought to have been caused by evil spirits or supernatural creatures coming into our dreams while we were asleep at night. Children, not being very strong-willed, were considered prime targets for such demons. As children tend to have many more such bad dreams than adults, that idea was borne out by simple observation. Or should I say that it was likely that the idea came about because children experience more nightmares and therefore are better targets for the night spirits that invade our dreams?

Then there's that old wive's tale (not so old . . . you still hear it today) that nightmares are caused by eating too much of a good thing (too many sweets, for example) or by eating the wrong thing, more or less our body's way of seeking revenge for stretching the stomach lining a bit too much.

So what are these dreams of disaster or monsters anyway? Many experts see nightmares as very intense dreams that play out some of our childhood fears and feelings of anxiety, others as dealing with the common fears, with archetypal fears, all people face. And there are several types of nocturnal incidents that people call nightmares.

The biggest split between two types of sleep-related terrifying incidents that occur is that between ''nightmares'' and ''night terrors.'' A nightmare is a bad dream; it occurs during REM sleep and may last more than a few minutes. There are all the qualities of any other dream, though in the nightmare we have particular fears, anxieties, frustrations, and perhaps even guilt feelings coming out. We are generally not able to move about while having a nightmare, being in that induced paralysis that accompanies REM-sleep and all other forms of dreams.

Night terrors, on the other hand, are situations in which we wake up, often covered with a cold sweat (missing from reactions to most nightmares), realizing we're terrified but not remembering why or whether it was because of a dream. In fact, it is very likely that we don't even wake up fully from a night terror, and we may scream, move about in bed, or even sleepwalk a bit due to the night terror. It occurs in the early part of the sleep period, and during non-REM stages of sleep, when we are not only not paralyzed, but *not dreaming*.

Both night terrors and nightmares are experienced more

frequently by children than by adults, since it appears that most of us outgrow these experiences, although they may both be experienced by adults (who, on the average, may have a nightmare a couple of times a year, with night terrors less frequently). Night terrors occur sometime within one to three hours after falling asleep, usually in the deepest stage of sleep, while nightmares, although they may happen in just about any REM-sleep period, occur generally in the later hours of the time you are asleep, when the REM stage lasts longer (the longer we sleep, the more the cycle of non-REM/REM reoccurs, the longer the REM stage).

Night terrors are a form of parasomia, sleep disorders, which are related to sleepwalking and even grinding your teeth while you sleep. Children who have night terrors often "wake up" screaming. Parents running into their rooms to see what's wrong may find them hard to calm down, limbs flailing as though the child is trying to escape something, eyes wide open and even glazed looking, and not recognizing that the parents are there, or possibly not recognizing the parents as who they are. The screaming, the hysterical fear, may last more than a few minutes or end as soon as the parents lay the child back down. If the child actually calms down and recognizes the parents, it's as if he/she is just waking up. Asked about what scared the child, he/she has no idea, no recall. Parents might simply think this is a nightmare, or might think, if the situation happens again, that the child has a psychological problem.

In fact, neither is the case. During the night terror, the child is simply *not awake, but still sleeping*. Given that the night terror occurs in the non-REM stages of sleep, the child is truly in the deepest stages of sleep, and may be more difficult to wake up right away after falling back to sleep. In this deepest state of sleep, we can sleep through just about anything, even through our own night terrors. There is no recall of what caused the night terror because the brain activity is very different than REM, from which we can recall imagery and content. We are, during night terrors, not dreaming . . . not creating signals that might dump into either long- or short-term memory.

Most night terrors occur in very young children, pre-schoolers according to some experts, though that may typically occur any time up until about eight years of age, they may occur in children as young as six months. According to some studies, night terrors occur more frequently in boys than in girls. Night terrors *do* occur in adults, though infrequently. As we grow up, we tend to outgrow the night terrors, as they seem related more to physical activity in the body and brain not related to mind, rather than the physical activity in the brain that stimulates mental processes in REM sleep.

In adults, the night terror is recognizably a different experience than a nightmare. A child may not wake at all during the night terror, yet may very well wake up during a nightmare. With little or no recall of having even had the night terror, there is no comparison to the nightmare. As adults, we may very well wake up in a cold sweat, our hearts pounding, breathing hard, and knowing we just had *something* happen to us in our sleep, something probably unsettling or even frightening, causing a feeling of terror or panic, but again with no recall of anything but that vague feeling. We can be disoriented and not fully awake, and sometimes not awake at all. We may have flailed our arms a bit, and the night terror might be accompanied by a bit of sleepwalking. It's as if our bodies react to something our minds can't quite get a grasp on, which seems to be exactly the case.

Night terrors may be more indicative of physiological and neurological imbalances than anything psychological, whether in children or adults. Children who are extremely tired may fall into that deepest stage of sleep in which night terrors occur (as might adults, for that matter). Night terrors in adults may be the result of stress, both physical and psychological (though it's been shown that psychological stress can cause physical problems). Unfortunately, night terrors are a part of childhood, although parents may consider them unusual and even worry when they happen more than once or twice. Most children will have at least one night terror as they grow up, but generally more than that. There is some evidence to indicate that frequent night terrors in children are genetically related, that such patterns of repetition of the night terrors run in families. This makes sense, given their phys-iologically-based nature.

Nightmares, on the other hand, are dreams, and as such provide information and imagery and emotion as other dreams do. The content of nightmares is often pulled from childhood fears. While we are children, we are effectively both vul-nerable (not capable of being fully functional in the world around us) and protected (by our parents). Such feelings of helplessness and vulnerability can cause fear and anxiety in us as children, and can certainly come up in our dreams as adults, even being related to our adult lives.

Have you ever felt helpless to affect a particular situation in your life, to remedy it to the better, whether that situation revolves around work, around your relationships, around money, and so on? Nightmares are dreams which can play out any helpless feelings, any fears or anxieties, whether relating to our fears or worries of failure or of being physically injured, or even left isolated and alone. Nightmares may be due to actual phobias (phobic nightmares), but are more often related to happenings in our lives, due to fears of being fired, recent accidents we have had (or seen), divorce, bankruptcy, and other negatives. Nightmares can even betray a fear of success, something that more than a few people experience.

While the majority of the nightmare-type dreams that we have do occur in childhood and we tend to outgrow them as we outgrow night terrors, nightmares do follow us into our adult lives. As mentioned earlier, we tend to have a couple every year, though experts have done studies which contend that one out of every 200 to 500 adults (discrepancy due to different study results) have them as often as once a week.

According to a national survey commissioned in 1982 by ABC Television and the *Washington Post* ("The American Dreams; Fear of Falling and Other Long National Night-mares" by Henry Allen, *Washington Post*, July 7, 1982), dreams of falling were the most frequent (71 percent), fol-lowed by dreams of seeing a loved one in danger or dead (59 percent) and dreams of "being chased and attacked" (56 percent). Other common themes reported by the survey were sexual experiences (54 percent), "accomplishing something great" (52 percent), flying or floating under one's own power (45 percent), paralysis or being "unable to run or scream" (42 percent . . . this one makes a lot of sense given our physical paralysis in REM sleep), taking exams (31 percent), missing a plane or train (28 percent), and being "naked in public" (15 percent).

Not all of the above dream themes can be considered nightmares, though there may be sensations of frustration accompanying a dream with such an occurrence. While the falling dreams may be most common in this survey, not everyone who has a falling dream may consider it a nightmare. The type of dream most often considered the common nightmare is that of being chased or attacked, and you often hear people talk about the nightmare they had of someone dying, or the one where they were in front of a group about to act or speak and suddenly noticed that they were stark naked, or the nightmare where you are in a crowd and can't get anyone to notice you. All of these betray feelings of vulnerability, of helplessness, and anxieties about not meeting our own expectations (or the expectations of others).

According to a leading researcher of nightmares, Dr. Ernest Hartmann, there are two types of nightmares. There is a "standard" nightmare, which is like any other dream, though with the additional label of "nightmare" because of its content. There are also "post-traumatic nightmares," a result of the experience of real events in one's life that may be stressful, scary, and even terrifying. Such events as being in an accident, an earthquake or some other disaster, or a soldier or law enforcement officer who is a participant in a violent scene may cause post-traumatic stress syndrome, which can often have long-term affects. Post-traumatic stress syndrome is being addressed more and more by psychotherapists as a cause of continuing psychological and emotional adjustment problems as people try to relate to their "normal" lives after experiencing something unsettling or horrible.

The post-traumatic nightmares are often a result of living through disasters or being witnesses to or victims of accidents or personal attacks. Such nightmares are often replays of the actual events, causing people to relive horrible, true experiences, rather than being related to other forms of fantasy-dream imagery. For example, I've spoken with people in the San Francisco Bay area that had nightmares for weeks related to their experience of the October 17, 1989 earthquake. Veterans of Vietnam and other wars, as well as police officers involved in shoot-outs, who have experienced situations where people die in front of them or where they (the dreamers) caused those peoples' deaths (whether justifiably defending themselves or not) may relive the experiences. In addition, such traumatic experiences may even show up in waking experience, as "daymares" (more on this later).

In looking at psychic experience in dreams, there are numerous reports of both precognitive and clairvoyant dreams of disasters that may affect the dreamer emotionally. If I somehow psychically pick up on the death and devastation caused by a major earthquake, I may react to that information in my dreams as though I had actually witnessed it. Since psychic perceptions tend to be very emotionally charged, one may receive precognitive/clairvoyant messages from both those who have been injured in the disaster as well as from the witnesses who look on in horror.

Unfortunately, the person experiencing such a psychic flow may actually have a recurring nightmare of the event, a form of psychically-induced post-traumatic nightmare. There appears to be less of an emotional attachment to the nightmare if it's recognized as a psychic dream, and it's likely that, on some level of awareness, there is that kind of recognition (that this is not a normal dream) and the nightmare will not re-occur. On the other hand, if the dreamer feels that what was experienced was a clear, precognitive dream, there may be an overwhelming sense that he/she should try to do something about the dreamed-about situation (warn people at least). In a later chapter, I'll discuss the issue of acting on such premonitions.

Such psychic dreams of disaster that may reoccur may also not be very clear. I've spoken with more than a few people, including a few psychics, who had non-specific dreams about the 1989 San Francisco quake. Only two people I've spoken with claimed to have had a vivid dream of the quake and its effect on the Bay area, and neither of them consider themselves "psychic." The psychics I've spoken with reported a general feeling of dread, that something bad was going to happen in the area, but no specifics. And most of them reported the sensation building in them or the dreams occurring within forty-eight hours before the quake. This may not be related to precognitive experience, but to a sensitivity to the geomagnetic field of the earth, or some other such physical variables that relate to earthquakes. More on that later.

In dealing with post-traumatic nightmares, feelings of guilt and helplessness may accompany the dreams. The best way to deal with such nightmares appears to be to talk about the nightmare and the events that the nightmare represents. Working through the feelings brought on by the original event appears to best alleviate trauma related to experiencing that event, whether the feelings keep coming back in nightmares or not.

What about the "standard" nightmare?

Again, these are dreams that go a bit further from any feeling of normal frustration or guilt of slight bits of fear. They are extreme in presenting the imagery in ways that induce "negative" emotional reactions which may spill over to our waking consciousness. Anxiety in nightmares may reflect some situation we saw as a failure in our waking lives, or may simply relate to not being able to function "normally" in our dreams, a sense of helplessness as the dream proceeds around us. Nightmares may reflect reactions to real events, essentially representations of anxiety or fear surrounding dealing with those events (divorce and other relationship issues, work problems, health problems, death in the family, accidents, and so on) where we feel that "normal" means of dealing with those situations are not effective.

Nightmares may be triggered by such stressful or traumatic situations as mentioned above or by any situation that may remind us of feelings of vulnerability or helplessness, such as what we felt when we were children. Nightmares may sometimes last longer than other dreams, as though the emotion carried by the dream takes time to build. Of course, what also appears to happen is that as the emotions build, we may react to them in that nightmare and wake up. If the nightmare brings on an intense reaction quickly, it will generally be a shorter dream.

The explanation of nightmares being caused by too much alcohol or too much food (or the wrong food) doesn't seem to hold much weight (although you may have a nightmare about eating too much food or drinking too much). The content of nightmares may relate to our waking state as much as any other dream. Our moods just before going to sleep do affect our dreams, and therefore may give cause to a dream being viewed as a nightmare. Scary movies or books may make us feel uneasy enough that it's not only tough to go to sleep, we end up with some of that scary imagery in our dreams.

Nightmares may be excellent indicators of problems we're facing in our lives. Looking at what goes on in a nightmare as an indication of an unresolved issue or as some way of telling ourselves that there's something wrong here may yield much information about ourselves. Nightmares may be warnings to the conscious mind by another part of ourselves, integrating information about ourselves or about situations in our waking lives, the outer world, that we're not consciously aware of. As all the information that comes through our senses is processed, there may be items that we miss on the conscious level, which we are made aware of through dreams and nightmares. Recurring nightmares can tell us as much about an issue that needs addressing as can any other recurring dream—it's recurring because we're not dealing with it, whatever "it" turns out to be.

And to bring it back to the psychic side of things, nightmares can be actual warnings of dangerous situations or individuals that will affect us or others. The key is to face the information in that nightmare and ask yourself "Why is that there? What can it be saying to me . . . or about me?"

There are many views on dealing with nightmares. Dr. Ernest Hartmann has written that we can avoid nightmares by figuring out what it is in our life that makes us afraid or feel helpless. Some awareness of what really frustrates us or stresses us out may help us recognize the nightmare imagery for what it is more easily. Dr. Stephen LaBerge and many others suggest facing up to that nightmare "monster" in the dream. Either through the use of lucid dreaming, or by "programming" yourself with the idea that you will turn and face whatever is "bad" in that nightmare, you may be able to confront the nightmare image and overcome it, or absorb it, or get information that may shed a light over what it represents.

"Why are you here? What do you represent? What do I need to be aware of in myself to change the outcome of the event represented by this image that frightens me?" Turning in the nightmare and facing up to your fears (rather than turning and running from them as we normally do in nightmares) may in itself be enough to alleviate the point of the nightmare, to allow you to recognize the image for what it really represents. Asking the above questions may take you a bit further in dealing with the issues in your waking life. It appears that facing up to these nightmares makes the most awful issues easy to deal with, and helps make sure they don't reoccur. Remember, it's typically the unresolved issues that cause recurrent nightmares.

You must acknowledge the nightmare images in order to deal with them. Some experts feel that to ignore or avoid these images that are trying to tell you something may send those feelings or other source issues deeper into your unconscious, to later reappear (possibly even stronger). Acknowledging the images, no matter how fearful they seem to be, as part of yourself, realizing that the monster you see in the nightmare is part of you, conjured up by you to "tell you something," can often be enough to end the nightmare. The belief that the image "has no power over me," whether occurring in a lucid dream where you are aware you're in a nightmare, or whether you simply believe that in your waking state helps overcome and work through the nightmares.

Facing up to the image may be the best way to go while in a lucid dream. Reactions in lucid dreams to nightmarish imagery may involve actively changing the dream to remove whatever that bad image is. In other words, if you are lucid in a nightmare, and aware that you have the "power" in that dream to change things, you may be tempted to simply whisk away the bad stuff and replace it with something else, or simply remove yourself from the scene, escaping in effect. According to Dr. Gayle Delaney, that might not always be the best way to go. This could cause the nightmare to reoccur simply because you are not dealing with or exploring what it is the images represent. The issues in the outer world, the waking world, that the images symbolize are not recognized or dealt with, and therefore the nightmares may continue.

Before you get too involved in worrying about how you're going to deal with your next nightmare, keep in mind that most of us rarely have nightmares, unless we end up in a situation where post-traumatic stress syndrome could cause them (or you really are buying into the fear provided by many horror films . . . though that type of nightmare rarely reoccurs). What about those people (the 1 in 200 to 500) who have nightmares frequently?

Dr. Ernest Hartmann (author of *The Nightmare: The Psychology and Biology of Terrifying Dreams*, Basic Books, 1984) has studied the types of people in this group, the frequent nightmare sufferers, and come to some conclusions. Hartmann talks in terms of people having "boundaries" between being awake and dreaming, and between reality and fantasy. People with "thin boundaries" between these states are most prone to nightmares in adulthood. They are people who are usually very sensitive (possibly hypersensitive) and trusting (sometimes overly so). There is often some ambiguity with regards to sexual identity, not being either strongly masculine or feminine, often recognizing both sides of themselves (though not necessarily or even generally homosexual or even bisexual). They may be prone to daydreaming. Many nightmare sufferers have difficulty waking up or gaining certainty that they are really awake (and not still asleep and dreaming).

And, interestingly enough, they are often people with very creative inclinations toward art, music, writing and other such endeavors. Besides Robert Louis Stevenson, who had a night-

mare that brought him "Dr. Jekyll and Mr. Hyde," Mary
Wollstonecroft Shelley wrote *Frankenstein* as a result of a
nightmare.

"Creative" people tend not to be rigid in their thinking
patterns, often looking at the world around them in a number
of ways to get different viewpoints. An ability to fantasize,
to merge reality and fantasy, obviously helps the creative
person, and may allow for more non-realistic imagery to come
through in dreams.

As we grow up, most of us learn to not only differentiate
between what is reality and what is fantasy, but to build
"boundaries" for ourselves separating the two. This not only
helps us from mixing up the two (fantasy and reality) on a
conscious level, it also helps protect us from potentially dam-
aging or frightening information that might keep pouring into
our dreams and conscious awareness. People with "thin
boundaries" may not have such well-developed defense
mechanisms, and therefore may end up with a spill-over of
fantasy-imagery in dreams and nightmares, as well as in daydreams.

Daydreaming, fantasizing while awake, is a natural state
for many people. Our minds tend to wander a bit into our
own memories every day, and may purposefully seek out
certain images because what is in front of us in reality is
pretty dull and boring. Daydreams tend to involve a replay
of events, perhaps with slightly different outcomes, or may
be a "practice" for an event about to happen (like asking
someone out on a date, or asking the boss for a raise). Daydreams tend to involve some emotion as well.

Most daydreams happen spontaneously, and are close to if
not exactly about everyday events. People can, however,
be deliberate about their daydreams, causing them to run a
certain course beyond their own lives (putting themselves
"in other people's shoes," so to speak) or even leap beyond
the bounds of "reality" as we know it. As a science fiction
and comic books reader, I realize there has to be a certain
amount of structure within someone's imaginings to create
the stories in the books I've read. Writing about fictional

characters at all involves a bit of daydreaming as you try to project the story in your mind and get it down on paper (or on disk).

Daydreaming can even be encouraged and guided by outside "forces." Guided visualization, where another person (or audio tape of another person) suggests a certain course for your daydream, can be of great benefit. Besides being a way to exercise the imagination, guided visualizations have been helpful in uncovering emotional problems and in doing a bit of self-healing; they are often quite beneficial to people. You might even consider such "outer-caused" daydreams as a form of meditation.

Unfortunately, with the good comes the bad, in this case in the form of a "daymare." Daymares are daydreams of disaster, of death, of accidents, or of other negative outcomes of events that could adversely affect you and others. People do have daymares caused by fears and worries ("what if my wife is cheating on me?" or "what if this plane I'm about to board blows an engine?"), and they can be quite similar to nightmares we have while asleep. Daymares may be replays of tragic events witnessed or participated in, and may be caused by post-traumatic stress syndrome, or simply by watching the evening news and worrying about what you see (which is often negative, violent imagery). They can result from stress at work or by socially emphasized problems (such as AIDS or the threat of nuclear war).

The differences between daymares and nightmares are often quite pronounced, as are similarities between the two. The same issues and experiences that cause nightmares may result in daymares. The differences, however, are important. With a nightmare, you are asleep, and unless you're in a lucid dream, have little conscious control over what goes on. With a daymare, you are awake, capable of consciously recognizing what's there, and capable of consciously ending the scenario, or of being distracted by other people or outside happenings (thereby ending the daymare). And the daymares relate more closely to virtual reality than do the fantastic images that may appear in a nightmare (although it may be quite unrealistic to daydream that your spouse is cheating on you, that's more realistic than dreaming your spouse has become a fifty-foot tall monster, isn't it?).

Fantasy-prone individuals may, of course, include quite unrealistic imagery in their daydreams and therefore in their daymares (do horror fiction writers have daymares or do they simply daydream since their own imagery doesn't generally frighten them?).

What about psi? Does this tie in? Actually, it does in a couple of ways.

There have been studies of what personality characteristics are included in people who are "more psychic" than others. One of those is creativity. In studies with artists, writers, and musicians as compared to control groups not in the creative arts, the creative types came out ahead, often significantly so, in results indicating psi ability in the tests. Creative types appear to be more psychic, yet that may be simply because they tend not to view the world in absolutes, but more in possibilities than others (though I know plenty of individuals who cross that line). They may be more open to psi or belief in psi, and therefore allow the experiences and information to flow rather than dismissing it as "not real" or blocking it out all together.

Psi experiences occur not only in dreams and nightmares, but also in daydreams and daymares. In fact, you might have a psychic experience with vivid imagery or information presented to you while awake, and dismiss it as a daydream, or there may be a sudden flash of a disaster occurring that you shake off as imagination (albeit negative).

How do you tell the difference? As you will see as you read on in this book, the difference tends to be in the quality of the experience—you just "know." Whether you act on that information, or even *can* act on it at all flows from whether you can even recognize the information as "real" and not "imagined." Unfortunately, this is not easy to do, especially when the information comes through while we are daydreaming; it seems easier to rationalize it away.

One other question comes up with regards to nightmares.

As mentioned, the original thought surrounding nightmares had to do with evil spirits invading our dreams, with probable intentions to do us harm. The entire *Nightmare on Elm Street* series has to do with the spirit of Freddy Kruger invading the dreams of the living and, basically, hurting or killing them in reality by affecting them in their dreams. In *Dreamscape*, we see the psychic characters capable of leaving their bodies and entering the dreams of others. Although the intention of the scientist in the film is to help people work through problems in their dreams (as with Dennis Quaid's character helping a young boy work through a recurring nightmare of a snake creature), the intention of the government overseer of the project is to use the psychics to kill others in their dreams, thereby killing them in reality.

What happens if you die in your dream or nightmare? From personal experience, I can say I have died in a couple of dreams and I'm still around. I did not, fortunately or unfortunately, continue on in my dream to an afterlife, although I remember one dream from college days where I dreamed of dying and haunting my roommates as a ghost (it was fun!). I've spoken to others who have also experienced death in their dreams, and I've continued that falling dream, as have others, until I actually hit the ground. Usually, I just got up and brushed myself off, having no damage to my (dream) body at all (eat your heart out, Wile E. Coyote!).

Do people die as a result of their nightmares? Probably not. The probably is only because if people really have died as a result of a nightmare, we have no information that the dream was the cause of death, no way of knowing since there's no one around to tell us. No ghosts, to my knowledge, have shown up claiming this to be the way they died. So, since many have reported dying in dreams and lived to tell about it, we can probably assume there's nothing to worry about.

We have much to learn from nightmares (and even daymares) as they truly betray what is bothering us, what our deep-seated fears and anxieties are, and what the unresolved issues are in our lives. Looking at nightmares as helpful tools, as indicators of those unresolved issues, may make them easier to live with. Then again, maybe you can use that nightmare to become the next Stephen King or Clive Barker. . . .

CHAPTER 5

Sleep, Dreams, and the Body/Mind Connection

In the first chapter, I discussed some of the views of REM sleep and dreaming, and promised to get a bit more into the connections between the brain and the mind and where dreams may fit in. That leads us to look first at sleep itself—what it is and what it's for.

To start with, there are no definite answers when it comes to the above questions about sleep and its function. Sleep is thought to be a survival mechanism developed in mammals millions of years ago, due to the higher brain functioning and bodily requirements that mammals have. It is more than simply our bodies requiring rest, since there are other ways besides sleep to get rest. In addition, given the pattern of activity in the brain during sleep, sleep must be more than just a rest-inducing function for mammals. According to Dr. J. Allan Hobson in his book *The Dreaming Brain* (Basic Books, 1988): ". . . we can fairly assume that it will be difficult to establish any functional hypothesis convincingly because the mechanisms of sleep are only beginning to be understood at the cellular and molecular level" (page 288).

In general, mammals such as human beings are on a biological clock setting which creates a day pattern for us that works out to approximately twenty-four hours, though some mammals are on a lunar and tidal period of 24.8 hours. Our rhythm of the day has us needing wake time and sleep time at an approximate ratio of two to one, which means that we should sleep about eight hours of every twenty-four. While most people play around with the amount of time spent sleeping, most experts agree that between seven-and-a-half and eight hours are about right to give the body the amount of sleep it needs.

Many of us hear that we *need* less sleep as we grow older, often because of the observation of the amount of time spent sleeping by infants being so much greater than that of adults. However, while it is true that human infants need more sleep, older children and adults (of any age) need about the same amount of sleep. What happens as we get older, though, is that our patterns change to accommodate scheduling for things like work and leisure activities. We tend to sleep less during the week when we have to get up for work than on the weekends when we don't. Many people (myself included) use the days off to "catch up on" sleep. Unfortunately, many experts agree that "catching up" really doesn't work that way (although sleeping an extra few hours on weekends sure feels good to me).

Sleep appears to be rest not only for the body, but also a necessary change in brain patterns. Some have suggested that it allows for processing information, to aid memory and learning of the day's events. While our ancestors saw sleep as a shutdown of bodily functions and even a state akin to death, the research results we do have about sleep indicate that it allows for both physiological and psychological "housekeeping" to go on.

Studies of sleep deprivation indicate some personality alteration the longer the person is awake beyond simple change in behavior because the individual is tired. Sleep deprivation seems to undermine decision-making ability, especially where creativity is concerned. We (most of us) apparently need at least five hours of sleep per night to avoid a loss of such creative abilities and to avoid some degree of forgetfulness. Of course, there are some people whose body clocks allow them the need for less sleep (and there are those who need more than the "normal" amount to be able to function well).

With increased hours of sleep deprivation may come some

degree of paranoia and irrational judgment and behavior. In fact, prolonged wakefulness can lead to hallucinations, to daymares that are more rightly related to REM-state imagery. Finally, some studies show that some individuals may exhibit psychotic behavior patterns if deprived of sleep for as long as 100 hours or more.

In studies looking at REM deprivation, where the individuals are awakened the moment they enter REM in order to abort the REM state (and therefore dreaming), the person's system generally attempts to get to REM as soon as the individual goes back to sleep. Lengthy deprivation of REM sleep (and therefore dreaming) may lead to waking dreams (hallucinations). When the dream-deprived individual can get back into the REM state, it may be a lengthy period of dreaming, as though the individual was "dream starved" and "binges" on dreaming when allowed to.

It was in 1953 that Eugene Aserinsky and Nathaniel Kleitman of the University of Chicago "discovered" REM sleep. William Dement, working under Kleitman, continued the important work that connected REM sleep with dreaming. It was discovered that when you wake a person up during the REM stage of sleep, they will report dreaming 85 percent of the time. In 1957, Dement and Kleitman introduced the criteria for sleep stages. In 1959, Michel Jouvet and Francois Michel of Lyon, France, first published their observations of the inhibition of muscle tone (though they looked at the inhibition of muscle tone in conjunction with brain-wave activity in the sleep stages of cats), related to the paralysis in REM sleep.

The REM state, if you'll recall, is not the deepest stage of sleep. We go through a total of four stages of sleep a number of times throughout a typical sleep period (though there is often a fuzzy line between the two deepest levels of sleep). From the time we are awake until we hit the first stage, we are often in a pre-sleep stage called the "hypnagogic state." This is a state in which body muscles are loose and we feel very relaxed, with people often reporting the sensation of floating. It is in this hypnagogic state that we often can hear noises in our homes and exaggerate them into imaginary burglars or disasters. It is in this state that our waking consciousness is a little fuzzy and may wander, daydream in effect. And it is in this hypnagogic state that OBEs often take place. In fact, some of the techniques talked about by people purporting to teach others "astral projection" may be relaxation techniques that lead to a hypnagogic state, and therefore may actually yield OBEs (more on OBEs in general in chapter seven).

Once we pass by this pre-sleep state, we enter stage one of sleep, a light-sleeping stage which we will re-enter later as our REM state. In this first stage we are more easily awakened (although that may not be the case later when we come back to it in REM). We go past stage one into an intermediate sleep, stage two; we are more relaxed and harder to awaken. We pass through this into stage three, a deep state of sleep, and finally to stage four, the deepest state of non-REM sleep. In this state our bodies are completely relaxed and conserving energy, and we are very difficult to awaken. Animals who hibernate do so in a state like the deepest sleep we enter into, where their bodily functions are conserving energy for perhaps months at a time.

After a time, we leave the deeper states of sleep and head back up to stage one and enter REM sleep; the whole cycle taking about ninety minutes. In a typical night, we enter REM sleep four or five times, with the REM period becoming longer as sleep continues uninterrupted. In a typical seven- to eight-hour sleep period, approximately 50 percent of our dreaming falls into the last two hours of sleep. This means that if we cut our sleep short, we may have less time dreaming as the longer REM sleep periods are cut off.

As mentioned earlier, it is in the deepest levels of sleep that sleep disorders such as night terrors and sleepwalking—somnambulism—occur. It is estimated that between two and seven million Americans might have a less than "good" night's sleep, being bothered by sleep disorders of one form or another. Besides night terror and sleepwalking, these disorders include sleeptalking, narcolepsy, insomnia, teeth grinding, bedwetting, and sleep apnea.

In stages three and four of sleep, our muscular system is

not paralyzed as it is in REM sleep. The body may respond, while we are asleep, to particular orders to move around, talk, or experience intense fears (as in night terrors). Sleep-talking may be a disorder some people suffer from, with the sleeptalker generally making little sense, and not capable of any sort of conversation as the brain has little activity, as it would in REM sleep (although I did have a roommate in college who answered questions intelligibly, and honestly— unfortunately for him—he may have been in REM at the time, since he did recall dreaming some of the conversations).

Sleepwalkers generally do not move around too much, unlike what we see in some comedy films. Many also suffer from night terrors, and the movements made during the sleep-walk may be related to the night terror being experienced. Sleepwalkers may do a bit of sleeptalking at the time they move about. There are, however, exceptional cases of activity during sleepwalking. Some sleepwalkers have been known to get out of bed and head for the kitchen. Sleep eaters, who generally don't suffer from waking eating disorders, often wake to find their kitchens messed up, with evidence that they ate quite a bit during the night.

In rare cases, otherwise fairly non-violent people may com-mit an act of extreme violence in their sleep. In a recent legal case, a man in Toronto was acquitted from a murder charge on the basis that he was sleepwalking at the time. He had (sleep) driven several miles to where his in-laws lived and killed his mother-in-law and almost killed his father-in-law. He then ended up turning himself in to the police with the claim that he was sleepwalking at the time (horrified, appar-ently, at what he had done in his sleep).

He was found innocent by the jury after evidence of his personal history of sleepwalking was revealed, along with observations of his sleepwalking while he was in jail. Physical examination provided evidence of brain-wave patterns indic-ative of sleepwalkers. This sort of violence is extremely rare, fortunately.

There is, however, a similar movement-related disorder that occurs during REM sleep. REM behavior disorder covers people who apparently physically act out their dreams, the paralysis of the body that normally accompanies REM sleep not working for them. Sufferers of the disorder apparently move about, sometimes violently so, during occurrence of their dreams. Spouses or others have been injured when they have been present during such occurrences of dream-induced movements. Studies of this disorder indicate that most of the sufferers are men, generally older than fifty, though some children have experienced the disorder as well.

Another non-REM disorder is sleep apnea, which relates to restricted breathing or stopping breathing during sleep. This disorder, which usually affects children and middle-aged (and older) men, affects the throat muscles, which tend to relax so much as to close off breathing. The discomfort and problem of the brain and body not getting enough oxygen generally causes the sleeper to wake up just enough so that the connections between brain and throat muscles are reinstated, causing them to work again. Such awakenings can disrupt sleep enough to cause the individual to be prone to sleepiness during waking hours.

On the other side of the deep-sleep coin is insomnia and narcolepsy. Millions of people suffer from insomnia of one form or another, having difficulty in either getting to sleep or in staying asleep. They may wake up continually through the night, or may wake up too early and not be able to get back to sleep.

Temporary insomnia may be a result of stress, worries, or even excitement in our daily lives. Such stresses and worries that keep us awake may simply relate to worrying about getting to sleep in the first place. For many, a self-perpetuating cycle of insomnia can occur, when they worry, after not being able to get to sleep, whether they can get to sleep at all. You can't sleep, so you worry about not sleeping, the worrying keeping you from sleeping, which continues the insomnia. Dealing with the stresses that may cause such temporary insomnia will usually rid us of that insomnia.

Chronic insomnia, on the other hand, may be a result of poor sleep habits or irregular sleep patterns. Perhaps the insomniac's sleep pattern is not a "regular" ninety-minute pattern in and out of the cycles. Or perhaps the person suffers from a sleep-phase syndrome, in which the body's internal clock is out of phase with what we consider "ordinary" sleep patterns, sleeping at night (they just can't sleep at night, because their biological clocks have them on a schedule where they ought to be awake at night and sleep during the day).

Drugs such as sleeping pills are often used by people to get to sleep when insomnia strikes. Unfortunately, that can lead to "drug dependency insomnia," where one cannot sleep without first taking the drug. Often, there are simple ways to deal with insomnia, from relaxation and meditative techniques, to simply staying out of bed for any reason other than sleep (and sex, of course). Too often the bed becomes a place of activity, from reading to watching television, and not just a place for sleeping. Making the major activity association between the bed and sleep seems to help a great deal in overcoming sleeplessness. Finally, adopting a regular schedule of sleep and waking time may reduce any unfortunate insomnia. For those suffering from sleep-phase syndrome, altering their schedules (so they are awake at night and asleep during the day) seems to work well.

Just as our dreams are affected by the events, moods, or thoughts of the day, stresses, whether psychologically induced or physically induced (such as illness) affect our sleep patterns. Insomnia may be caused by worrying or thinking too much about the thing that's bothering us that day, or by being in an unhappy situation (from a bad job to a split in a relationship). In addition, sleeping too much can affect us adversely. For example, sleeping very late on a Sunday morning (maybe into the early afternoon) may result in difficulty getting to sleep early on Sunday night (early because you have to work the next day).

An opposite sleep disorder from insomnia is that of narcolepsy, in which one tends to fall asleep at often inappropriate (and sometimes dangerous) times. This disorder, which appears to be genetically related, may afflict over a quarter of a million people in this country alone. Narcoleptics may fall asleep at work, at the wheel of a car, in a movie, or even during sexual intercourse. They may have a different pattern to their sleep, falling asleep for short periods of time and often immediately into the REM state, and may also tend to have hallucinations. Narcolepsy can be treated through the use of stimulants.

Finally, humans may have problematic sleep patterns due to post-traumatic stress syndrome. As discussed in the previous chapter, nightmares and night terrors can be related to living through a traumatic situation in our waking lives. Dreams and other reactions related to this syndrome can be merely symptoms of the syndrome which, according to therapists, should be addressed by working through the trauma. Other forms of anxiety dreams similar to post-traumatic, stress-induced dreams may play a key role in helping us to recover from emotional wounds (from relationship problems, grief due to death of a loved one, problems with work) other than those as dramatic as the physical events which cause the syndrome (such as seeing someone killed, being raped, living through a devastating natural disaster, and so on).

Dreams are often indicators of physical as well as psychological problems. In various studies, including one by Dr. Robert Smith of Michigan State University, it's been indicated that content and themes of dreams may reflect health problems, as in a study of cardiac patients which showed that those with "worse" heart disease had more dreams involving incidents of death or separation from family. Looking at our dreams may lead us to uncover physical ailment pointers. Part of us may be better able to recognize the signs of physical illness than our conscious minds, and may play out those "diagnoses" in our dreams. In addition, our dreams give us access to important, emotional issues in our lives, which could in turn affect our physical health.

Dreams may also have positive effects on the physical body. Studies of visualization techniques with healing indicate that such techniques may positively affect the body's pattern of healing. Dealing with illness in dreams may create a physical effect. Evidence indicates that visualized rehearsal of physical movements, from dance to sleight of hand, may at some level prepare the muscles for such activities. Dreams may yield physical solutions to problems, as evidenced by athletes like golfer Jack Nicklaus who dreamed a solution to a bad golf swing. Lucid dream studies with sexual activity going on in the dream state reveal physical arousal in the dreamer as though the dream sex were a real, objective experience.

Are dreams something separate from brain function or a result of it? In chapter one, I talked about the theories of J. Allan Hobson, Francis Crick, and Graeme Mitchison. Hobson's "activation synthesis model" has dreams as a by-product of activity in the brain stem. During REM sleep, there is activity in the brain stem that stimulates particular neurons using the chemical neurotransmitter acetylcholine. Neurons using acetylcholine are effectively "on" during REM sleep, while the neurotransmitters serotonin and norepinephrine are "off" during REM (and "on" during non-REM sleep). The random firings of the neurons during REM are interpreted by the cortex of the brain and woven into some kind of "story" to make some sense of the signals received. There is an indication that acetylcholine is related directly to dreaming, as injections of a similar chemical into animals yields REM sleep in those animals.

Hobson puts forward the idea that it is this activity in the brain stem that causes dreaming, that the brain then has to take the signals and achieve some kind of meaningful integration of them, and that the content can be read directly, rather than considered more symbolic of deep-seated wishes and issues that many consider the cause of the dreams. The brain activity, not the psychological issues, cause dreaming, and often its form. Excessive firings of the neurons related to our optic system cause more "visual" dreams. He does suggest that the brain may be creative in its creation of storylines for the dreams, and even just plain entertaining. Dreams may be simply there to be used for amusement, or may reflect some inner issues. Much of what we remember or make of our dreams may occur after the dream, using waking logic to construct something that makes sense to our conscious minds.

REM sleep, according to Hobson, may fulfill its place in us as a sort of maintenance program, even aiding in our development as human beings as we grow up. "Early in development, REM sleep could provide the brain with a highly organized program of internal action. This program is stereotyped, redundant, and reliable—all features useful to a developing system.'' (Hobson, *The Dreaming Brain*, page 292.)

According to Stephen LaBerge, the ''activation synthesis model'' may explain the physiological *how* we dream, but not the psychological *why* we dream (or why we dream *what* we dream). There is the added problem of lucid dreams, where we are effectively conscious in our dreams, indicating signals and information processing in the REM state that is anything but random.

What is REM and why don't we remember our dreams all the time? According to the controversial view held by Crick and Mitchison, dreams are not meant to be remembered, and may even be harmful to us if we remember them. REM sleep and dreaming is a way of processing the overload of information that our brains get in our waking state. In REM and dreaming, the brain is sorting through information in order to save the important stuff to long-term memory and flush out any garbage in the system. Remembering dreams may mean remembering garbage the brain is trying to get rid of.

If this sounds like the workings of a computer, that's fine, since the brain is effectively that. Christopher Evans, author of *Landscapes of the Night*, takes that analogy and puts it to good use. In large-scale computer systems, where there is an enormous amount of information added on any given day, there is often a need to ''take the system down'' or ''offline'' to add bulks of information, update files, scan for errors, do system building, and process that information and integrate it into the system's architecture. One might consider the brain as a computer, looking at REM sleep and dreaming as that ''off-line'' time period, given that normal body and brain functions are not going on at the time. As with a computer system, the normal demands on the system are shut out in sleep, allowing for some time periods (REM sleep) to process information and build/rebuild the system. Such a process may happen in a single REM session or extend over many periods if the issue or information being dealt with requires extensive attention.

In dreams, information gathered during the day may be compared and contrasted with information gathered in the past and stored in permanent, long-term memory. Some information may be similar to "duplicate files" in a computer, and therefore may be processed out of existence, or at least out of our conscious minds. Some may be "erased," as with perhaps some of the unnecessary "garbage" Crick and Mitchison talk about. However, most dream experts agree that the process is providing helpful information that can be, and perhaps should be, remembered. Dr. Rosalind Cartwright of the Rush-Presbyterian-St. Luke's Medical Center in Chicago, for example, believes that the processing of information to include comparison of the day's events with past memory occurs to put the information into perspective, to bring it in line with the personality of the individual.

Hobson has suggested that we forget our dreams not because they are meant to be forgotten, but because they are stored in short-term, rather than long-term memory (norepinephrine and serotonin, which are not being produced in REM sleep, are necessary for long-term memory). To continue the computer analogy, in dreams some (perhaps all) of the information is squeezed onto what I'll call "floppy disk memory" rather than "saved" to the "hard disk" of long-term memory.

As Hobson suggested, dreaming and REM sleep may be signs of processing of information, and therefore directly related to learning. The mechanism of REM sleep may stimulate higher centers of the brain, thereby having the functions of maintaining the central nervous system and helping it develop in children. Michel Jouvet of the University of Lyon proposed that during dreaming, we are practicing, rehearsing, trying out instinctual or genetically-programmed behaviors in a state in which our bodies are effectively paralyzed, and so without consequence. Such rehearsal may work for you in a physical way, as mentioned earlier, in getting your muscles ready for an unfamiliar activity. This may be why we dream so much in early stages of our lives and find there is a decrease of amount of time spent in REM and dreaming sleep when we become older.

To take the maintenance idea a step further, Dr. Ian Oswald of the University of Edinburgh has postulated that REM sleep occurs to allow the central nervous system to make repair to worn-down brain tissue and connections. During non-REM sleep, growth hormones are released that repair the body. REM sleep allows for the same to be done for the brain, with dreams occurring as a by-product.

REM sleep may be an evolutionary development of a mechanism needed to keep the brain efficiently operating. The brain may be processing information in REM and through dreams, and may be using this special state of activity to keep brain tissue in good working order, or as Oswald suggests, to repair it.

We know that both the body and the mind affect dreaming. Physical condition can affect the occurrence of REM sleep, as well as provide cues for the content and themes of dreams. Our physical state when we go to sleep may affect dreams, as well. While eating "bad" food or too much food may not cause "bad" dreams and nightmares, it may affect our dreams and their content because of the ways our bodies are affected by that food. The positions in which we sleep and whether we experience any cramping may affect the content of our dreams, and any signals from the "outside", from an alarm clock going off to a siren from a fire engine to an earth tremor, may cause a reaction in our dreams. Alcohol and drugs can affect our dreams, though they tend to decrease or even suppress REM sleep and dreaming.

The mind and what we think and feel affects dreaming. Emotional feelings and moods affect are dreams, intentions and expectations also come into play. Verbal messages and expressions heard during the day may be translated into visual imagery in dreams. According to Rosalind Cartwright, in an interview in *Health* magazine (July 1989): "Dreams perform important emotional homework . . . They review and revise our concept of who we are and rehearse where we are going. When life is tough, dreams provide a mechanism for repair."

Essentially, the functions of the body and brain seem to be tied to sleep in general and REM sleep in particular. There are effects of our physical and mental states on sleep and dreaming, as there are effects of our sleep patterns and dreams on our physical and mental states. We are still at the beginning of the pathway toward understanding the mind/brain connection in ourselves, and we know less than we'd like to admit.

Where psi and its place within our own functioning is concerned, we know very little, and in fact, a lot less than what we know about sleep and dreams. Psychic experiences are, unlike dreams, less than accepted in many societies, and have yet to be tied to a particular physical or mental state. Experimentation on psi moves on, with some research now being conducted in connecting such activity (if it even goes on within the biological framework) to particular areas of the brain, thanks to new techniques in brain-mapping (magnetic resonance imaging and neuro-magnetic mapping, for instance—using magnetic fields and computers to create a fuller, more highly defined picture of activity and structure in the body and brain).

Physiologically-based studies of both dreams and psi may eventually yield the definites of such mechanisms, the "hows" of those activities, but such studies may never yield the "whys." If, as many propose, dreams are a by-product of brain activity, where does that leave the intentional dream, the lucid dream? Good question, and one for which we have no answer at the moment.

So, let's wake up in our dreams for a time and see where that leads us. Let's go lucid.

CHAPTER 6

Conscious While Dreaming: Lucid Dreams

[Note: For extensive discussions of lucid dreaming, I recommend you read Stephen LaBerge's book, *Lucid Dreaming*, and *Control Your Dreams* by Jayne Gackenbach and Jane Bosveld, as well as other books listed in Appendix C of this book.]

A friend or loved one presents you with an interesting proposal for a weekend trip. Needing to take a day or two off from work to go on this trip, you say "Let me go home and sleep on it." That night you sleep and begin to dream. In the dream, you suddenly realize you're completely aware you are in a dream. In the dreamworld, you can explore the possible benefits and consequences of the trip and taking the time off from work. You go through the possibilities, come to a decision, and remind yourself to remember the dream when you wake up. That day, you call your friend and pass on your decision, feeling good because you literally "slept on it."

Aware in your dreams? Conscious it *is* a *dream*?

This is lucid dreaming, a particular kind of dream state for which we have evidence in the historical record going back as far as we have records of dreams themselves. While the lucid dream is not one everyone experiences, it is, according to many experts, one everyone can ease into or learn, and it is a particular dream state that has only recently gained acceptance (recent as far as the entire history of dreams is concerned).

The term "lucid" as applied to dreams is credited to the Dutch physician Frederik Willems Van Eeden in 1913, who coined and presented it in a paper to the British Society for Psychical Research (SPR), the world's oldest formal society studying psychic phenomena from a scientific standpoint (the second oldest being the American Society for Psychical Research—ASPR—in New York). However, while the coining of the term and recognition of the state of lucidity goes back to 1913, and the historical record of such experiences much further, lucid dreaming has had to travel a rocky road to acceptance.

After Van Eeden, Celia Green, a British parapsychologist, was the first to extensively discuss the dream state in her book *Lucid Dreams* in the 1960s. A scholarly work, it unfortunately did nothing for the acceptance of lucid dreams as a real dream experience. It was perhaps the association of lucid dreams to psychic phenomena that created such acceptance problems.

Psychic experience and parapsychology have for a long time faced acceptance problems, with a great deal of denial by the scientific "establishment." That the lucid dream got its "name" in a paper to the SPR and the first scholarly treatment in a book by a parapsychologist, even though lucidity in dreams is not a psychic phenomenon, did nothing to interest the psychological community that was ignoring and often lambasting anything to do with parapsychology, psychic phenomena, or the popular "occult."

While Green's work saw little acceptance, there was a growing interest in the sixties to look at altered states of consciousness. Dr. Charles Tart's work with altered states did much for the interest in them, and by association the interest in dream states. (Tart is perhaps best known to others with respect to his work in parapsychology—there's that connection again.)

The writings of Patricia Garfield, Ph.D., a San Francisco therapist (see her book *Creative Dreaming*), and Ann Faraday, Ph.D. (*Dream Power, The Dream Game*) in the seventies worked wonders with introducing many concepts having to do with dream-work and lucid dreams into the general public's consciousness. The writings of Carlos Castaneda have also been credited as having a great impact on awareness of altered states, dreaming, and lucid dreaming.

However, it is the experimental work on lucidity in dreams at Stanford University by LaBerge and others in the late seventies that finally brought the beginnings of acceptance, although the first papers were turned down for publication due to, it appears, philosophical problems ("It," whatever "it" happens to be at the time, "is impossible, and therefore can't and doesn't happen."). "Belief system" conflicts have plagued science since the beginning, and both physical and social scientists are guilty of the offense of non-acceptance (or even non-consideration) of a paper, view, theory, or finding simply on the grounds that it "must be impossible." After finally getting their paper published, there was a positive response, and the study of lucid dreaming was off and running (although it had already been running at Stanford).

The early work at Stanford on lucid dreams came from the angle of communication from the dream state. If you were "aware" and "conscious" in the dream state, and the rapid eye movements could be correlated to particular movements of the dreamer within the dream, a code of sorts could be worked out and communication could take place. LaBerge, himself skilled at lucid dreaming, and others so skilled (whom he has called "oneironauts"), were able to communicate from within their dream states, thus showing that such a conscious dream state does exist.

It's interesting to note that while the folks at Stanford were working on their lucid dream studies in the late seventies, Keith Hearne at the University of Hull in England was working with lucid dreamer Alan Worsley, also using eye movements as communication from the lucid dream state. While Hearne published first, it is to the group at Stanford that credit for gaining acceptance of lucid dreaming goes to. But the parallel idea of using eye movements with the lucid dream and REM state as a communication ploy was obviously the right one.

Particular patterns of eye movements were agreed upon and carried out by the oneironauts, and that led to other studies and findings. Through eye signals and playing at counting and singing in the dream, it has been established that elapsed time in the dream state is approximately the same as that in "real life," in the world outside the dream. The old tale of dreams allowing you to cover vast amounts of time within the dream, as though time itself were compressed, has been shown to be untrue. Part of the reason this time compression may not be *able* to work relates to the time it takes the pathways of the brain to send signals and do anything with them. No matter how fast we think, we can't keep track of significantly small fragments of a second. For full months to actually occur as minutes, something would have to change in the speed at which we process that information. So, as mentioned earlier, it's been suggested that we make use of techniques similar to the movies or theater in "compressing" time.

The time issue is one that has been leveled at some of the conceptual framework around ESP. Most talk in terms of "instantaneous" knowing or transmission of information from one place or mind to another human mind at some distance away. However, given the speed of light and the time it takes information to be processed, a signal from thousands of miles away would get to us in less time than it would take us to realize we even received the message. It would seem instantaneous, since it would take us a moment to react to it.

Studies of lucid dreams indicate that the imagery produced in such a dream is often "more real" than what we see in the physical world. Colors are more vivid, everything is in sharper focus, and it seems ultra-real. Recognition of that, in itself, may be a way a person "wakes up" in the dream. Imagery in such dreams is reported to be more like reality than any imagery we can produce in visualization practices while awake.

How do we become "lucid" in our dreams? Generally this happens spontaneously, and people often remember such single-occurrence lucid dreams, though they appear to be infrequent or really one-time occurrences. Lucid dreaming on a more-than-once-in-a-great-while basis seems to be a natural occurrence in 5 to 10 percent of the population. Dr. Jayne Gackenbach and others have suggested that lucid dreamers are less likely to be neurotic or depressed personalities.

Most lucid dreams are "dream-initiated," and occur because something within the dream alerts the dreamer that it *is* a dream. Thoughts within the dream such as "Isn't this odd?" or "This can't really be happening, can it?" or a recognition that what's going on bears little resemblance to real experience can seemingly jog the consciousness of the dreamer to come to the conclusion of "Oh, I must be dreaming."

Memory or recognition of a situation being one we've experienced before can spark lucidity. For example, let's say you're having a dream of going on vacation. You board the plane, arrive at the destination, and suddenly realize you'd been there before with the same people; it's like a déjà vu experience in the dream. This may bring on a realization that it is, in fact, a memory, that some aspects of the experience seem too real or maybe unreal, and bring on a questioning of yourself about whether you're dreaming or not. Questioning the reality of the dream is a first step to lucidity in that dream, as it will put you toward some detachment within the dream, where you are now examining the "reality" in which you find yourself a bit more closely, looking for other signs that it is a dream.

To stay lucid in the dream, we apparently need some degree of detachment, as though we continue to remind our (dream) selves that we are dreaming, that what is being observed and participated in is just a dream. This "self" in the dream is a construct of oneself, whether it's "you" or some version of yourself you create or even another character role. Remembering that the "role" is just that so you don't get too involved in "playing the part" appears to be important. Forgetting it's a dream might end the lucidity of it.

If you feel yourself falling out of the lucid state within your dream, you might try to focus your (dream) attention on an object or individual in the dream. Garfield suggests that a constant state of alertness in the lucid dream may be necessary to stay lucid, while "there is a danger that excitement over the joy of your freedom and power will wake you" (Garfield, *Creative Dreaming*, Ballantine Books, 1989, page 120). Somehow, you have to strike a happy medium. In addition, you can program yourself, while awake or while in the dream, to remember you are dreaming. "I will remember I'm dreaming" might be a good mantra to repeat before sleep or while in the dream. LaBerge has suggested that if you feel yourself falling out of lucidity, you spin your dream self around like a top or like a small child would. This spinning technique apparently keeps you on your own focused, conscious awareness of the dream.

While we seem to be able to perform miracles in lucid dreams, there is some degree of equivalence to our "real" physical selves as far as what we can do or accomplish in the dream state, as though there are still some limits on our own abilities. However, such limitations may be stronger with regard to mental achievements than physical ones. Controlling the dream (or your imagination) so you picture yourself as Superman knocking an asteroid off its collision course with Earth would be easier than, say, dreaming (or imagining) what it's like to be a super-genius.

There appears to be some internally consistent logic being applied, so that miracles are "possible," given the "physical laws" of the dream world you've created. Science fiction differs from fantasy fiction in that true science fiction is based on the "laws" of our universe and extrapolations from those laws. There is often a bending of such laws to allow for plot devices such as faster-than-light travel or time travel (which may not be impossible even by current laws of physics), and certainly extraterrestrial life is plausible. These are tales based on science. Fantasy, on the other hand, usually involves magic or supernatural forces that can play with the fabric of reality and supersede the laws of physics. Good fantasy fiction, however, also creates its own laws, so that even magic works according to the rules, which are usually logical when related to one another.

Our dreams, therefore, may create new rules to play by, but are still limited to internal logic and to how much our imaginations can do.

There are, however, limitations to other mental activities. For example, most lucid dreamers find reading impossible, if not very hard to do. You might try reading as a test to see if you are dreaming or not. If you pick up a book and can read it, you are generally awake. If you can't read it, or you turn away and back and it now says something different (the text has changed), you are undoubtedly dreaming (and that realization may be enough to cause you to be completely lucid in the dream).

In discussing psychic abilities with psychics, and specifically with people who are good at remote viewing, they've mentioned that reading is often difficult if not impossible when receiving information clairvoyantly. Visual images make much better targets for psychics, and one might make the analogy to the translation of verbal information (spoken or read while awake) into images while dreaming.

In general, our own actions in the dreams are similar to those in waking life. According to LaBerge, we walk around in life and in lucid dreams with some actions that are "reflexive" (actions which are carried out in response to a situation purely from a reflex standpoint, such as keeping our balance), "instinctive" (actions or reactions to stimuli in life and in the dream state which are programmed into us, such as running from a dangerous situation out of fear), "habitual" (based on patterns we've developed in ourselves over our lifetime), and "deliberate" (where we can consciously choose to act/react in a very deliberate fashion, whether awake or in a lucid dream).

Since our own non-deliberate actions tend to follow along within certain boundaries in dream, deliberate, conscious action applied within the lucid dream (when applied to using the dreams for problem-solving or some other applications) should bear some resemblance to reality. In confronting a problem situation, such as making a decision about going away for the weekend and having to miss a day of work, throwing in a "magical" or "miraculous" solution (such as, say, having someone in the dream hand you a check for a million dollars so you can quit your job, or stopping time in the dream so you can go without missing a day of work) will not help too much when applying the dream solutions to real-life conditions. And while destroying the "evil ogre" that is your boss may be cathartic in the dream and help you feel better, you certainly won't go far when faced with the real-life boss (not unless you know any magic sword dealers).

What good are lucid dreams if you can't play with reality in order to get to solutions? First of all, looking for solutions to real-life conflict in a lucid dream does not mean you can't be creative in how you play with the possible solutions. Running through a series of possible scenarios based on different decisions still allows a great deal of play with "reality." By expressing some degree of control in your dream, the solution presented to any problem or issue is based on your ability to think through the problem and possible solutions, rather than on reflex action (as might be presented in a "normal" dream).

You can even look for creative solutions to physical problems or for ways to rehearse physical movements, as mentioned in the last chapter. As a magician, I've learned several sleight-of-hand moves by rehearsing them over and over in my (waking) mind. Somehow, that has made performing the effect much easier even the first time, and made it look a lot better to my audience (since, mentally, I can view the effect as it is seen from the audience's perspective). In lucid dreams, the imagery is much more akin to reality than in waking visualizations.

So, within the lucid dream world, you can take a better look at problems you're having and observe what the benefits or consequences of any chain of events you set into motion might be, almost as if you are both scriptwriter and director of the film that is your dream. At a moment's notice, you can change the script, add or subtract characters, and redirect the actions toward new conclusions. Engaging dream characters in conversation will enable the "you" that is creating the dream to interact with the "you" that is lucid in the dream.

As an aid to decision-making, the lucid dream can therefore be invaluable in weighing all possibilities. In addition, you can be creative in your approach to problems and innovative in looking for solutions, all without worrying about what anyone else is going to think or how anyone else will be affected (since it all occurs within your own dreamworld).

Lucid dreaming may be the perfect state for artists to see what a new painting or sculpture being imagined might look like, for architects to check out new designs, or for scientists to play out experiments. It may be the perfect way for a screenwriter to see how the movie will "look" or a musician to "listen" to a new piece. In essence, lucid dreaming may be the best place for people to be creative without having to extend themselves in reality. You can purposefully play out ideas with extremely vivid imagery and few boundaries. Perhaps this is why so many writers have been able to gain ideas from their dreams, since the dream state, lucid or not, allows much greater freedom in creativity than the waking state.

Facing up to your fears and nightmares, to conflict, is another application of lucid dreaming. There are, however, a couple of schools of thought where this is concerned. Some who work with lucid dreams express the idea of manipulating the "reality" of the dreamworld in which conflict occurs, of changing the dream so the nightmare images either go away or are purposefully overcome. Changing the dream, fighting and overcoming the monsters, may not always work to your benefit.

Facing and overcoming the monster in a dream may work in some cases. However, as we discussed with nightmares, asking the menacing thing "What are you here for?" or "Who or what are you?" usually brings about a response and often a transformation of the image into something friendly. Remember that the images come from within yourself and therefore are representative of you. Taking advantage of lucidity in this situation will allow you to more or less be your own therapist, to identify and even work through problem areas in your life. Just remember that while this may be good for you, you may still need to deal with deep-set issues with a real therapist.

Hiding conflict or escaping from it is often a way we deny our own aggressive tendencies. According to Gayle Delaney: "To confront and understand threatening or perplexing dream images is, in my opinion, the best way to approach dream guidance, because the rewards of loving and understanding your enemies seems far greater than those of demolishing them." (*Living Your Dreams*, page 172).

Reduction of anxiety by working through situations that cause such worries is very workable in lucid dreams. As the director of your own dream, you can push things in various appropriate directions to show yourself that some anxieties are unfounded, while situations that cause others can be lived with or "fixed" in waking life.

Phobias have been dealt with by people in their dreams. As controller of the dream world, you might bring in the thing you are afraid of, and set up situations where you become more used to it, finally becoming somewhat comfortable. For example, if you are claustrophobic, you might place your dream self in a setting that is just closed in enough to feel anxious. However, realizing you are in complete control of the "reality" you're in, you can begin to work with smaller and smaller enclosed spaces, until your comfort level with enclosures is enough that you can face the real world with new confidence that such a setting will not adversely affect you. You are effectively healing a phobia, by becoming immune to the situation that causes the "illness."

Healing the body may be an application of lucid dream imagery. Studies involving waking visualization techniques, such as Carl Simonton's work with cancer patients, indicate that positive imagery can help some people overcome illness or somehow instigate a speedier healing process within the body. Carrying that further to the lucid dream state, where just about anything is possible, the imagery and effect may be stronger than waking visualization techniques. You may be able to use the signals the body is giving you through your unconscious to recognize an illness and start the healing process; that our minds have an effect on the health of our bodies has been established. Just how the mind can work its wonders to heal us (or make us ill, for that matter) is still not understood. However, lucid dreaming may provide a more direct access to the internal workings of the mind/body connection, and therefore a valuable tool in healing ourselves.

And from the more "selfish" end of things, lucid dreaming can be applied to simple, conscious wish-fulfillment. Want to have a date (or more) with that famous movie star? Want to "play" at being James Bond? Want to captain the starship Enterprise and "boldly go where no one has gone before?" Lucid dreaming . . . yeah, that's the ticket. It may be the ultimate form of entertainment, as it is bound only by our imagination and is (or at least seems) participatory.

Of course, we do not have to control our lucid dreams to get something out of them. Often, merely being a conscious observer in a dream will allow us to learn more about ourselves and ask ourselves important questions. Being an "outside observer" in a dream is like consciously watching a play, albeit one about our inner workings, and being able to analyze it as it goes along. We can learn much, even without direct participation (and probably can even "rewind" and see the "instant replay" if we miss something the first time).

So can we train ourselves to have a lucid dream? If so, how?

There are several techniques for achieving lucidity in your dreams. There also appear to be some requirements for lucid dreaming. One of them relates to how you feel about lucid dreaming. You must be motivated to have such dreams, as you must be motivated if you wish to remember your dreams. You must intend to remember them and be lucid in them. Dream recall, memory of your dreams, is important. If you can't remember you had a lucid dream, how can you tell if you did (or did not)? We'll talk about dream recall more a bit later.

LaBerge has mentioned that even asking yourself while awake, "How do I know I'm not dreaming now?" on a regular basis can program you to ask the same question while in a dream. That suspicion, that recognition that it *may* be a dream is often enough to make you lucid in your dreams. Reminding yourself that you will both remember your dreams and be awake in them helps as well, and repeating such reminders at bedtime will often have a great impact.

There are a few methods that researchers have relayed that seem to help induce lucid dreams. Often, the asking of the question above is a starting point. Rehearsal of a dream you'd like to have, or incubating, pondering a question with the intent of waking up in a dream to deal with it can help program your dream-state to allow for lucidity. Most crucial, however, seems to be the *intention* to be awake in your dreams, recognition of what is real and what is a dream even while awake, and dream recall to reinforce the patterns of lucid dreaming. Using remembered dreams, going over them in your mind with the added image of you being awake or lucid in those dreams, can help set you toward that actually happening with subsequent dreams.

Keith Harary and Pamela Weintraub have also developed a practical program to work toward lucid dreaming. Published as *Lucid Dreams in 30 Days: The Creative Dream Program* (St. Martin's Press, 1989), the program allows you to train yourself to wake up in your dreams at a slow pace so as not to force the issue, and covers dream recall as part of that process. According to Harary, the idea of a thirty-day program allows for gradual development of the ability to have lucid dreams on a regular basis, and to allow yourself to get adjusted to the process of dreaming in a conscious fashion.

Lucid dreaming may allow for a conscious recognition of the extra information that may come into our minds which we've deemed "psychic." If you are aware you are dreaming, you may be able to isolate psychic information or even initiate the retrieval of such information. ESP in lucid dreams is an interesting prospect, and one not really researched as yet.

If you do learn lucid dreaming, you might even attempt telepathic contact with the dreams or conscious mind of another, as in the movie *Dreamscape* (get the feeling I liked this movie?). Once in a lucid dream, you might suggest or state to yourself that you are powerfully psychic, and proceed to seek out information on specific problems or questions using this new-found "lucid dreaming psi." In the lucid dream, for example, act as though you have telepathy and try to contact a friend or relative, or use clairvoyance/remote viewing to peek in on an event at another location, or watch a movie you've never seen or visit a location you've never been to. Then, once awake, check the results of the dream experience with the physical reality. If the physical reality matches the dreamed information, congratulate yourself. You may have just learned how to become instantly psychic, if only in that lucid dream state. And that ability, even dreamed up, may put you one step closer toward conscious psychic experience.

One particular form of experience connected to psi that often comes up in a discussion of lucid dreaming is the out of body experience. LaBerge and and a few others see the OBE as a very vivid form of lucid dreaming, one in which the self-image is placed outside the body and in the real world, yet where all is still a dream. The idea that the OBE may be simply a clairvoyant experience where we merely *think* we're not in our bodies may have support in the lucid dream where psi-derived information is brought in to the dream world. On the other hand, Harary's view (which I and many others looking at OBEs share) is that the lucid dream and the OBE are two different states. You can have an OBE while in a lucid dream, but having such experience does not mean you are dreaming, lucid or not.

In a paper presented at the 1989 Parapsychological Association, Rex Stanford discussed a study which indicated a correlation between lucid dreaming and OBEs that take place in the dream state; There was no correlation of lucid dreaming to OBEs as they occur in the hypnagogic or waking state. It was proposed, however, that lucidity may be some kind of launching point or bridge for the OBE, allowing the "whatever it is that leaves the body" to leave. In the next chapter, I'll discuss the OBE/dream connection more fully.

It is possible that the lucid dream state gives us access to some of our own psychokinetic ability. It was in lucid dreams that George Orr, the main character of Ursula K. LeGuin's *The Lathe of Heaven* programmed his dreams to change the world, changes that came into effect as he awoke. There are no studies to my knowledge of attempted psychokinetic effects on the waking world from a lucid dream state, and I really haven't heard of any such experiences, but who knows.

There are also those lucid dreams which may even transcend our awareness of the material world. Called "high lucid" dreams, these provide glimpses of what the human consciousness might evolve to through spiritual transformation, through a sense of true freedom, a oneness with the universe, and/or a "knowing," a "cosmic awareness" (to quote more than a few Marvel Comics).

Lucid dreams should not be taken lightly. As mentioned by Gackenbach and Bosveld, in and of itself, lucid dreaming is more or less a hollow accomplishment. If you don't use it for anything, what good is it? Since it may provide incredible insight into ourselves, use it for work within yourself.

In the lucid dream, we are aware of being in a dream. This may be the only "definite" we can get out of any state of our existence. Can we really say we are truly "awake" while our bodies are not asleep? At least in the lucid dream, we can say we are truly "dreaming" and mean it. Or is there more to the lucid dream, to dreams in general? Are we leaving behind the body and entering a dream realm or even re-entering, in an "astral form," the real world?

Let's go out of body and see, shall we?

CHAPTER 7

Dreaming Your Way Out Of Your Body

Have you ever had a dream that you floated out of your body? Maybe one in which you flew to another place, either a place where you "saw" friends or relatives, or a place you'd never been before? Ever think that maybe somehow the dream was true, that you really went there somehow?

How about this: Ever have the sensation while awake that you were somehow "out" of your body? Maybe you even felt, while awake, that you were somehow floating above your own body?

Both scenarios, the experience occurring while dreaming and the experience while awake might be considered out of body experiences (OBEs).

As mentioned in chapter three, the OBE is not strictly a psychic experience, but rather a psychological one; simply the *experience* that you somehow felt yourself *out*side your own body. It's when you can somehow remember what you just observed while in the out-of-body state, and that information, which is not already in your memory and not available to you through your normal senses or logical inference, checks out as true.

Whether something actually leaves the body is a question left unanswered at this time. Occultists (and old books on psychical research) often use the phrase "astral projection" since they describe the projection of some "astral body" or form or spirit. This astral body somehow leaves the corporeal body behind and can travel elsewhere, without the constraints of the physical body, and observe other locations and people, bringing the memories back to the body. The astral body is often described by writers on astral projection as being tethered to the physical form by a "silver cord," to prevent the astral spirit from being lost or cut off. If the cord breaks, according to these occult experts on astral projection, the astral body may not find its way back to the physical body, and the body may die or become inhabited (possessed) by another "free" spirit.

But since the out of body experiences that people have (and I include psychics who claim OBEs more pointedly in this group) don't fit the occultist mode of the astral double, we really can't just accept the soul-leaves-body concept at face value. In fact, most people who have an OBE do not report a silver cord (or any color cord) at all, and some have even noted their surprise at *not* "seeing" a cord during an OBE. So what's really going on here?

I also mentioned in chapter three the parallels between a clairvoyant or remote viewing experience and the OBE. The only difference appears to be that in the clairvoyant viewing of a distant location, we don't visit the scene, the view comes to us. In the OBE, the same information may be attainable, but somehow part of us goes there to do the viewing. There may be little or no difference in these psychic experiences except in how the viewer perceives the way the information is gathered.

Let's say we have a person who is capable of remote-viewing a distant locale like the island of Moorea in French Polynesia (off the island of Tahiti). Let's say that the "psychic" has a problem in accepting what's happening when he gets the "view" of Moorea, maybe he just has a hard time accepting that the information "just comes to him." But maybe he wouldn't have such a hard time accepting the information if he could actually be there to somehow to observe the scenery. So, his mind more or less clothes the information in an OBE; it adds the sensation that he left his body behind, visited Moorea, and brought back the information in the form of in-person observations (and while he was there, I'm sure he had a marvelous time).

So, is the psychic OBE an instance where something actually leaves the body, or is it the clairvoyant experience of someone who has a hard time taking in psychically-derived observations without the act of "being there?" We don't really know for sure.

There is also some crossover with telepathic experience. In some dream-related OBEs, people have reported seeing others who apparently have "invaded" their dreams, as they (the "invaders") later report seeing the dreamer (the one reporting the incident) while also dreaming. This may be an instance of a shared dream, a telepathic experience where the dreamers tap into the same "dreamworld." In the film *Dreamscape*, Dennis Quaid's character was capable of leaving his body and entering, and interacting with, the dream of another. Whether you classify this as an OBE or a telepathic experience is mostly a matter of semantics.

Did Quaid's character actually have to leave his body to enter that other person's dream? Possibly, although since any harm he would come to in the dream of that other person would be reflected in his physical body, one could make a stronger case for a telepathic bond. In the *Nightmare on Elm Street* series, Freddie Kruger is without a body altogether (he died in a fire)—that makes his existence a ghostly one, a permanent OBE. He is able to jump into and influence the dreams of others, which in turn influences their physical bodies. Again, there is a case to be made for telepathy, since it is the mind/spirit or consciousness of Freddie which enters the dream through a mental connection with the dreamer, as with Quaid's character in *Dreamscape*.

Of course, several psychics have talked about the possibility of folks having OBEs being able to see each other when outside their bodies. Telepathy or OBE? Clairvoyance or OBE? Hard to say.

There have been experiments in the field of parapsychology looking at the main question of whether it's ESP or OBE. In one experimental series conducted by Robert Morris, the subject of the experiment, Keith Harary, was to "visit" his kittens (who were in another room) while "out" of his body. The behavior of one of the kittens during these "visits" correlated with its behavior when Keith was physically present. Did the kitten actually sense Keith's presence while in the OB state, or was the kitten somehow aware Keith was thinking of being there, and responding accordingly? Again, we can't say for sure (although it would seem from this and other experiments that there *was* something "leaving" the body). Keith, by the way, has not only written about lucid dreams, but also OBEs (*Have An Out-of-Body Experience In 30 Days*, by Keith Harary and Pamela Weintraub, St. Martin's Press, 1989).

The American Society for Psychical Research (ASPR) conducted a series of experiments looking at OBEs for many years. The late Alex Tanous, a psychic who had had OBEs since he was a child, was involved in those experiments from 1968 through the 1980s. The ASPR experiments, conducted by Dr. Karlis Osis (now retired) and Donna McCormick, used both targets for Alex to perceive as well as physical measurements that Alex tried to affect while in the OB state, with some degree of success.

This, as well as other results of the experiments seem to suggest that "something" leaves the body. Alex's own definition of the OBE included the idea that some part of his consciousness (but not his soul or spirit) left his body. During an interview conducted by Marvin Scott of Independent Network News (through WPIX TV in New York) in 1982 at the ASPR, Alex defined the OBE (as far as his experience was concerned) as a "separation of my consciousness from my body which is able to perceive on its own." In other words, some part of Alex's consciousness or mind would split off and "go anywhere in the world and perceive what is there and bring back the information" to his physical body. Many psychics supposedly capable of an active OBE agree with Alex on that point, and have said that only part of themselves, part of their consciousness or spirit, splits off, sort of like a space probe or psychic double. It is that "double" that goes elsewhere, makes observations, and returns with those memories.

Surveys of OBEs reveal interesting statistics. Less than 5 percent of people having had an OBE have observed that silver cord connection back to their bodies. 44 percent of the experiences take place during sleep, though probably not in a deep sleep, as in a dream state. Experiencers having the OBE while asleep don't usually confuse the experience with a dream; they report that they "feel" different that normal dreams. Some OBEs in dreams may be, as Stephen LaBerge suggests, a form of a lucid dream. However, others with sleeping/OBE experiences say that while they have the OBE during a dream, and the OBE feels different than a normal dream, they are not necessarily conscious of being in a dream-state or even asleep, as the definition of a lucid dream necessitates. In fact, what often tells such people that they (their bodies, at least) are asleep is that as they leave their bodies, they look down upon themselves and "see" themselves sleeping peacefully.

About 32 percent of the OBEs reported take place while the experiencers are awake but relaxed. Parapsychologist Dr. John Palmer has reported that about 28 percent take place in the hypnagogic state. A number of OBEs take place while the experiencer is under extreme stress, such as in surgery, in a physical accident, during illness, during a near-death experience, or even while under severe emotional duress.

The most typical OBE, whether occurring asleep-and-dreaming or awake-but-relaxed or in the almost-asleep state, is described as a floating sensation, often a sensation that one is floating up near the ceiling, and often the sight of one's own body from a point floating in the air or standing by the bed. Such descriptions often come out of dreams, where the dreamer may not even classify that experience as an OBE.

Going back to Alex Tanous's definition, whatever it is that leaves the body (let's call it the "OB Something") is capable of going elsewhere in the world, without the physical body, and is capable of perceiving surroundings and events, bringing that information back to the body. That the OBE can occur while awake or asleep-and-dreaming does not diminish its capabilities in observing events and bringing information back. However, whether one can recall the OBE and the information brought back by the "OB Something" may clearly depend on whether one is in a dream state or not while having the OBE. If it occurs while awake or even in the hypnagogic state, there may be a greater likelihood that you will remember what you "perceived" while you were out (of body). If the OBE occurs during dreaming, you may not recall much or any of the information, or it may be remembered along with (and confused with) other dream imagery, and therefore not recognized for what it was. Working on good dream recall will help with this process of determining whether you had an OBE (or other psychic experience) and with recognizing the information from the outside.

Are there other OBEs in dreams that have some sort of objective correlation to what's happening in the world outside the person having the dream OBE?

There have been reports of OBEs during which the individual having the OBE is actually seen at a location other than where his or her physical body resides. This particular out of body experience is sometimes called "Bilocation," as the person having the OBE is physically (bodily) in one location while being observed at the location he or she is visiting in that "out of body" state.

These are very interesting experiences, since when they are corroborated by the witnesses at both locations, they indicate that something quite unusual and anomalous is going on. Alex Tanous, who had been the subject of more than a decade of OBE research by the ASPR had reported such experiences where eyewitness testimony corroborated the experience.

I've had my own experience with this as well, which ties in to dreams and OBEs. Back when I was working at the ASPR in 1982, I was also teaching parapsychology adult education courses. I became good friends with one of my students and her daughter, and she (the student) claimed a bit of her own psychic ability. One morning I woke up having had a very vivid dream of "being" at her house, which was about forty miles away, late at night and talking with her and her daughter. A couple of days later, this same friend/student asked me if I had a dream about visiting her house on the night in question (the night I actually had the dream).

When I replied "yes" with a bit of puzzlement, she said that I had actually shown up there in the house when she was having a conversation with her daughter. I was seen and even somehow touched by them (and their dog reacted to me as well) at the time I was also home asleep (unless I had started sleep-driving). They were aware I was home asleep (I apparently told them) and asked me to leave. I promptly "vanished."

(I was a bit embarassed about the experience, but not as much as I would have been if I hadn't been wearing anything when I went to sleep that night, since they were able to describe what I was wearing!)

This OBE/bilocation experience was followed two weeks later by a second one with the same friend, though in that case I was in a waking (though bored) state when I experienced the OBE. Again, I was seemingly in two places at once.

Do such bilocational OBEs prove that something actually leaves the body? Unfortunately not. It is just as "likely" that the "other" me was a telepathic projection, an "image" projected directly into the minds of the perceivers that had visual, auditory, and even tactile (touch) components so that it seemed as though I was physically there.

That the first time it happened to me was when I was dreaming was very interesting. Many people have seen apparitions (apparent ghosts) of people who were really still alive. In some of those living apparitional sightings, it has been reported that the subject of the apparition was asleep at the time they were seen. Some people have related such stories to me, and included that they remembered dreaming about visiting that friend or relative (who saw them).

These could be situations where someone awake telepathically picks up on the dreams of someone asleep, rather than the other way around. I'll discuss this a bit more in the chapter on telepathic dreams.

In general, most OBEs that occur while someone is dreaming are not bilocation or apparitional experiences. There is rarely someone at "the other end" who "sees" the OB traveler. These are exceptions rather than the rule.

The general experiences connecting dreams and OBEs include more observation on the part of the dreamer, information coming in from that distant location arrived at through an OBE. And these locations are not always true representations of the actual place. People have reported many odd "extras" when describing Paris or New York or wherever else they had "traveled" to in the dream OBE. Somehow the places are modified.

In fact, the "places" people "travel" to while in the OBE are not always true physical locations. People have reported "strange" worlds or settings, which often sound similar to the kind of imagery one would have in a dream. Some people find themselves in worlds similar to but slightly different than their normal physical surroundings, or sometimes somehow capable of making changes to their surroundings, of manipulating whatever reality they seem to have entered in the OB state.

Have they truly entered other realities, an "astral plane," or maybe traveled through time itself? Have they entered parallel worlds just slightly different than our own? Or are these perceptions of "different realities" merely reflections of a dream state? Such imagery does make it difficult to decide where the OBE leaves off and the dream takes precedence, if there is an OBE at all.

In a recent discussion with my good friend and colleague Keith Harary, we talked about the connection and confusion between OBEs and dreams, more specifically lucid dreams. Consider this conversation between the two of us as a union of this chapter and the previous one.

LA: Do people often confuse the two states, enough to have two books? Were your two books an attempt to help people understand them as two experiences?

KH: Many people confuse lucid dreams and out of body experiences, and to present both experiences clearly would be a worthwhile way to go. We tried very hard with the out of body book to not make any assumptions or occult claims or anything like that, which we don't do, but just to say here's an interesting state of mind if you want to get into it. Here's everything we know about how to encourage or induce this experience, without joining with some cult or going off the deep end. People do join cults to explore their mental abilities, then get taken advantage of in all kinds of ways. We wanted to put something out there that's very simple. A book that's $5.95 is better than spending thousands of dollars on some kind of cult and getting sucked in.

So the idea was to present out of body experiences clearly and simply and then lucid dreams clearly and simply. And they are two different states of mind.

Now there's a big controversy, some people say, over their not being two different states. There's a whole philosophical and scientific controversy over whether out of body experiences are dreams, or something quite different from dreams. What I've found is that people define dreams in all kinds of ways, and some of those definitions seem to include out of body experiences. If they say "Well, anything that happens when you're not in a conscious waking state and experiencing the outside world the way it supposedly really is, or the way we're familiar with it, is a dream." If you define dreams in those terms, then how can anyone argue that point? I think that OBEs and dreams are two different states of mind, but that we also don't know enough about what makes them different. Experientially they're different, but I also realize that people definitely confuse the two states.

Sometimes people report what they believe to be an out of body experience but they may be reporting a dream. And it's like an out of body experience to them, so it's probably defined as such in their continuum of experiences.

LA: Are you defining the out of body experience as feeling like you're out of your body?

KH: You feel subjectively like your body is in one place and you, whatever you happen to be, however you define yourself, experience yourself as being some place independent of your body. Some people would say that's a particular kind of dream. We don't really know that for sure. It's almost a theoretical or rhetorical argument.

Some researchers will say "Well, sometimes when people are having rapid eye movement in dreams they're reporting things that sound like out of body experiences." In the laboratory, experiments were conducted in which eye movements apparently decreased during out of body experiences. "Well," some will point out, "not all dreams happen in REM sleep." Again, a lot depends upon exactly how you define dreams. You could argue all those points. So perhaps sometimes people have dreams or something like dreams when they're not in REM sleep. All of that may be true. It still doesn't mean that a strictly defined, operationally defined dream and an operationally defined OBE are exactly the same thing.

The trouble is that it's very hard when you're dealing with those subjective states, and there's been so little research to distinguish them and base that distinction on objective data. You might distinguish them by the one overwhelming subjective quality of an out of body experience: you feel like you're out of your body. Then some future researchers can sort out later whether that's just a special kind of dream, whether you're really leaving your body, or whether there is some other explanation for your experience. I have no idea if you're even in your body in the first place, and what that specific concept means, or what consciousness is, or whether consciousness is something that can truly be defined as being "inside" of anything else. I don't claim to have those answers, but there's definitely a particular kind of subjective experience associated with what we typically call an OBE.

I've had lots and lots of lucid dreams and lots and lots of out of body experiences; I do subjectively distinguish the two states. I don't think we know enough about either state, though, to operationally be able to define a physiological difference. There is a subjective difference, and there are definitely things you can explore about an out of body experience that you can't explore in a lucid dream, as we typically define it, and vice versa.

LA: In a lucid dream where you know you're dreaming, psychic content might be obvious or not. It still doesn't have to be obvious since the dream may not be one in which you're trying to elicit psychic information. The same question of "is it psychic?" or not can come up in an OBE.

KH: First, there's the whole question of what is "psychic" information, if there is such a thing. I don't even use that word. I use terms like "extended perception" or "extended functioning" or "extended abilities." The point is, the subconscious mind has a lot of underlying abilities to process information that we know very little about. A lot of that may be a deeper level of analysis that we can't even fathom. It may look to us on the surface as though something really incredibly psychic has happened here, because we can't figure how we could know the thing that just popped up into the dream or whatever. That doesn't mean that it's psychic. Just because we don't know where the information came from doesn't mean that it came from beyond.

LA: We have a lot of information coming into us on a daily basis that we're not aware of, and some of this can be a speculation on information that's already there.

KH: And it doesn't have to be a conscious speculation. It could be an unconscious thing. There's also the whole business of drawing conclusions after the fact; sorting out information which strikes you as "Boy, look at that. This dream looks like it came true" and ignoring all the ones that didn't.

For example, there's a vivid example which we point out in the lucid dream book. These are two people who spend a lot of time together, they're in a couple's relationship and share a lot in common to begin with—you would expect those people to have many subjectively shared dreams. In other words, they would think there are times when they both seem to dream about the same thing, the same subject, maybe even the same imagery in their dreams, depending upon their respective psychological backgrounds. That's not necessarily a psychic event at all. Of course they're going to have similarities in their dreams if they have similarities in their waking lives which sort of bleed over into the dreamworld. And they're no doubt also working on certain problems together so sometimes ideas and images that emerge in their dreams can look psychic, or appear to them to represent telepathic experiences, when that isn't what is really occurring at all.

The research studies that were done with randomly chosen targets are worth looking at for evidence. In the real world, it's just too messy to try to figure it out, even though many people will say "There's no way I could have known this. I'm sorry, you can make your scientific arguments all you want, but I know what happened to me." Fine, that's a legitimate point of view. It doesn't carry any weight in the scientific world, but it's a legitimate point of view, and many people who have that point of view often don't care if it carries any weight in the scientific world.

So, I think that there is a tendency to assume that certain abilities exist, like psychic abilities, and to use that as an easy explanation for a lot of what we experience, when in fact, if it is ever a legitimate explanation for what happens, that may be the case in very few circumstances, relatively speaking. On the other hand, it may not be. We don't know enough about what we think we mean when we use words like "psychic" to know for sure when it is and when it isn't. You're never going to figure it out based purely upon a subjective analysis.

I've had dreams that strike me as subjectively raising the question "How could I possibly have known that?" Further, I've often had the experience of apparently knowing about something that's going to happen, which I don't appear to have any way of knowing at the time and later on it seems to happen pretty much as it was in the dream. But is this a conclusion that I'm drawing subjectively after the fact, filling in the blanks. . . .

LA: And misremembering the dream.

KH: Yes, who knows? If you write it all down in detail, then compare it, basically, you'd have to have had a whole dream log all along and see what works and what doesn't. There's also the factor of coincidence in there.

LA: Right, and the question may become, when someone tells another about a dream that comes true later, what does that really mean? Is it precognition, is it coincidence, did he somehow dream this and put himself in the position of making that dream come true?

KH: That's a really good question. Then you get into the

whole question of free will and destiny and those are not questions that I feel equipped to answer, though I'm amazed at the number of people who *do* feel equipped to answer them.

LA: There's the inevitable question of how do you know the dream is psychic, or how do you know that what you got through the OBE is psychic? The experience is generally going to feel different and the information that comes through is what you need to look at. If it was important enough to call your attention, it means you should pay attention to it. But it doesn't have to be psychic.

KH: Your unconscious intellect may say that "the only way Loyd is going to listen to me is if I convince him he's having a psychic experience. So I'll present this to him as though it's a revelation and maybe he'll listen. I know it intellectually, but if I say that right out he'll discount it on a conscious, intellectual level. So I'll present it to him as a revelation." Then again, revelation may just be a natural language of the unconscious mind.

You may never know what's going on deep beneath the surface of your conscious mind. So then, you have this feeling or image and say "Whoa, a psychic experience" and maybe you pay attention to it, or maybe you don't.

LA: That's a good way of putting it because a lot of other kinds of experiences, such as channeling, are probably exactly that, the subconscious creating a vehicle or other personality through which such information can be presented through you to others in a way that those others will listen for a change.

Going back to out of body experiences, there's that strict definition that's used that the OBE is not a psychic experience unless there is other information coming in that you technically couldn't otherwise know. But here, you go back to that question "how could I have known that?" and the multitude of possibilities to answer that.

KH: Exactly, how could you know? There were the experiments we did at Duke University that tried to get at that question. There were some curious things that happened in those experiments that, at the moment, I don't have an easy explanation for, and again I'm not pushing for any particular point of view here. There were times when something very curious appeared to be happening, and if there is a mundane, readily available explanation for that, great—I'd like to know what it is; I'm listening.

But that's how I approach this whole area. If it turns out that there's no such thing as psychic abilities, which I would say is a possibility that I'm open-minded about, I think that would be really fascinating. In fact it might be more fascinating if there aren't psychic abilities, because then I would want to know what it is about the human mind that makes people feel that's what is going on. How do people get sucked into that if such abilities really don't exist?

LA: One of the things you hear about out of body experiences is that you often have them while you're dreaming, that you have traveling dreams. The question becomes, again, if you're visiting places you've never been to before, and bring back a detailed description of the location, as with remote viewing experiences, then what's going on there?

KH: Some researchers would come up with a statement like "Well, that's just a psychic dream that looks like an out of body experience," like that's an explanation of something. Give me a break. Now you add layers of complexity onto it. I don't know what's going on there, but like so many other things, my intuitive feeling is that ultimately there will be a simple explanation. And honestly, if the explanation is not simple, then it's probably not accurate. Human beings are complicated, but they're also pretty simple creatures. It's a kind of paradox.

I'll make it more complicated for you. What does it mean when people have out of body experiences while they're dreaming, and while the dream continues they are aware, subjectively, that their body is "over there," that associated with the experience of their body is the experience of an ongoing dream, while they feel that they're "over here" watching that situation from a distance, and having a completely different experience? And people have also reported experiences where while that's going on they also feel as though they're in a third place in a sort of transpersonal state observing this whole thing from an even more "distant" additional perspective.

I haven't seen anyone in the literature dealing with that level of the experience. It's usually an either/or type of focus, but there are many instances in which there seem to be simultaneous things happening, almost as though you've compartmentalized your overall consciousness experience. The dream "doesn't terminate" while the out of body experience continues. What do you call that? I don't know, but I know that it happens, and it would be interesting to know in that situation what the experient's physiology is doing. I wouldn't be surprised to find rapid eye movements. After all, the person is subjectively experiencing dreaming and somebody who says that out of body experiences are simply dreams would say "they're having a dream and that includes all of these components."

That may be a simple explanation, something completely different is going on there that we don't as yet understand. Maybe we are able to compartmentalize our subjective experiences in some literal way—different aspects of your consciousness or your brain, however your personal world view puts it, different aspects that are able to have different experiences. In that sense perhaps you can be in two places at once, if not literally, then psychologically.

Don't you already do that? Don't you drive along the freeway chewing gum while you're consciously thinking about making love with your girlfriend back home? What's that all about?

LA: Or even the situation where you're driving along and you're suddenly at your destination without being conscious of having driven all that distance. Where were "you" when you were driving there?

KH: It only makes sense to talk about where you were psychologically. To say that a person literally checks out of their body, well that assumes so many things about what the experience of being in your body is all about that it can't be dealt with at this point.

Darlene, my wife, pointed this out to me. Do you experience yourself as being in your body? You don't really. You don't necessarily feel as though you're experiencing the world from inside your body. And even when you are walking down the street looking at the trees, you often sort of experience yourself with the trees. Your everyday waking experience is not even one of feeling totally focused on your body, and experiencing the world from "within" it. So, are we talking about a continuum of carrying that far enough so that you ultimately have an out of body experience? Maybe. Some people would say it's just a subjective state. Well, subjective states sometimes occur because of objective phenomena.

LA: And we accept subjective states where there may be something objective going on.

KH: If you stick your finger in a wall socket, you will have a shocking experience. You will probably feel surprised, subjectively, and even experience some subjective pain. You may even feel as though you're out of your body, subjectively. But there is something objectively going on there, that is "helping" you to create that subjective experience.

LA: Not to mention the shock you'll experience when you look in the mirror and see that you've been given a permanent.

KH: [Laughter] Yes.

LA: In speaking of paranormal experiences, for the most part we're talking about what Vernon Neppe has called the subjective paranormal experience, since we have no way to objectify most of our experiences.

KH: Vernon is a creative thinker; I understand what he is getting at. I refer to apparent psychic experiences, but I'm not sure if that's really the best term. "Apparent psychic experience" simply means that an experience seems psychic to the person having it. That doesn't mean that it is or it isn't really "psychic" and leaves open the question of how the term psychic should be defined. Most people have their own definitions.

LA: And culturally we're told that the experience is a paranormal one as opposed to a normal one.

KH: It's always relative to what you view as everyday reality.

LA: That's right. A paranormal experience in this culture would be very different from one in the culture of the Australian Aborigines, where their reality contains other viewpoints.

KH: Whereas if we were to live within their culture we might view ourselves as having experiences that are paranormal but that they would consider "everyday." And they wouldn't necessarily consider those experiences psychic. If you can look at the ground and tell what animal was there four hours ago, that's a pretty interesting ability. Some of it is just analysis; it looks intuitive but it's not even that. You just notice that the sand is a certain way, and draw what you experience as an objective, analytical conclusion.

You kind of get that way out in the desert, when you're paying attention to every footstep, every breeze, every movement. You can be climbing a cliff and notice a rock moving just a little bit and know to hit the wall and get out of the way. You get very sensitized to your environment when your survival depends upon it.

LA: In lucid dreams people are paying much more attention to what's going on in the dreams, because they're dreaming and they are aware of that.

KH: The thing is, people can get carried away with that, too. You can have a lot of lucid dreams and really become sort of a junkie on that. Some people do get overly focused on the idea of manipulating their state of mind. I don't think it's a good thing to do all the time. In fact, Pamela and I suggest that when you learn how to induce lucid dreams, you experiment with it, you see what it can do for you, and you also include a lot of what we call free dreaming. Just let yourself go. Nobody really knows what dreaming is really for or all about, so it's probably a good idea to just let yourself go on a regular basis. Just dream as you always would, and even allow yourself to have lucid dreams in which you just watch the dream and see what you can get out of it, without necessarily trying to change it around, unless that's going to help.

For example, if you have a recurring dream and it's really bothering you, and you can do something within that dream to either resolve it or understand it better, that may help you. On the other hand, the problem that you are dealing with in that dream, or trying to deal with, may not go away, but may show up in another dream that you're able to better understand and eventually deal with in a better fashion.

So if you're caught in a kind of loop, if your unconscious mind keeps repeating a dream because you're not getting the message, why not do something that encourages your mind to present that particular revelation in a way that you will more readily comprehend?

So, in essence, while it may be very difficult to tease the OBE away from the dream as a separate experience (when the OBE occurs during sleep), it may not really matter. In the end, it would be wonderful if we could really understand that the OBE is or isn't a situation in which something actually leaves the body. At the present, however, we are stuck with really not knowing this.

Add to that dilemma the OBE as it occurs within a dream, and you place that experience in a setting which further confounds the question. No longer is it "simply" a matter of "Is the OBE a clairvoyant experience dressed up as a venture outside the physical body or is it a case of the 'astral body' or 'spirit' or 'consciousness' actually separating from the physical body?" When the OBE occurs within the dream state, we add to that question the imagery of the unconscious, which can dress up psychic information and deep memory as a psychic experience or an excursion to another place or time.

The ultimate question for our time, since we really have no objective means to discover whether "something" truly leaves the body or not, is "Does it matter?"

In all cases, whether the information is coming from "traveling clairvoyance" or the OBE or a "psychic" dream dressed up as a voyage to another location, it is presented in a way that is saying to us "Hey, take a look at this. . . . It may be important to you!"

So, what you might do when you have such dreams which may or may not be OBEs is to simply consider the information presented and its usefulness to you. It may be that the information seems frivolous and not very useful. Well then, maybe it was fun info, your mind just throwing you something to make you smile, or it may have been frightening, and indicative of some other deep problem or question in your life.

In any case, the information bears paying attention to, regardless of how it bubbled up through the layers of your consciousness, or whether you had to "go" out of your body to get it. And if the OBE is some form of clairvoyance, a disguise for another form of psychic experience, do we experience clairvoyance differently? Or do we have the out of body sensation when we gain information from other locations?

The answer is in the absence of that sensation, as you'll see very soon. Let's move on to staying in our bodies but connecting with the dreaming and waking minds of others. . .-.

CHAPTER 8

Telepathic Dreaming

Telepathy is one of those abilities used and abused by the movies, television, in science fiction and comic books, as well as by speculators of military applications of psi. The idea that one person can gain an awareness of what's in another's mind is at the same time both more and less than what most people think of when they hear the word "telepathy." In other words, it's not "mind reading" and it's not, as it often appears in science fiction, a direct communications link-up of two minds. No one can directly access the mind, the thoughts, the emotions of another, at least as far as we know. If such a person were to exist, it's unlikely that he or she would step forward to disclose that ability. It would probably freak most of us out.

Experiences of telepathy seem to revolve around a basic awareness of the general contents of another's thought or emotion. In other words, there's no actual mind reading involved, merely a kind of jump of thought. One person (the sender) is having a particular train of thought or maybe is in a particular emotional state, and the other person (the receiver) has a sudden "knowing" of this, gets the gist of what the sender is thinking or feeling.

People are interested in such connections between people, especially people related to one another (such as mother and child or twins) or very close emotionally (husband and wife or lovers). There are a couple of considerations when looking at the apparent telepathic experiences of people who are so close.

First of all, one must always consider the non-psychic connection. People who have lived together for a long time (not just in a relationship . . . this also fits the twins and the parent/child connections), or who simply have really gotten to know each other well in certain situations, can often predict how each other will respond in similar situations. I frequently hear "We often know what each other is thinking . . . sometimes I can start a sentence and s/he can finish it." Well, one must always consider that two people who know each other well, who have been through many kinds of situations together, might really know just how each other will respond in a particular situation, even to understanding basically what the other would say in that situation. This is not usually a conscious thing.

The other point to take into consideration is that emotion seems to play a big part in psychic experience in general. Two (or more) people emotionally involved often seem to share some sort of above-average psychic link-up. It's not just that twins are more psychic because of the genetics involved, but rather because of an emotional tie between them.

Telepathic information rears its head in many situations. For example, there are many stories of people knowing when someone close to them is in a crisis, in danger, or even when such a person has died. It may be that the person in crisis sends out a telepathic cry of alarm. Those who get it clearest (if at all) are generally the same people who are normally empathetic about friends, lovers, and relatives.

Telepathic information-sharing also seems to occur when in the dream state. Not only do people sometimes dream of others they know in particular situations, later to find that those situations were actually going on at the time of the dream (or were thought about by the person dreamt about), but there are reports of shared dreams, of two people having the same dream.

There has been much work in the field of parapsychology on telepathic dreams. The seminal work, recently out in a second edition, is *Dream Telepathy* by Montague Ullman and

Stanley Krippner, with Alan Vaughan. The work was conducted at Maimonides Medical Center in New York during
the sixties, although analyses of telepathic dreaming continue
today, and are reported in parapsychological journals from
time to time (*The Journal of Parapsychology, The Journal
of the American Society For Psychical Research, and The
Journal of the Society For Psychical Research*). The work at
Maimonides stands as an exceptionally rich body of experimental data that supports a psi hypothesis.

Experiments conducted in dream telepathy have typically
included protocols similar to other psi experiments, though
with the addition of the sleep/dream factor. Subjects designated as "receivers" were asleep at the time the "senders"
were focusing on the targets. By monitoring the sleep stages
of the "receivers," the researchers were able to watch for
the dreaming (REM sleep), then wake up the "receivers"
after that stage. Since it is most likely that people can remember their dreams when awakened just after REM, the
subjects were able to describe their dreams for the researchers,
often in great detail. In the Maimonides experiments, the
verbal descriptions were recorded and later transcribed. The
description of the dream would be matched up by judges with
the targets. In many instances, the connections between the
detailed descriptions and the targets were obvious.

One of the difficulties in doing any "free response" experiments, where there is no forced target as with card guessing, is the addition of details or the attempt to identify imagery
and other information by the mind of the "receiver." While
there may be several similarities between what the "receiver"
describes and what the target is, the target is often placed
into the context of a dream, sometimes making it difficult to
tease apart the actual target from the additional detail of the
dream, the dream imagery masking the psi signal.

For example, let's say the "target," Bob, is concentrating
on a picture of a robin perching on the limb of a tree. The
"receiver," Fred, has a dream about Batman and Robin, both
looking over Gotham City by standing (perching?) on the
ledge of a building. Is this a correct "guess"? Well, while
it may seem obvious to you that there is a connection between

the picture of a robin and the dream of Batman's partner, Robin, "perched" on the edge of something, we might have to look at other possibilities.

Did Fred recently see the film *Batman*? (Even though Robin never appeared, most people wondered where the Boy Wonder was in that film.) Does Fred read comic books? Has he had other dreams about superheroes, or specifically about Batman and Robin?

Even if any of these others sources of dream information are pertinent, the timing of the dream in connection with the timing of that particular target suggestion still may yield statistical significance. There may, however, be another problem. If the judges looking at target pictures end up with targets that include a robin and a picture of, say, Batman or some other superhero, the judge may have difficulty in choosing between the two potential targets. How would you choose if the dream was of Batman and Robin, and your target choices were a picture of a robin and a picture of a superhero?

So, you can see that unless one is careful about target selection and judging, we might have a problem in deciding on an impartial basis that any particular target had a connection with a particular dream. Fred's mind might have simply received the picture of the robin (bird) and processed it into a dream about Robin (the Boy Wonder). That doesn't mean that Fred did not *get* the correct target, just that the process of dreaming may embellish the information, placing it into totally different contexts.

On top of all this, you have the added problem of whether this is truly telepathy or really clairvoyance. Is the source of information the "sender's" mind or is it the target itself? This is, at this point in time, difficult if not impossible to answer. But, once again, does it really matter if it's telepathy or clairvoyance? There is psi happening here, and that may be the only truly important consideration. Later, when researchers in parapsychology have a handle on the process of these two abilities (if they are in fact separate abilities), this question will be of more importance, and perhaps easier to answer.

So what is a "true" telepathic experience? Couldn't any

experience be clairvoyant? To a great degree, the answer to the second question is "yes," in that if there is an event or experience, a stimulus in physical reality that causes the "sender" to think or "send" that information, the "receiver" may be focusing on the stimulus rather than the mind of the "sender." If the information is simply mental, if what is being "sent" is simply a thought or emotion or memory, with no relation to the "sender's" environment, then we can say we're probably dealing with telepathy and telepathy alone.

Deanna Troi, the counselor aboard the starship *Enterprise* on *Star Trek: The Next Generation* is a member of a people who are true telepaths. In episodes where Troi's mother shows up, communication between mother and daughter is presented as purely mental discussion, though Troi typically insists that they verbalize (telepathy can apparently be considered rude behavior by those of us who can't do it). Troi, however, had a father from Earth, a non-telepathic human. Consequently, unlike her mother and other Betazoids, her abilities are genetically diluted. She cannot pick up stray thoughts from other non-telepathic people. She can, however, pick up emotional states, even over a great distance (such as from people in another starship). This empathic ability to pick up emotions from others, makes her an excellent counselor for folks with emotional or psychological disturbances, or even just for people who have a hard time with a particular decision.

Star Trek has illustrated many such examples of telepathic ability, as has science fiction in general. Even more "normal" films and shows have done this, such as the film *Ghost Dad*, in which Bill Cosby's character's spirit can be seen in darkened rooms, but has to communicate by telepathy.

Telepathy as mind-to-mind communication is far from a desired form of interaction the way we experience it today. We cannot simply "think" a message to others and expect it to be received. Our subconscious minds, however, or whatever it is in us that controls psi, apparently do use telepathy from time to time as a form of communication. In daily life, there are instances where perhaps the reason you and another person thought the same thing at the same time was because of telepathy. Or maybe you knew who was on the other end of that ringing phone because you picked up on that person's thoughts centering on you. Or maybe the reason why that long-lost buddy of yours even called you to begin with was because you were thinking of him and he picked up on that (or vice versa . . . you picked up on his thoughts of you, leading you to think of him, leading to an awareness of "that's Fred calling now").

Since direct communication from mind to mind is considered telepathy, it may be that one person's dream can be recognized as possibly telepathic by another. For example, Carl Jung (and other therapists since Jung, including Nandor Fodor and Jule Eisenbud) have reported clients' dreams that seemingly tap into the therapist's life. This seems almost as if the client is telepathically picking up on some of the thoughts, emotions, and concerns of the therapist. The information is revealed to the client by including it in a dream. The fact that the only way the dream can be pegged as potentially psychic is by the therapist him/herself to whom the dream is told and not by the client who dreamed it is very interesting from a psychological point of view.

You might have all sorts of interesting dreams about friends or relatives, yet not consider them anything out of the ordinary until you reveal that dream to the other person, who might respond with "Hey, that just happened to me!" or "I had the same, exact dream!" Because we learn that dreams are just typically that, dreams, we often may not connect the information in a dream to a real event until after we discuss the dream with another person.

In many cases, however, you might learn of a telepathic connection without discussing a dream with another person. It may just be that the description of a situation in the life of another is enough to register that. Here are a couple of letters that illustrate this. The first two come from Joanne Mied of Psychogenic Research, a psychic practitioner in northern California.

> My friend Tricia and I were sleeping in the same bed one night. I had this dream about these two people

who were my parents, who weren't actually my parents. She, at the time, was having trouble with her marriage, which was why she was staying with me. In the dream, her parents were very unhappy and were scolding her about it. Actually, they were scolding me about it. When I woke up, I said to her "Gee, I just had this really strange dream and these people were scolding me." I was a single person at the time, so it didn't make any sense to me.

She said, "So what did these people look like?" I described the woman, who was small, and the father, who had gray hair, and I can actually see them in my mind's eye right now. They were her parents. It was her dream.

In this dream, it would appear that Joanne's proximity to her friend Tricia, may have placed her in the position of picking up further information, in this case that Tricia's parents were not thrilled with what was happening and were scolding her about it. Here's another from Joanne:

I worked with this woman, Yvette, and I dreamt one night that she had moved to Oregon. We were having dinner at her house, and there was this beautiful stream and a waterfall right outside the window. She really liked living there, she had lost weight, she didn't work, she could stay home all the time, and she was really happy.

The next morning, I came in and said "Hey, Yvette, I had this dream about you." She said that that night her husband had come home and told her that this company had been thinking about moving to Oregon. If they moved there, she wouldn't have to work.

It turns out the company is not moving, so that makes it a telepathic dream, not a precognitive one. Joanne apparently picked up on Yvette's husband's announcement about Oregon and played it back to herself through a dream.

Here's one with a bit of a practical value.

I was supposed to meet my mother in town. I overslept and "awoke" to a dream of my mother knocking on my window and telling me to "come on, R—, come on."

When I awoke, I looked at my watch. The time was 10:15 A.M. As soon as I got to the meeting, my mom told me that at about 10:15 she had gone outside and repeatedly said "Come on, R—, come on."

—C.R.N., Montclair, CA

It's possible that the timing of the dream and when C.R.N.'s mother said she'd gone outside to wait for him and effectively call to him was purely coincidental. It is, however, interesting to note the reported wording of the message that appeared in the dream and in real life, and that the dream was potent enough to wake C.R.N. up, which meant that while C.R.N. was going to be late, he wasn't going to miss the meeting altogether.

After my ex-husband and I were separated for five months, I dreamt that he came to see me. About a week before he actually came, I started having the dream again. He came three days before Christmas and left the day before Christmas. I asked him why he didn't call before he came and he just said "You knew I would be coming anyway." I dismissed any thought of what I had been having as a premonition simply because it was the holidays and he wanted to see his son (not quite two years old yet).

May came along and the same things happened as with Christmas. I dismissed the idea because it was his son's birthday on the 24th May. He came a few days before his birthday, then, again the beginning of the next month. Each time I asked him why he didn't call and his response was the same.

A year had passed with no visits and no dreams. In June of the following year I began having the dreams again. Father's Day was coming up and I knew he'd be here. He never wrote or called beforehand, nor had I received any previous letters except two cards and a present for my son last Christmas.

My son and I packed up and went to Green Bay the weekend of Father's Day. When we returned, we heard my ex in the house. He was here looking for us.

I haven't had the dreams since 1979, nor has there been a visit from my ex since. I think my psychic abilities died with any feelings I had for him, though I think I would know if *he* died. I hoped he would never come to visit after that last visit.

I think he knew we had a psychic connection between us, but we never discussed it.

—R.A., Wisconsin

R.A. may very well have had a psychic connection with her ex-husband. Her awareness of his visits may actually have coincided with his planning such trips, mentally, if not in fact. There may be other factors at work here, since the dreams occurred for a bit before each visit. A very telling pointer here is her lack of dreams in connection with her lack of visits. Emotional bonds appear to create psychic ties between people. Breaking or weakening those emotions may eradicate the psychic connection.

Here's one that's a bit different, taking us to a whole other area of telepathic experience and dreams.

On April 11 1982, I dreamed I was in an area resembling a World War II army camp, with one-story, wooden barracks. As I stood outside of the building, Bob, a man I had been engaged to fourteen years earlier, walked out the door accompanied by several people I did not clearly see. He paused and looked at me in a sad, wistful manner, then slowly turned and walked away.

On the night of April 12, I had the same dream, repeated in exact detail.

On the night of April 13, the dream was repeated to the point of him pausing to look at me. In this one he said "Sorry, honey, but this time you will be the one left behind and hurt." He turned and vanished.

In October of that year, I learned that he had been ill and died in a V.A. hospital on April 13, 1982.

—S.F., Rock Island, WA

Was this a case of an apparition visiting a dream of a living person? Or was this a telepathic "good-bye" between two old friends?

In this case, as it was a repeated dream, it would appear that Bob, who lay ill in the V.A. hospital connected somehow with S.F.'s dreams. The day he died, the dream's detail shifted slightly, as though it was his way of providing a final exit line. It would be advantageous to know the time of Bob's death in relation to when S.F. dreamed the message in order to place the dream either before or after Bob actually died.

One of the major categories of the sightings of apparitions, ghosts, or spirits relates to timing, to when the person seen actually died in relation to when their apparition is seen. Most apparitions of people who have died are sighted within the first twenty-four hours after death (actually less than twelve hours in most cases). They are generally visions of people known to those seeing them, and are often close friends or relatives. In some instances, these sightings have actually shown up in dreams, as though the apparition is appearing in the dream because the person the ghost wishes to visit is already asleep. In such cases, it may just be that the apparition, for want of a way to wake up the sleeper (no self-respecting ghost carries clanking chains anymore), somehow appears in the dreams of the sleeper. According to the experiences of those seeing such apparitions, most of these visitors are showing up to deliver a last message or to say good-bye to friends or relatives. Such good-byes can often be a comfort to the "living," as they may help reduce grief.

What's all this to do with telepathy in dreams? *Ghost Dad* is a film that illustrates some of this very well, in that the ghost in question has to communicate verbally through the use of telepathy. Many questions have come up over the years with regard to apparitional sightings. Although some may seem a bit silly, they are actually worth wondering about.

Some of them are: "Why do ghosts have clothes on and where do they get them from?" or "How is it I can see the ghost but not everyone can?" or "If the ghost is immaterial, how is it he/she can speak, since talking involves air forced through vocal cords?" or "How is it the ghost can change appearance to some degree, appearing at different ages each day?" These questions all have to do with the actual essence of what an apparition is.

Fantasy, horror films, and fiction (including some myths and legends) have told us that ghosts can manifest themselves out of something called "ectoplasm" and that they can materialize or dematerialize at will, pass through walls, fly, and do all sorts of other things. Yet the actual reports of the behaviors of apparitions provide a different picture. Apparitions appear to look like the people they were in life, and in fact may be apparitions of living people, some form of an OBE.

Ghost Dad was such a situation, where the living body of Bill Cosby's character lay somewhere while his spirit moved about out of his body. Unfortunately, Cosby's character wasn't aware that he could have changed clothes by simply thinking about it; that his clothes were as much a projection of spirit as the rest of him. Or so we think from other such cases. Apparitions behave like the people they were (are) in life, and many encounters with apparitions indicate that for some reason the ghosts refuse to acknowledge that they're dead, or are unaware of it altogether.

In a case I investigated a few years ago in Livermore, California, a young boy was communicating with a ghost named Lois, who was the previous owner of the house built in 1917. Lois had lived in that house all her life and died in it as well. Why was she in the house? According to the boy, she was there because she loved her house and didn't see the need to go anywhere else. She appeared to him as an old woman, a pre-teen, a teenager, and a woman in her twenties, often wearing different clothing on different days. He was a bright kid, and had the presence of mind to ask how that was possible. Her answer fits with some theories about apparitions. She appeared to him in the way she wanted, in whatever her self-image was for that day, projecting that information directly into his mind.

In other words, how she felt on a given day (as a teenager, an old woman, etc.) affected what she "sent" as her appearance. Her "voice" was part of this projection. Telepathically, there was a connection between the boy and Lois, one for which she was somehow responsible.

What are apparitions? They appear to be some form of consciousness, (or mind, spirit, soul, or whatever you want to call it) that is capable of telepathically sending detailed information into another mind. We perceive with our minds, as our brains translate the information received through our senses into signals which are then decoded by the brain and the mind. Having an hallucination does not mean you're crazy, disturbed, or out in the desert with no food or water. Outside stimuli can create very different images of reality than what is actually there (a fact magicians are very well aware of).

If some part of the human consciousness survives the death of the body, then the normal channels of communication have been cut off. No physical body is there to be seen or heard, so telepathy seems the next likely possibility for communication. In the original run of the *Star Trek* television series, there was a race of beings called Organians (an episode called "Errand of Mercy"). They were energy beings, existing only as free-floating minds capable of telepathic communication with others. They were also capable of projecting the image that they were simple, physical, humanoid, peasant-types until the time was right for them to reveal themselves.

Apparitions seem to appear the same way, though with apparently less control of their appearance than the Organians had. The self-image, the way a person sees himself or herself, is apparently what is projected by the apparition. As most of us have a self-image that involves clothing, the apparition appears fully clothed.

Sightings of the apparitions of people who have just died or are in the process of dying may be spurred on by either the desire of the apparition to appear to friends or relatives, or by the wishes of the person being "visited" (some part of that person wanting to know when that friend or relative has died). Most people think in terms of the intention being on the part of the apparition, though there is no direct evidence of this (mainly assumptions and of course the commentary by psychics and other people who may have a whole different insight into the matter).

Whether the apparition appears in the waking state of the observer, or in a dream, the mode of communication would appear to be telepathy. In the dream situations, what may happen is something like this: Susan goes to sleep one night. Unbeknownst to her, her grandfather has a heart attack and dies during that time period. Susan wakes up, remembering a dream in which her grandfather came to visit her. In the dream it was nighttime, and she was in bed. Her grandfather appeared to her and smiled as he looked down on her. He waved good-bye and said, "Don't you worry about me. I'm headed somewhere wonderful." He vanishes. Upon learning of her grandfather's death during the night, Susan is surprised, but feels that it really was her grandfather saying good-bye. While she grieves, she isn't overcome with grief, feeling he really is at rest somewhere "wonderful."

In some of the dreams of this type, the setting of the dream is much like reality, the bedroom or sleeping place of the dreamer. In others, as with S.F.'s above, the apparition appears in a dream with some other scene or surroundings more appropriate to a dream. However, there is usually an explicit or implied message that the person represented in the dream is dead or is going away somehow.

Is it possible that the apparitions of these people are tapping into the dreams of others? If you accept the possibility of apparitions at all, or the possibility that OBEs are representative of "something" leaving the body, then it follows that an apparition's presence can be registered by the mind in a conscious state or by the subconscious, dreaming part of the mind. The apparition projects his/her image or message into the mind of the dreamer, as he/she would into the mind of a conscious individual. The subconscious then takes over, placing the projected information into the context of a dream.

The other side of the coin here is that the telepathy of the dreamer registers the thoughts of the person dying. That person may have thought of a number of close friends and relatives before death and sent out a kind of telepathic farewell. The person(s) receiving the information processes it and places it into some context that can be accepted. If receiving it while awake, the percipient may "see" or experience the information as an apparition, or simply a feeling that "something" has happened to the person who has just died. If receiving it while asleep, the information may be integrated into the imagery of a dream, or may even cause a particular dream to happen.

The appearance of such apparitions in dreams or in the waking state may also signal injury or accident. You may dream of a friend, relative, or lover getting into an accident and awaken with that firmly imprinted in your mind. The information may be useful in that you are not only sure the dream was a cry for help, but you even know where to go to find that hurt friend. Such incidents have been reported in the past.

As I'll discuss in a later chapter, such an awareness of an accident or even of a pleasant event in the life of someone you know that occurs while you're dreaming could be a telepathic experience or a clairvoyant one. We come back to the question of "What is the source of the information . . . mind or event?" And again, there is no absolute answer. There may be no way of telling, short of the feeling that you, the dreamer, have when you recall the dream. Did it feel as though you were watching an event happen or did it feel as though there was an intent, a thought, a cry for help or attention involved?

What you do to assimilate such information into your life is the important issue. When you have such experiences, look to what they say to you, the dreamer. They may be telling you simply that the person was thinking of you, or that you were capable of picking up information from the other person's mind. Or they may be providing you with an emotional outlet, a preparation for some event already in the awareness of the person who "sent" the message. Or perhaps they provide information to be acted upon, like "Help me . . . here's where I am" or "You're late . . . wake up and get over here quick" or "I'm thinking of you and want you to call me."

There's no quick test to see if a particular dream is telepathic or not. Compare your dreams with those of others who may have a connection to what you dream about. Check with people you dream about and see if there is some correlation to what you dreamed, something that may say why you dreamed it. And pay attention to how the dream feels to you, whether it feels like a connection to others or something else.

Human beings, like other social animals, have a need for affiliation with others. If this affiliation comes out as a connection in our dreams, terrific. It all boils down to the idea that we are all more alike than different, that communication does flow, whether verbally or telepathically, from one mind to another and back.

CHAPTER 9

Dreams of Days Past

Have you ever had a dream of being in some past time, some historical setting? Ever wonder where it came from, or whether somehow you could really have been there?

There is much discussion these days of past lives and reincarnation, as this is often a central discussion point of "new age" thought. Our wisdom or lack thereof, our likes and dislikes, and even our problems are, according to proponents of the past life idea, related to our past lives. Psychics and channelers are asked routinely to describe who their clients were in past lives. Hypnosis is used to regress people to their previous existences. And our dreams, we are told, often let information about such past lives slip into our consciousness.

Ever wonder why people often find out they were some person of historical significance (which may merely mean you were somebody you could look up in historical records)? Or if not somebody making it into historical records, that the prior life was either extremely good or extremely bad to them? Or maybe that they lived in ancient (now-defunct) lands like Atlantis (which is not verifiable)? Or that they were extraterrestrials in past lives (yes, I have heard that one more than once)? Rarely, it seems, have people been poor schlubs from the Dark Ages, or slaves in Egypt or the American south. Given the population of the world today, if we've all been born before, there's too many of us to have all had even one past lifetime, let alone more than one (unless we consider that Atlantis had one heck of a large populace, or we can really consider other lifeforms, terrestrial or extraterrestrial).

So, what's the scoop from parapsychology about reincarnation, and where does it tie into dreams?

Reincarnation, the idea that our soul, spirit, or consciousness can be reborn in a new body and given a fresh start, is not new. In fact, the idea is right up there with any other idea of an afterlife, and whole religions (such as Hinduism) make it a central belief, often including the idea that one can "come back" not only as a human, but as any living creature under the sun (or under the ground or sea, for that matter).

The belief was even part of early Christian teachings. According to some scholars of the many versions of the Bible, the belief in reincarnation was excised from the teachings of Christ and the Apostles in the fourth century A.D. by the second Catholic Congress convened by the Emperor Theodosius; a political decision, not necessarily a religious one. Apparently, belief in a "second chance" after one dies makes it difficult to control people (from a political standpoint). In other words, "if you sin in this life, you still get another chance" is not a concept that helps keep people as well-behaved as "if you sin in this life you will suffer eternal damnation."

So, the idea's been around (and reborn into more than a few cultures and religions from time to time). The question of "evidence" and "proof" arises when one studies the concept.

There are a few "proof" sources cited by people who believe in reincarnation. One is the idea that the religions that teach its existence are correct, and that it does happen, thanks to God or the gods or whomever else one's religion says may be in charge of the universe. "So it is written" is a familiar argument for a lot of religious ideas. Arguing against such belief system "proof" sources is just about impossible, unless one can prove or disprove the idea of a particular god or gods or God.

A more common "proof" source brought up in today's new age is the idea of past life regression, or using hypnosis or other techniques to regress a person's memories to a time before conception. Many people have remembered some kind of existence in the fairly recent or extremely distant past. Most of these past identities are either unverifiable or too verifiable. How do you verify if there was a wise-man from Atlantis named Arion if we can't even verify the existence of Atlantis as a real, though sunken, place? And how can there be several people running around all claiming to be Cleopatra in a past life? (Maybe Cleo was a multiple personality and each was born into somebody different today? Nah, I don't think so.)

The big problem with hypnotic regression is "information contamination." There is no way to absolutely exclude all a person has read, seen, heard, or experienced as far as information about the past is concerned. Someone who swears never to have read or heard anything about County Cork in Ireland in the late nineteenth century, yet remembers a fairly convincing past life (complete with accent) may have come into contact with such information without remembering the information source.

We all gather relatively "useless" information from the environment on a daily basis. Conversations from others around us do enter our ears and lodge in long-term (though undoubtedly submerged) memory, whether we are conscious of hearing that information or not. And who among us can truly and honestly say that we can remember *everything* we ever read or saw on TV or in a movie, especially while we were children? Or can we truly remember that Irish neighbor of ours from the time we were three years old, the one who used to babysit and tell us bedtime stories of her life in County Cork?

Information lodged in our subconscious memory is still retrievable information, especially while in an altered state of consciousness such as a hypnotic trance. For whatever reason (often the suggestion of the hypnotherapist that we really did have a past life), our minds come up with that information, creating a past life that sounds interesting to us (and certainly to the hypnotherapist).

Past life regression is not valid proof of reincarnation. In fact, because of the problem of information contamination, it stinks from a parapsychological viewpoint. It's interesting, but not very useful. There are uses for it, however.

As a therapeutic tool, past life regression may be very valuable. For some people, getting at what bugs us is a problem. If we can set the cause of problems in the context of "it was an issue in a past life that is causing problems today," we can remove ourselves from any responsibility for that problem. "I have relationship problems today because of what happened to me in my last lifetime." Such discussion of the past life and problems can reveal much to a therapist, in the way any sort of association or storytelling therapy might work (such as Jungian sand tray therapy).

People visiting psychics and channelers are often told about their past lives. Assuming the psychic or channeler is truly psychic, what they are picking up may be real information or not. Maybe they are capable of focusing on some part of you that reveals who you were in the past, and maybe not. Again, verification is extremely difficult if you are told you were an Egyptian slave or a dolphin in that past life. Or maybe what the psychic/channeler is doing is picking up on problems or concerns of your life today, revealing that information to you in the form of a metaphor, a story with something to say about what you need to do with your life right *now*. All I can say is that you might discard the "clothing" or "window-dressing" of the story of the past life, and look closely at the actual advice being given. If it doesn't sound right, think twice about it (and please use good old common sense, as well as your own intuition).

So are there good cases of reincarnation? Yes, there are, but they're only strongly suggestive, not absolute proof. To avoid the kind of lifetime information contamination mentioned above, young children, not yet full of teachings, are often the best sources of such cases. There are literally thousands of cases of children under the age of five that suddenly and spontaneously remember having lived before as someone else. The vast majority of reported cases come from countries such as India, Burma, Thailand, and others where reincarnation is part of the actual belief system. This is more than likely because in cultures that don't recognize reincarnation, the parents of a three-year-old speaking about a past life would undoubtedly first assume that the child's imagination is at work, rather than literally believe what the child is saying.

Dr. Ian Stevenson of the University of Virginia, is the preeminent researcher/writer in this area. There are cases with the children providing rich detail of that past life that have been investigated by researchers under Stevenson's auspices. Checking the information for accuracy, then checking for possible information contamination is part of this investigative process.

Children (the younger the better) are good sources for such cases, since the chances of contamination are much less and the "memories" may be stronger simply because the child hasn't grown up enough to establish a personality or self-identity. And in some cases, the children have been able to speak in the dialect or language of the person whom they supposedly were in that past life.

The information coming from such children is far and away much more suggestive of reincarnation than either hypnotic regression or information from psychics. Adding in the dialect/language matches makes it even better. A person capable of remembering a past life (in hypnosis or spontaneously) who is also capable of speaking and *conversing* in the language or dialect of both the geographic location and the time period adds much to overcome the information contamination possibility (the same could be said for any channeler who could not only channel the spirit of someone from England in the tenth century, but also speak Old English of that time period, which most of us could never understand).

Adults often report such spontaneous rememberances, but due to the increased chance of contamination, as well as the possibility of some form of multiple personality disorder which feeds off information from the subconscious, as well as a psychic possibility, such cases are relatively low on the "proof" totem pole. However, that psychic possibility, retrocognition (reaching into the past for information of which you are not aware), may be responsible for a number of these cases, including many of the cases involving children.

Retrocognition is a natural outgrowth of the idea of precognition, awareness of the future. After all, even though there are many concepts of how time works with regards to the future, we know (or at least we think we know) that there is a past to gain information from.

Cases of reincarnation may be cases of retrocognition, of reaching back for detailed information. Once the information is received, the mind may "clothe" that information in a neat package of "memory," in much the same way information gained by clairvoyance is turned into an out of body experience. Your mind has a hard time accepting the observations of that past event unless "you were there," so it creates the context of a past life to provide a vehicle for passing the information on to you.

It is unlikely even in the case of retrocognition that language could be received to such a degree as to make the person conversant. While such cases are rare in the reincarnation literature, they're not unheard of. These cases, above all the others, are more strongly suggestive of reincarnation, and less so of retrocognition. Unfortunately, they are also extremely rare.

If there are records or information in existence that allow us to check the "memories" of a past life against historical fact, it is also possible that ostensible cases of reincarnation and even retrocognition are real-time clairvoyance of those records, not memories of a past life or retrocognition of past events.

Such information comes out in a variety of ways. For example, let's say that you had an acquaintance living in a very old house (Revolutionary War period) in the northeast U.S. You visit that person for dinner, discussing a number of things, but little or nothing about the house and its history. That night, you have a dream which you remember the next morning. In the dream, you observed several people looting the house after taking away the inhabitants at gunpoint. They were all dressed in clothing of the eighteenth century. In the dream, you "saw" the man taken from the house try to run, to escape, and "watched" as he was shot down.

Sometime in the next few days, you speak with the acquaintance who lives in the house, and relate the dream to him (starting out with a typical "I had a wonderful time, and I even had a weird dream about the house"). The person you're relating this to is puzzled. He didn't remember telling you about the house's history, or that the original owner's family were Tories and arrested by the Continental Army, or that the owner tried to escape and was shot. You and all others at that dinner also agree that there was no such discussion. So how did you know? And why do you suddenly feel like Rod Serling is looking over your shoulder?

Most people are aware of psychics who apparently can "read" the history of an object by holding it in their hands. Sometimes called psychometry, this is an offshoot of clairvoyance. Somehow, it appears that objects can record information, that happenings around an object are imprinted, and can be deciphered by our brains. The information can be "played back" in a variety of ways, and may be far from complete. But in many reported experiences, the "playback" may be like that of a VCR, with the psychic "watching" the events from the past as though watching a film on videotape. Of course, it's not just self-professed psychics who have these experiences. Most of us have such experiences many times in our lives.

Ever go into a house for the first time and feel like you were very much at home there, that it felt like a good place? Or the reverse, you felt very uncomfortable, like something "bad" had happened there (which may have simply been the folks living there having very emotional fights)? Picking up on the "vibes" of a house or other location or even such perceptions of antiques or other previously owned items seems to point to our capability to receive information apparently "imprinted" on that object.

There is little difference between perceiving the history of a hand-held object or a house you walk into. What is a house but a large object?

When we pick up specific information "recorded" in the environment of a location, it comes out in a variety of ways. Feeling good or bad is just one of these ways. We may "hear" footsteps or voices, we may "see" cloudy or out-of-focus or transparent or sharp images of people or objects that may have been in the house or building previously. We might simply get a warm feeling or a cold chill. We might "smell" perfume or cologne or something foul, even after the house has been aired or fumigated.

All this might take place during waking consciousness, or be perceived and taken in through our subconscious, only to come out during sleep and dreaming. Why come out in dreams?

Most people who see transparent or even solid images which apparently do not fit with the reality of the location will dismiss them as hallucinations or become afraid, since they are "obviously" in a "haunted house." Hauntings tend to relate to these types of experiences, a playback of an event involving people which was "recorded" by the environment of the house sometime in the past.

Our culture and religions often tell us that such hauntings are indications of evil spirits or demons, and as such should be feared. In fact, if you are perceiving such clear images, consider yourself lucky. You may be looking backward to a time before VCRs and even photographs. But because we're taught such things are indicators of psychological disturbance (which they typically are not, especially when there are many witnesses to such "recordings"), or indicators of evil ghosts and ghoulies, we tend to ignore what we're receiving.

So the subconscious mind, which has this great information to relay to us, chooses another avenue which the conscious mind can deal with: dreams. Placing the information in a dream allows for either acceptance of the information as is, as having been picked up from the house or object. It more often allows you to dismiss the information as "just a dream," which is much less threatening.

In any event, whether a single dream is a case of retro-cognition, of viewing the past, or of some clairvoyant, real-time reading of the information picked up by an object or location is impossible to determine at the present time. And again, it doesn't matter what label we place on it. If the information is useful or interesting, make use of it, enjoy the experience. Whether there is a direct link with the past or whether you're decoding existing information really only matters to the people studying the experiences. If all retrocognition is psychometry or clairvoyance of records, it may mean we cannot psychically pick up information through time (at least to the past). That helps researchers and theorists in looking for and understanding psi processes, but probably doesn't mean a whole lot as far as the person having the experience is concerned.

From a spiritual perspective, whether we're remembering an actual past life through our dreams or conscious experience, or whether we're having psychic access to information in the past or recorded in the past, it does matter to what's happening here. Unfortunately, you've seen that there are too many unanswered questions and alternate interpretations to have an answer to what's happening here.

In their dreams, people do have remembrances or experiences of being someone else. So, too, do they occasionally bring forth information about past events. In fact, dreams can work well as a vehicle for our memories to remind us of something important we may not be able to dredge up consciously. If there is real-time clairvoyance going on in addition to this memory retrieval, the reason is undoubtedly also to be seen in the dream.

The important lesson to be learned is that these memories, these experiences, these dreams, may have much to tell us about ourselves and how we need to view ourselves and our connections with other people in our lives today. It's the information's validity and applicability that we need to concern ourselves with, not whether we lived before in Atlantis. After all, as far as Atlantis is concerned, you really can't go home again . . . except in your dreams.

The past is what we call the present after it has happened. The present is when we live now. Psychic experiences of the present are therefore easier to look at, since we're there. . . .

CHAPTER 10

Dreams of the Here and Now

How do we tell if the psychic information is of the present (clairvoyance), of the past (retrocognition), or of the future (precognition)? That depends on the feedback you receive. If you have an experience you classify as psychic, and you later determine that information was correct, if you really need to classify that experience as precognitive or clairvoyant or even retrocognitive, you need to relate the time you had the experience to the actual time of the event. If the event happened before your experience, it was retrocognitive. If it happened after, precognitive. If it happened at the same time, clairvoyant.

But again, with many experiences it may be virtually impossible to determine if the information crossed time as well as space. If the time difference between the perception of the information and the actual event was large (say hours, days or even years), it wouldn't be difficult to classify that experience. If the time difference were, say, minutes or even seconds, unless that event actually happened where you were standing (or sitting) there would be no way of determining that it was not a clairvoyant, real-time experience.

Labels, classifications, words like clairvoyance, retrocognition, and precognition are a help as well a hindrance. Getting too caught up in them confuses the issue and can make something very interesting too much trouble to deal with.

With dreams, those labels can be even more confusing. If

a psi-viewed event occurs while you're sleeping, not knowing just when during that specific sleep period the dream happened means that you can't determine at all whether the dream was real-time, or of the past or future. More importantly, even if you feel the dream was unusual and even perhaps psychic, it still may not be a dream you can immediately relate to an event.

Clairvoyance is very easy to test in the laboratory, as the idea of a subject picking up on a target "now" is much simpler than trying to establish the conceptual grounds for a subject (or researcher) to consider grasping information through time (in addition to simply going through space). One need simply have the target selected (randomly, and without anyone knowing the nature of that randomly assigned and hidden target), the subject make a guess, and the guess compared to the actual target.

When you add in another person staring at or concentrating on the target, the possibility that telepathy is involved comes up (did the information come from the person's mind or from the target?). Conversely, if you try to set up a telepathy experiment where a "sender" concentrates on a target and a "receiver" tries to describe it, you again confound the experiment: Is the receiver getting the information from the mind of the sender (telepathy) or from the target alone (clairvoyance)?

One of the most productive forms of experiments for clairvoyance (and precognition) research has been that of "remote perception" or "remote viewing." Remote viewing experiments conducted in the past have used a couple of methodologies. In one, a person is sent out to the randomly selected location at the time the "viewer" is to receive impressions of that location. This outbound observer or "beacon" spends time walking around the location, noting details and focusing on what he or she observes. The "viewer" reveals what kinds of impressions are received from the location of the beacon.

In another remote viewing methodology, experimenters randomly select coordinates of a location for the "viewer" and simply ask the "viewer" to describe that location.

In the first methodology, the remote viewing session includes information from a location with an observer. With such a situation, the information received by the "viewer" could have come from either the location (clairvoyance) or the mind of the observer (telepathy) or both. In the second, we presuppose that not having an observer, a beacon, eliminates the telepathy possibility. This may not be the case, for if there are any people (or maybe even animals) in the vicinity of the selected location, the information received could have also come from them.

The real question is, does it matter? If the information comes in through a process that doesn't involve the "normal" senses or intuitive or logical inference or deduction, then we may have a psi process occurring, regardless of whether we can tease it apart as telepathy or clairvoyance (which are, after all, only arbitrary framing labels). Labels or jargon seem to often be a problem in having people conceptualize just what it is to be "psychic." People are often more caught up in whether that psi experience was telepathy or clairvoyance, rather than simply whether something unusual and informative, perhaps something psychic, did occur.

This confusion between telepathy and clairvoyance has even carried over to clairvoyance of future events, to precognition. Several experiments have been conducted in precognitive remote viewing, where the beacon is sent out to a location randomly selected *after* the "viewer" has made his/her descriptions. In some instances, the observer sent out is the actual "viewer."

As far as psychic dreams are concerned, this same "confusion" could occur if you try to label or classify the dream so as to be "strictly telepathy" or "strictly clairvoyance."

For example, let's say I had a dream that a major world leader was being attacked. I wake up, remembering the dream, and listen to the news. I learn that an attack, such as the one I dreamed, actually took place during the night. Did I pick up that information from the actual event (clairvoyance) or from the mind of the attacker (telepathy) or even from the mind(s) of a witness or two (also telepathy)? The information, in other words, was accurate, but the mode of communication is in question (from "viewing" the event—clairvoyance—or from receiving information from the mind(s) of person(s) present—telepathy—or even both?).

Does it really matter which, as long as the information works? That's the real question, as the words we use to categorize experiences and abilities we call telepathy or clairvoyance or even precognition are just arbitrary in the grand scheme of things.

In other precognitive remote viewing studies, a potential event (such as the outcome of a horse race or commodities trade) is given a symbol to associate with (say, a particular fruit for each of the potential winning horses). The "viewer" doesn't so much "view" the event in the future as the piece of fruit he or she will be given based on the outcome of the event. If horse number one is associated with a watermelon, and the "viewer" sees himself eating a watermelon after the race, the experimenters would note that the "viewer" has "seen" horse number one win. If that horse does win, the experimenters must provide the "viewer" with a piece of watermelon, to close the loop, so to speak.

So, was that precognition of the fruit that would be provided or of the event itself, or did the "viewer" somehow telepathically connect with a version of himself from the future? When we precognize future events and then receive the feedback that such an event actually has happened, are we then sending that information into the past to ourselves?

Again, does it matter? You make use of the information or not. If not, what good is it? Labels and categories can easily confuse the greater issue of "is the information valuable and useable?" since we can get so wrapped up in classifications such as "remote viewing" that we forget to apply the messages received.

> Often I have dreams and don't realize their significance until the actual event takes place. In one case, I saw an entire murder take place. I described the house and clothing of the victims. The faces were

fuzzy, but I later learned my friend was shot by her husband who also killed himself. I was never in her house, but described the room down to the detail of a bloody mirror.

—K.W., North Wildwood, NJ

The above dream is a good example of how the time factor leaves you in the cold in trying to determine just what kind of psychic dream this was. The murder could have occurred at the same time as the dream, earlier, or later. K.W., not knowing that the dream was truly significant, would not have tried to deal with whether the dream occurred at the same time, or before, or after. K.W. did not even determine just where the event dreamed about could have occurred, because of incomplete information.

Such dreams can make us feel incomplete, because of the nagging feeling that we should have been able to do something. This is not always the case. If the dream occurs at the same time as the event, or the event happens during the sleep period in which the dream occurs, there is nothing to be done, except perhaps reveal the dreamed information to interested parties who might be able to make use of it (Police, for example, if the information could help in an investigation).

On March 19 1982, I had a dream that my brother was driving his car at a very high speed. Then I saw his head explode and there was blood all over the front and side windows.

On March 20 1982 at about 11:00 A.M., a policeman came to the door and told us that my brother had shot himself in the head while driving 100 miles an hour.

—J.L., Anchorage, AK

This is a classic example of a percipient receiving very clear information about a very specific event. The information was verified and the time factor of the event essentially related to the sleep period of the dreamer.

Why did J.L. have that dream if there was nothing to be done to save the brother? In such instances, as with cases in which a person sees the apparition of a relative or loved one at the time of (or just after) the death of the individual represented by the apparition, this may be the mind of the "viewer" bringing in the information to help relieve the grief, to prepare the "viewer" for the news that is to come.

> I dreamt that my brother was down in a deep hole reaching for my help. I tried to help him, but before I could, I woke up.
> The next morning I felt very strange and disturbed about the dream. I told my wife that Bill was in an accident and was hurt very badly.
> About noon, my mother and sister came by with the news that Bill was in a serious accident and was all broken up. The truck in which he was riding (in the back) got hit in the back by a tractor-trailer carrying logs. The accident happened on a bridge just before the river, and Bill was thrown down an embankment some fifty feet below the highway. Eight people were in the back of the covered pick-up. One was killed, and my brother was the most seriously injured.

> —E.F., Norfolk, VA

Dreams like this one and the previous one might also hold a bit of important information that is helpful. There have, in the past, been reports of people who have been hurt in accidents yet not found at the scene of the accident. Dreams of accident sites can be carriers of life-saving information if the dreamer (or someone told about the dream) can use that dreamed information to rescue to injured party. Psychics have had experiences in being able to find lost and injured people, and this information can be provided to psychics and to us "normal" folks in or out of the dream state.

Around October, I had a vivid dream in color about a house which I described to my mother when I got up in the morning. The description I gave included carpets, drapes, furniture, etc. Color schemes in each room, as well as the exact location of the rooms was very detailed.

Two weeks before Christmas, my aunt's family moved into their new home. We went to visit on Christmas Eve. I had never even been aware of the location of the house, being on the unfamiliar side of town from their old rural home in a city far from where I lived. Mom and I walked into the house, a four-level maze of rooms and stairways, and both of us were awe-struck. This *was* the house in my dream down to the last detail, including the new furniture neither one of us knew my aunt had purchased.

—B.C., West Valley City, UT

Life saving? Grief preventing? Important? No, not really, yet this dream is a fairly common variety. We often dream about very mundane or very exciting events which are neither life-threatening or life-altering. This doesn't make them any less "psychic" or any less interesting. In fact, they may be more useful than many other types of psychic dreams since they may simply be a way for the mind to let us know that we have a bigger connection to the world around us than what we have with our "normal" senses and sensibilities.

People interested in psychic dreams (such as you, I assume, since you're reading this book) are often interested in keeping track of those psychic dreams, in determining which are the psychic dreams and which are not, and in doing something with the information from those dreams. In a later chapter, I'll discuss working with your dreams a bit more, so for the time being let me discuss with you something very basic you should do.

Keep a dream log or journal. As you recall dreams, write them down or tape-record them. Some people keep a cassette recorder next to their beds, others simply a pad and pen. The time we best remember dreams is just as we wake up. Granted, it isn't easy to be awake enough to take down any information, yet not awake enough to have forgotten what you dreamed (just waking up can be an ordeal in itself, as I am well aware). Record (on paper or on tape) the dream and note any special feeling you have toward the dream. Does it seem different than other dreams? Might it be related to a real event?

Make sure you include the date, and even the time you woke up remembering the dream. This will help somewhat when if you try to pin the dream down to a time span.

Then, as you learn of events that have an apparent relationship to what you dreamed about, go back over that dream and note which of the contents of the dream were actually related to the events. Note also the timing of the event, and see how that relates to the timing of the dream.

If you can only connect the dream to the event within the time span of your sleep that night, don't place too much weight on it being precognitive (or retrocognitive). Remember, a real-time clairvoyant dream is just as interesting as a precognitive one, even though there's not much you can do to affect an event that has already occurred. The information provided by the dream could shed quite a bit of light on the event itself, helping you intellectually understand what happened, or helping you emotionally deal with the consequences of that event.

Even though psychic experiences are difficult for people to accept in general (until they happen to you, and even then they're tough to handle sometimes), it's somehow less difficult to accept psi perceptions of events occurring in the present, in the here-and-now, than it is to accept those of the distant past or of the future.

On the other hand, from a usefulness standpoint, most people would feel that a warning of a coming event is more important than information of an event that has already happened. Is this really true? Are precognitions more useful than clairvoyant experiences?

They are if that's what you believe. As you'll see in the next chapter, the future appears to be changable, elastic to some extent. The usefulness of a precognition therefore depends on what use you make of the information. If I foresee an accident for myself and stay out of the situation that I foresaw, there is no accident. That's good. But if I had that same "vision" and did nothing about it, thinking that the future cannot be changed, what good is that precognition except as something for me to get worried about?

Since the events are occurring at approximately the time we have a clairvoyant "view" of a situation, there's little if anything we can do to alter that situation. But once again, we could use that information in follow-up activities, rescuing people we have just "seen" injured, stopping or arresting criminals we have just "seen" commit a crime, and aiding people we have just "seen" fall ill. Just think about the possibilities if fire fighters, rescue workers, police, or paramedics could be aware of situations that need their attention as the situations happen; there wouldn't be any sort of time lag between the event, the reporting of the event (say, by a witness calling 911) and action by the appropriate people in helping with that situation. They could be on their way immediately.

Of course, if there were any way to be more precise about precognitive information, if we knew the accident or crime was to happen before it actually happened, the police, fire fighters, or rescue folks could be on the scene as the incident happens or even sometimes before in order to prevent it.

Once again, we have the basic problem of the inadequacy of detail in psychic experience. Without knowing just when an event is about to happen (not to mention exactly where), there's no way to judge where (and when) to place the people who could help best (or prevent the situation from coming about). As the future tends to be mutable, not fixed, there are too many unknown variables which could affect the efficiency of such prevention attempts.

On the other hand, with clairvoyant information, you have the added benefit that the event is happening as you get the information. This enables you to make an attempt to relate that information to an event that is real in the here and now. Any information on location or description of the event, coupled with the feeling or knowledge that the event has already happened, can provide more confidence in the possibility that you can do something about the event's results.

On *Star Trek* (both versions) as well as in a number of other science fiction films, TV shows, novels, and stories, there are technological devices which can pinpoint life-forms on a planet's surface (or in other starships for that matter). These sensors enable the characters to perform precision rescues and contacts where they'd otherwise be guessing as to where hurt crew-people are or where the greatest concentration of a sentient life-form is for contact.

While we have no transporters as on *Star Trek* with which to perform rescues, information that could pinpoint where there is danger, where there are living people trapped in a fire or under debris, can cut down the time spent searching for such people and watching out for dangers.

Much of the potential applicability of information we receive in the fashion we now call "psychic" is in such follow-up activities. Awareness of real-time situations, from the rescue and crime scenarios to perceptions of design flaws in products (and perhaps in buildings) are used today, though information is gathered through the use of the "normal" perceptions and through technological means. Add to the ways we collect such information "normally," any new information we might gather instantly (at the time or shortly after the event or inspection) we might otherwise not get so immediately (or perhaps ever), and we have greater efficiency in saving lives, preventing tragedy, keeping quality control where otherwise there might be little, and helping people understand the circumstances around them that affect them both physically and psychologically.

The potential for real-time psi is incredible. I should mention that there is a potential danger as well. If you have such an experience of receiving information which you connect to a real-time event, there is always the possibility that you are wrong about it. Time can therefore be wasted in trying to do something about an event that hasn't actually happened. Or the information could be incomplete so that it is severely misinterpreted, putting you on to the wrong place or the wrong situation. Or the information is correct but is not actually psychic. It is possible that what you perceived in or out of that dream was a situation that you "knew" about purely by coincidence. And there's always the possibility that information already in your memory about that event (that it was going to happen) was buried deep enough that you didn't know you already knew it.

We come again to the recurring problem of "How do I know it's a psychic experience?" On an absolute level, we can never be 100 percent sure that it was psychic, that it wasn't intuitive leaps of logic using half-memories or deeply buried ones, or that it wasn't coincidence. You can, however, be closer to an assumption that it was information beyond normal perceptions or buried memory if the event you perceive is one removed from your own experience.

Let's say, for example, you dreamed of a small child lost in Yosemite National Park, a place you'd never visited (but perhaps seen pictures of), complete with details as to where the child was (landmarks, for example). You woke up and watched the morning news, which included the story of a little boy lost overnight in Yosemite, and still missing in the morning. The event hadn't yet happened or been reported to the news media at the time you went to sleep, yet here it was. When the boy is found, the news coverage includes video footage of the area surrounding the boy's location, and it closely matches your dream imagery.

Buried memory, intuitive inference, or logical deduction? Very unlikely, perhaps to the point of being improbable. Coincidence? Hard to eliminate, but an absolutely incredible coincidence (on several levels) if that is what it was. Psychic or paranormal or extended perception? As long as you are not one of those people who say such experiences or perceptions are patently impossible, then this is the likeliest possibility.

Again, you also need to look at your own feelings about that dream. Did it seem "different" from other dreams (beyond simply the ability to remember it clearly, where you may not remember most of your dreams that clearly)? How did it feel? Did it "feel" right?

What do we do with seemingly clairvoyant information? A good deal of time, reported experiences lack enough detail or description of a real-time event to be able to connect the information from that experience to one particular event. Lack of detail is the bane of a psychic's existence (and a parapsychologist's as well). I could dream about a real murder occurring and get a clear view of the murderer, but nothing else. I could be absolutely positive that the dream was real. Unfortunately, knowing what a killer looks like without being able to tie him or her to a location somewhere in the world or to a particular murder means that the information is virtually useless. Unless, of course, I were to run into that person sometime in my life. In that case, if I really felt my dream was a true representation of this person now in front of me, that she/he was a murderer, I'd use that information as advice that I should steer clear of this person. I simply do not have enough information to do anything.

In such situations, people who have the experiences need to understand that there may be absolutely nothing to be done with that experience or information. This can be extremely frustrating, and people can even become obsessed with such an experience. It is important to "let it go," rather than feel "I should have done something about it." Better to think that when you see an actual crime being committed, where there is something you can do (like report it to the police, testify, and so on). Psychics report that they have to "get used to" not being able to do something with all the information they get, just as we all have to do this on a daily basis.

One other point to remember is that no matter how clear such experiences might be, how detailed they are, when the "vision" comes to you in a dream, you may have to look carefully at that dream. Imagery from your subconscious might very well be mixed in with the clairvoyant (or other psychic) information. In addition, as with any psychic experience, in life or in a laboratory, it is important to not read too deeply into the "picture."

If you "see" in your dream a tall, cylindrical, pointed shape, you might try to identify it with a landmark you've seen before, or your subconscious might fill in missing details so that an incomplete, vague shape now looks more like the Eiffel Tower. This often creates a real problem, since that shape may be accurate, but the identification is not. It wasn't the Eiffel Tower, but a tall salt or pepper shaker.

Point of view can distort what we get out of these experiences. We're used to seeing with our eyes, and we've learned to see things proportionally. However, if a shape or image appears in a "vision" or dream without anything near it to provide a frame of reference, a tall, pointed, salt shaker floating on a background field of a solid color might actually look bigger than it is. Or part of a car might not look like part of a car, because the image fills your whole field of "vision."

If all this sounds like there may be more problems here than it's worth, you could look at it that way. What I mean to say, however, is that you need to be aware that the imagery or information coming through on such channels can be incomplete or provided from a different frame of reference. If you feel that information coming through in a dream or psychic "vision" is truly psychic, try to look at it as just a few pieces of a puzzle laid on a big piece of white paper. If you can piece together the puzzle, great. If not, then the pieces might fit with what you already know about a dozen different situations. Figuring which of those situations is the right one may be difficult if you try to think about it too much. You might simply go with your hunches or feelings as to how this information relates to reality. With that, you might find greater relevance of that dreamed information to your life.

Can real problems be caused by such psychic dreams? Unfortunately, the answer is yes. Running your life solely on the basis of what these dreams or waking experiences seem to tell you may leave you unconnected with the real world. Pay attention to what's really going on around you (stay grounded, to put it another way).

Clairvoyant and precognitive dreams can cause problems in other ways. There have been a few cases which have made it to court of someone dreaming of a murder. Feeling civic-minded, the dreamer reports the dream, which came with very detailed information, to the police. For want of a better suspect, the dreamer is arrested, the police viewing the dream as a kind of confession to the crime. In some instances, such reports really do turn out to be confessions—in some cases the "dreamer" really is the killer. But in other cases, the dreamer was an innocent bystander, someone who somehow "knew" about the incident. In those cases, the police have little or no evidence which could even be stretched to cover the dreamer. In a couple of cases, however, the fact that the dreamer was the only suspect (simply because of an attitude of "She/he had to have done it. How else could she/he have known so much about it?") was enough to hold the dreamer over for trial.

Dreams of such detail are generally rare. Police typically have to find hard evidence upon which to build a case before following through on arresting someone who had a dream. They're more likely to believe the dreamer was an eyewitness and proceed from there. In fact, there are also cases on record where a "witness" to a crime or situation later comes forward and admits that what was seen was actually from a dream, rather than physical perception.

In addition, there are police departments and individual officers and detectives who have worked with psychics on criminal cases, which indicates an openness to such experiences as the dream of an "average" person being possibly psychic rather than an indicator that the dreamer had something to do with the crime.

Also consider that "psychic" may not be a word in the vocabulary of the people you report the information to. If you do report such information anonymously, you may also have to contend with how to present it. "I dreamed about a murder" will probably be less accepted than "I have information relating to a murder."

Therein, again, lies the problem of "packaging" psychic information, whether clairvoyant, precognitive, or of other forms. Our society in the western hemisphere says that these experiences are not "normal." Therefore, to get the information across to the people who need to know, you sometimes have to rephrase the way you want to talk about it.

Real-time psi perceptions of events apparently occur in our lives, regardless of whether we consider ourselves psychic or not. Many immediately label them with the word "coincidence" or the phrase "lucky guess." Others assume that all similar experiences, psychic or not when you look carefully at them, are psychic. We can go to extremes in either direction. What's important to remember is that the information coming to our conscious minds from dreams, from memory, psychically or not, are being flagged as important. Paying attention to it may provide solutions to problems in our lives. Dismissing the experiences as invalid information because the vehicle of the information, an apparently psychic dream or waking experience, is not considered "normal" or even "possible" by some is to do ourselves a great injustice.

The majority of people who have dreams we can classify as "clairvoyant" or "real-time psychic" dreams, have dreams a lot less "exciting" than those that might deal with murder or other crimes, or even those that deal with disasters happening in the here and now. Most reported clairvoyant dreams (and waking-clairvoyance experiences) tend to have to do with our own lives or the lives of those in our immediate range of experience. By that I mean relatives, friends, or people we know quite a bit about (such as political figures, people prevalent in sports or entertainment, or locals we know about but may not know personally). Clairvoyant dreams can be quite unsatisfying, since unless there's something we can do about the situation we "see" in our dreams, we might as well be watching a news report on TV or reading an account in the newspaper. And that, of course, may be the very reason our minds bring in the information, as a simple news report. Why do we read the paper and watch/listen to TV/radio news? Because we have a curiosity about the world around us (and the immediate events and people that may affect our lives). Or such dreams and experiences may be very satisfying for that reason, allowing us to know about events as they are happening rather than having to wait for the actual report in the news.

If your experience in or out of dreams says "Here's something that's happening right now, or just happened," follow up on it, within reason of course. See if it happened and think about how such information may affect your own life, or the lives of those around you. You may be surprised at just how much you're really connecting with the world around you. Or you may learn that the psychic/clairvoyant part of you is simply very good at keeping you abreast of local, national, and world events, happening in the now.

As for the future, that's coming up next. . . .

CHAPTER 11

Future Dreaming

Can information come to us from a future, either one that is predetermined or one that is probable? Can anything, whether it be information or objects or people travel from the future to the present, or the present to the past?

We usually think in terms of cause and effect with regard to things happening, where the event (the cause) brings about a particular happening or outcome (the effect). With precognition, it is suggested that the effect (the precognitive experience) *precedes* the cause (the predicted event in the future). Is this possible?

Abraham Lincoln had a dream. In his dream, he found himself walking through the halls of the White House. He came upon mourners and a funeral. When he asked "Who is dead in the White House?" the reply was "The president . . . he was killed by an assassin." This occurred in March of 1865. In April, this dream, which he had discussed with several people, came true—Abraham Lincoln was dead, killed by assassin John Wilkes Booth.

Since the time humankind could think and develop our own rituals, religions, and explanations for the way the universe works, we have been interested in, if not obsessed with, two areas covered by the field of parapsychology: the idea that there is some existence after death, and the notion that some specially gifted people have access to the way the future is to be.

Divination techniques used by people, primitive and modern, to "read" the future run a wide gamut from utilizing the movement of the stars to studying rune stones, from watching the flights of birds or migration patterns of animals to "reading" animal entrails, from throwing sticks to staring into a crystal ball. But all of these require "special" talents or learned skills, or so we're told by the practitioners themselves.

Everyone dreams, and so the future as it appears in the dreams of everyday folk is more accessible to us all through that state. While it is true that some cultures may raise certain individuals above others for more frequent dreams of future events, we all seem capable of somehow receiving information across time, whether in the dream-state or simply through hunches, intuitive flashes, or so-called "visions."

Precognition as a studied "ability" in parapsychological research is not difficult to test for. You set up a test or experiment for which the target has not yet been selected. Your "subject" makes a selection or "prediction" or "guess" and then you randomly select the target (or a computer randomly selects it). You check to see if the target matches the call. Sounds easy, but there are inherent problems, both from the standpoint of other "psychic" explanations (do we use precognition to "see" the future, or psychokinesis to "influence" the future) and from the philosophical and physical end (how is it possible to gain information across time, and is there even a "definite" future for us to access?).

There has been much discussion in recent years as to just what an experimental series dealing with precognition means. Most experiments are conducted utilizing random event generators (mentioned back in chapter three) or computers which randomly select the target after the calls are made. Statistical analysis is applied to the results to see if there are significant numbers of correct calls or hits (significant above what you'd expect by chance). Participants are usually given the option of beginning the run when they feel ready; this causes a couple of potential problems.

First of all, psychokinesis can enter into the picture. Experiments indicate that people may be able to affect the random output of a computer or other Random Event Generator (REG). If this is so, it may be that the person making the "guesses" utilizes his/her psychokinesis to cause the REG to come up with matching results. In other words, instead of guessing what the machine will choose in the future, you affect the machine so that what it chooses matches your guesses.

Can we know for sure that this isn't happening in a given experiment? I don't think so. Even if you check for psychokinetic ability (giving the same person a PK test before the precognition experiment) and that person does well, there's no way to tell whether PK has or has not influenced the machine in the precognition experiment. We have no detection devices to look for PK "energy" as yet. There is also the added (and dreaded) possibility that the experimenter, wishing for certain results, uses his or her own PK to cause the subject's test results to be a certain way.

Of course, there are enough stories about people about "knowing" future events that precognition is at least a possibility. That supports the idea that the precognition experiments are feasible, that they don't have to be psychokinetic. In addition, precognition of a slightly non-random bunch of targets may simulate psychokinesis. Even with a random event generator, there are times that the output may be less random (more heads than tails in flips of a coin)—sort of some nice runs of good luck. If you knew when to start, when the run of less random targets began, it might look like you were influencing the outcomes. In other words, instead of influencing the output of the REG, you are using precognition to choose just when to press the "start" button to begin the test (which is when that run of less random targets starts), not when to actually start influencing the machine.

For example, let's say you went to a casino and decided to play the slots. With psychokinetic ability, you might be able to influence the slot machines to pay off, to come up with the right results after pulling the lever. On the other hand, you might roam around the casino until your precognition told you that a certain machine would pay off after three more pulls. Knowing this, you know just *when* to try each of the machines so that they pay off.

See the problem?

In looking at dreams, this is not such a big problem. The issue of psychokinesis (creating the future) vs. precognition (knowing the future) is less serious. Unlike the character of George Orr in LeGuin's *The Lathe of Heaven*, who could affect the whole world with his dreams, it looks as though we don't have that kind of major PK ability. If we did, we'd all be wreaking havoc with reality on a daily basis. So if we're not playing with reality like George Orr, there must be some consensus of how the world looks and runs, some guidelines that keep things going as they are. Then again, maybe we could affect a major change if we all decided on it. One of the "Eternal Champion" characters of fantasy and science fiction writer Michael Moorcock spoke of the "fact" that the world *was* flat until humanity decided otherwise.

But this leaves us with a bigger problem: Is it possible for our awareness to reach into the future? Is there even a future for us to reach into? What is time and how does it relate to dreaming?

J.W. Dunne, with his extensive study of his own dreams written up in his 1927 book *An Experiment With Time*, brought a couple of ideas into the public eye. In his book, he detailed an extensive study of his own dreams, looking for dreams that transcend time itself, for evidence of pre-cognitive information in normal dream states. Until that time, others had asked for dreams and other experiences that might be subjected to analysis for psychic correlations, but Dunne went a step further in taking a pool of his own dreams rather than a grouping of the experiences of others. Dunne is to be commended for this, according to playwright and writer J.B. Priestly in *Man & Time*, and for bringing dreams and the act of remembering, recording, and analyzing one's own dreams into focus for the general public.

The other contribution of Dunne in that book and later ones, including *The Serial Universe*, deals with time itself, as he extensively explored ideas of the structure of time and its relation to space. While Priestly and others have problems with some of Dunne's ideas, and while Dunne's theoretical discussions are often difficult to follow, our notions of time today (numerous as they may be) owe quite a bit to Dunne's work.

There has been much discussion of the idea of time itself. As much discussion as there is, there are only some things we know about the way it (probably) works. I'll discuss just a few of the ideas of future time here. There are a number of books you might consider reading if you are interested in time, including those of Dunne and Priestly; check the appendix for their titles. You might also read lots of science fiction, especially time travel novels, or those dealing with the structure of time (One science fiction novel I recommend is *Jack of Eagles* by James Blish, as it deals with the ideas of J.W. Dunne).

Time is changeable. We know this from two areas of science—physics and psychology. Albert Einstein dealt with the concept of time dilation as part of relativity, a concept proven by experimentation. Time dilation deals with both rate of time passing as well as how fast one moves through space. The faster you go (in relation to the rest of the universe), the slower time proceeds for you.

For example, if someone were to travel in a spacecraft close to the speed of light, and take a grand tour of our solar system, depending on how far one traveled, you could return in a few months or a couple of years, as far as the people you left behind were concerned. To you, traveling near the speed of light, perhaps a few days would have passed. Time would proceed at its "normal" pace here on Earth, while on the ship, it would slow to a crawl. And since time itself slows for the ship, so does perception of time. You would not even notice how or if time has changed until you stepped off the spacecraft back on Earth. Your watch/calendar would say that a few days had gone by, while the calendar on Earth would say differently.

What this means is that time's passage can be physically slowed down or even sped up. Time is not a steady, straight arrow thing. It is really only our western cultural concept that time flows into the future on a straight path at a steady rate, not actual reality. The more you hear or read about time as a concept, the more confused you might get, as you learn that the more you study time, the less you realize you know. This doesn't say that we can get information from the future, merely that time is not a constant.

Psychologists have learned that one can change a person's perception of time. Experiments with people isolated from time-keeping devices (including the rising and setting of the sun) have shown that even the person's body-clock, which is basically on a twenty-four-hour cycle, can be affected, and can change by even tens of hours (how'd you like to be living a fifty-six-hour day without discomfort?).

Is there a future? Well, we know there's a past (we've been there) and a present (we're there now), but a future? We never really get there, since as we progress through time, our present becomes the past, and the future becomes the present. Let's look at ideas of time with that in mind.

One concept is that time and destiny are one and the same—we are predestined to live our lives in a particular way; the future is already written "in stone." If there is an objective future already laid out for us, maybe it is possible to somehow reach into it and "see" the definites of tomorrow or next month. However, this appears to remove all free will and decision-making power from us. If we are destined to do a particular thing tomorrow, whether we like it or not, then we are merely puppets of some universal puppeteer, characters in the Book of Life. Maybe we could flip through the pages ahead to the ending of our particular story as our own awareness of the present shifts from one page to the next. Unfortunately, if we get information from an inevitable future, that raises a particular question: What good is it? If I see I'm to die tomorrow, and I know I can't change that, what's the point?

Predestination is an idea that many, especially scientists dealing with time and with subatomic physics have a hard time accepting. In quantum physics, in the "world" below the level of atom-sized particles, the world works more in probabilities than definites. We don't know the outcome to some event until there is an observer there to witness the outcome. ("Does a tree falling in the woods make a sound when there's no one there to hear it?")

So, there is the idea of "probable futures." This is the concept that there are a few, perhaps many, future paths likely to occur, depending on certain events or decisions happening in the present. If you've seen *Back to the Future*, and especially *Back to the Future II* and *Back to the Future III*, or read time travel science fiction (or DC or Marvel Comics), you are probably familiar with the idea of going back in time and doing something that changes the future.

For example, in *Back to the Future*, Marty McFly (Michael J. Fox) accidentally changes the past, then has to rectify the error. If his parents don't fall in love, he's not going to be born. In "fixing" things, George McFly (Marty's dad) hauls off and hits Biff, the town bully. When Marty returns to 1985, his father is no longer a wimp—he's a successful science fiction writer. And by warning Doc Brown (the scientist who invents the time machine, played by Christopher Lloyd), Marty enables that character to have the foreknowledge to wear a bulletproof vest on a particular night in 1985, thereby saving his life.

Back to the Future II seemed, to many, a bit confusing to follow, as Marty McFly and company deal with major changes and alternating timelines thanks to a little more time-tampering. Marty heads off into the future to help his kids, only to find that an almanac of sports scores gets sent back to 1955 to Biff, who proceeds to make himself rich based on the information in the almanac (knowing all the sports scores for the coming fifty or so years gave him a distinct advantage when gambling). This sets off a chain of events that alters Marty's timeline, sending him and Doc Brown back again to 1955, where he (and the audience) gets to watch himself on his first visit to the 50s. Sound confusing?

Well, luckily, all is fixed in *Back to the Future III*. Marty McFly gets a chance to go back further into the past where he rescues Doc Brown from a future in which he's gunned down by (who else?) the town bully, an ancestor of Biff's. By the end of the film, all is right with the timestream, although the present Marty returns to is (fortunately for him) the happier one with his folks being successful. More importantly, we see that Marty has learned from his experiences and is able to make a choice about his own future based on what he learned in his time travels. The choice is one that will keep him whole and happy.

One reviewer of *Back to the Future III* seemed to have a problem with the timestream changing as it did. The stimulus prompting Marty to go back to the Old West to rescue Doc is a tombstone indicating that he died in a gunfight shortly after arriving there. Marty changes things when he goes back to 1885, and the tombstone vanishes. The reviewer found major fault with that—how could Doc Brown die before the time machine was even invented?

Time travel is confusing, as is any idea of mucking around with probable futures. If the movie reviewer went back in time to centuries before he was born and lived out his life there, dying, in effect, "before" he was born, would he be born in the first place? Of course he would, since the reviewer's subjective time span had nothing at all to do with what year he lived in (unless, of course, he did something to screw up his ancestors).

An episode of *Star Trek: The Next Generation* first broadcast in February, 1990 (entitled "Yesterday's *Enterprise*") also dealt with a change in time. A previous incarnation of the starship *Enterprise* escapes a battle with the Romulans through a time warp bringing it twenty-two years into its future (to the time of Captain Picard's *Enterprise*). This disappearance of a Federation vessel from a crucial point in time changes things. The Federation is, from the perspective of the TV viewer, suddenly at war with the Klingons, a dead crew member suddenly lives (Tasha Yar, security chief), and others are no longer aboard (Worf, who, as a Klingon, would now be at war with the Federation).

It is only through the urging of the character Guinan (Whoopi Goldberg) that the other *Enterprise* is sent back to rectify things. In fact, if not for Guinan's recognition that "something's not right" with their time, that there'd been a change of some kind, the new *Enterprise* would have been destroyed by Klingons. Apparently, Guinan's race of beings is sensitive to time, and therefore to any changes in it. Why did no one else notice? Because if there were a change in the past, everything from that point forward, including all memory of everyone who lived at that point and after, would be dependent on the time-altering event and what came after for facts. New timeline . . . new events . . . new memories.

All this, of course, is science fiction: a character traveling to an already existent past and changing his own present.

If we knew of something supposed to happen tomorrow that didn't quite suit us, we might do something to prevent it. If the event then doesn't happen, we're happy. We may make a guess about what is likely to happen tomorrow when we go to work and then make a decision to change our own behaviors to create a less likely outcome. The future that would *probably* happen doesn't.

Perhaps what precognition might be is our minds telling us what is "probably" going to happen in the future, given what we know now. Our brains become computers, calculating the odds of certain events happening in the future given what's been happening in the present and what's happened in the past. We make a "guess" or "prediction" of that "probable future." If it doesn't happen, because of chance or because someone made a non-probable decision, our prediction fails. If we move to prevent the prediction from coming true, that future never comes about.

We may be using clairvoyant ability to gather more information about things happening in the present, so that our brains have more data to make an educated guess of the future. Once again, though, that "probable future" is just that: probable, not definite. When it doesn't happen for the reasons named above, the prediction is invalid, no matter how good the guess was. Human decision-making can cause such probabilities to change at a moment's notice.

Let's assume there is some kind of objective future, and that it is changeable ("always in motion," to quote Yoda from *The Empire Strikes Back*). Perhaps precognitive experience, assuming psi abilities work at all, is an awareness of a "probable future," the one *most likely to occur*. When a prediction is made, then actions change (either because of the prediction or other factors that show up later), the probability changes and another future, another outcome becomes "most likely."

This brings up the idea of the "intervention paradox," which looks at altering outcomes of events perceived by precognition. Think about this: I have a precognitive experience during which I "see" myself in a car accident at a certain intersection tomorrow when a car runs a red light. I decide not to drive at all, and to stay away from that intersection in general. The next evening, I hear about a car running a red light at that intersection, narrowly missing a bus. I also learn that the time it happened was about the time I would regularly drive through the intersection. The event happens, though not as predicted. No accident, especially not one with me involved.

I intervened in my daily routine because of that prediction. The information came to me from the future, yet by acting on that information, I avoided that future all together. By intervening, I caused a time paradox: How could I get information from a future that never comes to be? There's an effect (the psychic experience) without a cause (the accident).

Another example: Let's say the current president of the United States (whoever or whenever he is) is told that there is to be an assassination attempt on his life on a particular day, and that the psychic who "saw" this attempt, also "saw" the president die. Perhaps that particular president decides to listen, and wears a bulletproof vest that day (and puts more Secret Service folks on the job). The assassin attempts to get near the president, but is scared off by the extra security. The assassin, a suspicious-looking individual, is noticed by a Secret Service agent, who stops him, frisks him, finds the gun, and arrests him. No attempt, no death, yet a real threat that could have happened.

Intervention due to the extra information not only saved the president, but also changed the psychic's vision of the way the future was to go. Some would say the psychic was wrong, others would say the psychic enabled the Secret Service to change which became the "most likely" Future.

Of course, the psychic's "prediction" may have resulted from the psychic somehow telepathically picking up the intent to assassinate the president from the mind of the assassin, as well as the assassin's plans to try it on a certain day at a certain location. It is not always necessary to say the information comes from the future. It may be "extra" information from the here and now.

Physicists have postulated that some particles may actually travel backward in time. Suggestions for such particles have included the idea that tachyons, theoretical particles which can only travel *faster* than the speed of light, can travel backward in time. Another idea bandied about is that antiparticles, such as positrons (an electron with a positive, rather than negative, charge), are actually particles traveling backward in time, which is why their charges look opposite to what we'd expect. Whether these particles can actually carry information to a human mind is a whole different question.

Can the future actually affect the present or the past? We really don't know. That's unfortunately the best answer I can give, although many will offer more definite answers (especially many self-professed psychics). It appears that sometimes there is information about the future that shows up unannounced, and that this information comes true. And sometimes that information can be used to make other choices, and to effectively alter that envisioned future. And of course, there is also the aspect of coincidence to consider (though the role of that in a given, apparent precognitive experience is difficult, if not impossible to assess).

When one has a psychic "flash" or "vision" or "gut feeling" about the future, the information content varies from simply a feeling that something (good or bad) is about to happen to a clear picture/message of what is going to happen. Knowledge of a future being spotty may mean not being able to directly connect the "vision" to the event until after the event happens. Of course at that point there's not a lot you can do to affect that event. Specific information about a future event, when it is recognized as such, can be helpful. But first the experiment must decide that the information is about a future event and that the information *can* be utilized at all.

If the experient believes in an inevitable future, he may do nothing but wait it out. On the other hand, even a helpful psychic who knows to use precognitive information can't be too helpful without specifics.

People have had precognitive experiences about all sorts of disasters. If an individual got information that a DC-10 was going to crash tomorrow in Chicago, with enough detail as to what was wrong with the plane, that doesn't mean anything can be done. Without airline information, and considering the hundreds of flights going in and out of O'Hare airport on a given day, it would be next to impossible to figure out just which flight to ground. Incomplete information can be extremely frustrating in this respect.

In dreams, there is the added complication of dream imagery that could effectively "pollute" the precognitive information. Not only is there the difficult process of remembering the fine details of a dream, but also the problem of separating out from a dream just what is psychic information and what has been added by the subconscious to make the dream more interesting.

Nancy Sondow, in the January 1988 issue of *The Journal of the American Society For Psychical Research* ("The Decline of Precognized Events with the Passage of Time: Evidence from Spontaneous Dreams"), recreated with her own dreams J.W. Dunne's precognition experiment. In the journal article, she discussed a finding of her experiment which coincided with that of other precognitive studies and observations of spontaneous precognitive experiences. What she found was that most of her dreams that could have been considered precognitive came true within a day of the dream. There tends to be a falling off of how accurate the premonitions are the further down the line into the future the events are. Sondow brings up the point that if what we are "reading" of the future comes from the branching of possible futures, the further into the future one tries to "see," the more likelihood that you could be picking up on the wrong "branch."

She also discussed a couple of objections to any analysis of spontaneous dream precognitions which can affect the drop-off rate. One, from Dunne, is one I've discussed previously. Given all the possible things one might dream about, if you wait long enough and wade through enough dreams, the dreamed event may happen, or a real event will merely be connected to the dreamed event by the person doing the analysis. If I predict that I will someday soon come into some money, one might connect that prediction to anything from my receiving a bonus at work (which I expected anyway) to finding a coin or dollar bill lying in the street. Coincidence, two events related to one another by an observer, is responsible if you wait long enough. So, if the event dreamed about happens very soon after the dream, there is much less chance that the dream-connection to the event was coincidence.

The other objection is one she calls the "memory-artifact interpretation," which has to do with the length of time since a dream occurs and the decay of memory (forgetting) of details that might otherwise be connected as precognized bits of information. The longer you wait for the event to occur, the better the chance that you'll forget some details that might allow you to connect the dream to the actual event.

Of course, there are some features of precognitive and other psychic dreams that often set them apart from other kinds of dreams. One is the quality of the dream imagery, which might be more vivid and evocative that other dreams. You remember it more clearly and somehow may "know" it relates to real events. The other is a feeling that occurs for people when they come to the event earlier dreamed about, a sense of déjà vu, that the event is truly familiar because they dreamed about it.

Besides the fall-off due to attempts at picking out the correct future "branch," Sondow also discusses the idea that there may be this decline in precognition due to the way we deal with the future. The immediate future tends to be more important to us than a time further down the road. Therefore, this immediate future, which is also less subject to extensive branching off, may be more often targeted by our psi. Sondow brings in the point, however, that we do sometimes dream of people or events other than ourselves, people and events not as important to us, so this argument may be less effective than a fall-off due to further branching possible futures.

Such precognitive dreams as those of disasters, while not necessarily affecting us directly, may be "important" to us because of their intensity of the emotions they create. On October 21 1966, a coal deposit on the side of a mountain in Aberfan, Wales, slid down on top of a school house. Over 100 people were killed, mostly children. This event caused a very emotional response in many who heard of it. Before the event, many people apparently felt feelings of dread, of something awful about to happen (precognition). There were similar responses similarly felt at the time of the disaster (clairvoyance). Dr. J. C. Barker, a psychiatrist, solicited dreams about the disaster, and found some potentially precognitive ones. These included a report that one of the girls who died in the disaster spoke to her mother about a dream of something that was to happen (and about death) two weeks before the disaster.

Unlike the dream of this little girl, most of the others had no direct connection to the coal accident. The issue of "importance" seems to hold little weight in light of situations like the Aberfan disaster, or with cases of people dreaming of other such situations that they themselves are not going to be directly involved in.

Let's look at a few dream experiences reported to me.

> I knew of my father's death before I was told the following morning. I was eight years old.
>
> —W.S., Shawnee, KS

This is a very typical statement made by people to others they know are interested in psychic phenomena. The questions one must ask about such a statement would illuminate whether this was truly a precognitive dream, or probably not. The major question is "How did he die?" If the death was sudden and unexpected, by accident, then perhaps so. It is, however, possible that the dream created awareness based on knowledge that the father was ill, had already been in an accident (though had not yet died), or even that the event happened just before or at the same time as awareness in the dream, making this a real-time (clairvoyant) psychic dream rather than a precognitive one.

There is also the possibility that another in the household got the call that the father was dead while W.S. was asleep, and that there was discussion of the death that the sleeping W.S. overheard, though not consciously. That information could still bleed over into the dreamstate.

> I dreamt about going to buy something in a store, then before making the purchase, discovering that my checkbook was empty. The dream came true the next day.
>
> —T.J., Littletown, CO

Once again, this dream could be precognitive or could simply be based on the knowledge that T.J. was planning to shop the next day, and the non-remembered emptiness of the checkbook. If T.J. had been the one to tear the last check out, leaving the checkbook empty, that fact could show up as a reminder in a dream. T.J. should have looked in the checkbook before shopping.

> I had a dream about my mother's friend. I dreamed that she had on a dark blue T-shirt and she held up a check, saying that she got her income tax return on a Monday.
> The next day, she went over to my mother's house, had on a navy blue T-shirt, and it was Monday. She had just gotten her income tax check.
>
> —D.C., Laconia, NH

Here we have a very straightforward dream. Unless D.C. knew that the mother's friend was due over to her mother's home, and that the friend had been expecting that income tax check to come, and that the friend tends to wear navy blue T-shirts (either in general, or specifically on Mondays), then we might judge this precognitive.

These next two dreams are also fairly specific, though in each case, the information is not 100 percent right on all points.

> I had a very vivid dream of hitting a deer with my car on my way to mail Mother's Day cards at a post office three towns away. The next week, in that particular town, I hit a deer with my car—on Mother's Day.
>
> —M.A., Highland Lakes, NJ

In the above dream, the Mother's Day cards (which, I presume, would never be mailed *on* Mother's Day) represent the date of the deer accident, rather than the actuality of mailing the cards. Otherwise, the town and accident are on point.

> I dreamt that a person I didn't know left money to me in a will, the sum of $22,000 a year for ten years. The next day, my friend's mother found her deceased husband's will in a safe, (I never met the husband), and with it a bill of sale from a ranch he'd sold. My friend's mother was to receive $22,000 a year for ten years.
>
> —K.F., Nampa, ID

In K.F.'s dream, a person she didn't know (the deceased man) left $22,000 for ten years to his living wife in a will. While the money was not left to K.F., the information otherwise proved true. You can, however, make a case that this was not a precognitive dream. Since the will existed in real-time, K.F. may have picked up the information from the will, rather than from the friend's mother's discovery of the will. That would make this a clairvoyant dream.

> About sixteen and a half years ago both my parents died. My mom, forty-eight years old, died in late

January of 1973 and my dad, sixty-four years old, died in early March of the same year. I was twenty-three years old at the time; my brother was twenty-four years old. The death of my parents was a total shock to my relatives and to my brother who eventually had an emotional breakdown. I, on the other hand, "knew." I had dreams for three months prior to their deaths. I thought I was losing my mind. I cried for three months. I tried to "warn" my mom "something terrible was going to happen!" When it finally came to pass it was like a rerun of a bad movie. I was now part of the dream and wanted to wake up. I lived through everything that happened.

It was a week before my mother's death that I physically went through her final physical pain. I could not breathe; my dad helped my walk through the long hallway to the front door and opened it. I eventually was able to take deep breaths and it passed. It was a horrible feeling of drowning.

It was a week to that night my mother took the same, painful walk, unable to breathe, her lungs full of water. She never made it to the hospital. She was Dead On Arrival. I had begged my mom to go to the doctor; she was on high blood pressure medication and was careful of her diet. She also had hypertension. The doctor said she had a massive cardiac arrest.

My dad mourned terribly for weeks, crying. He worked long, hard hours. He promised me he would never leave me, but I knew when he left for work that Friday morning it would be the last time I would see him. The night before he was so happy; he had dreamt of my mom. He died on the job—it was a massive heart attack. He collapsed getting off the bulldozer and someone caught him as he fell. The paramedics revived him, he opened his eyes for a brief moment, smiled, and closed them. My cousin told me all this as he was at the scene, having worked at a firehouse in the area.

When I got his call to come to the hospital I knew! I told my boss that there was no point in going to the hospital because my dad was dead, even though no one told me at the time. I just simply knew.

I was physically fine, but not too sure of reality. I was hoping I would eventually wake up from a horrid dream. The funeral director who took charge of both my parents' wakes took me aside and told me he had never seen the kind of smiles both my parents had when they left this world. His experience with my parents had him amazed, and he actually had to lessen the smiles because it filled their faces.

As they lay in their coffins I knew exactly how they were going to be dressed. I had nothing to do with it, as my mother's sister had bought my mother's final outfit. My mom was dressed in a blue, satin dress; my mom did not like blue. I saw this in my dream, even down to the single red rose one of my cousins put on her chest. My dad and I were closer so I did have some say as to what he would have wanted.

My dreams were a scrapbook of some sort. I don't know why I had foreseen all of this. Perhaps it was so I could be prepared. I have lived with guilt and felt that perhaps I had not done enough to alter things. Reading your book has made me feel better coping with my feelings.

—C.R., Brooklyn, NY

One of the key ideas as to why people have precognitive dreams about disastrous events we are unable to change is brought up in the previous letter. "Perhaps it was so I could be prepared," said C.R. The idea that such an experience can prepare us to better cope with grief has also been connected with sightings of apparitions of relatives and friends who have just died. We become aware of the death somehow before the normal means of communication are used to advise us of the events so we can be psychologically prepared to deal with that forthcoming knowledge.

C.R. attempted to get her mother to go to a doctor before she died. The warning was not heeded, but that is to be expected. Most people would not base their next movements on information presented to them from someone else's dream. However, it makes good sense that when someone tells you that an illness or medical problem is going to get worse, if you in fact are not feeling up to normal or you already know you're a "little" ill, to go to the doctor to get yourself checked out. This makes good sense whether the person telling you to do so had a dream or not.

> I had a series of dreams while in my teens which indicated that my mother's life was running out (a time bomb), and of her being taken out of this world on a spaceship—which was a death symbol. I woke up crying like I was in grief. These dreams occurred around 1972–73. She was not at this time showing symptoms of the cancer that later caused her death.
>
> In 1975, she started to get sick, and got worse until she was diagnosed by U. of M.[ichigan] hospital in 1976 as having multiple myeloma. The doctor said it could have been present in her bone marrow for a long time, but not causing trouble until it spread. He compared it to a time bomb.
>
> She died in May 1983, at age 56.
>
> —L.S., Southgate, MI

Here again we have a dream involving perceived and predicted illness, this time presented in a symbolic form, though recognized as such by L.S. The dream could have been clairvoyant or precognitive. Even though the symptoms were not showing at the time of the dreams, it is possible that there was cancer in her mother's system, and that this was perceived by L.S. at the time of the dreams.

In any event, the idea of the purpose of the dream comes up. There was little, if anything, that could be done after the

symptoms started showing. If L.S. had more specific information, such as that the dream indicated that her mother had
a current medical problem that needed to be checked out,
perhaps something could have been done (provided she could
have convinced her mother of the need to see a doctor). Then
again, the dream may simply have been a preparatory one,
to get L.S. ready for what was happening with her mother.

> I had a dream that my sister went for a long drive.
> While she was driving, her car began to swerve all
> over the road. She lost control and went off a cliff. I
> could see that her front tires had metal sticking
> through the rubber.
>   When I told her of my dream, she remembered
> that some of my other dreams had come true. She
> took her car to a gas station and found out that the
> steel belts in her tires were broken and coming
> through the rubber.
>
> ——J.L., Anchorage, AK

The above dream is an example of the dream that is heeded
having a direct effect on the future perceived. There was a
real problem with the tires. J.L. perceived that the future,
with those tire problems, could cause dire consequences for
the sister. Luckily, the sister heeded the dream and headed
for a gas station (maybe just to be on the safe side). Did it
hurt anybody to check out the tires? No. Even if there'd been
nothing wrong, having tires checked is an easy thing to do.
In this case, it presumably saved a life.

Once again we can look at the source of the information:
Did J.L. gain the insight of the accident directly from the
future or was it a real-time psychic perception of the problems
with the tires (plus a little supposition that such problems
with tires would lead to an accident)? Does it matter whether
it's a prediction or real-time perception? Not really (unless
you're a parapsychologist going crazy trying to figure all this
stuff out).

Here's a couple of experiences where the premonitions

were heeded and changes in predicted futures made. The first is a precognitive dream experience, the second a "feeling" that something was to happen. Both come from the personal experiences of Joanne Mied of Psychogenic Solutions in Novato, California.

Once I was working at a resort and dreamed that one of the older buildings caught on fire. Interestingly enough, when the staff was alerted, two other people reported dreams of fires in the resort buildings within the preceding days. The fire extinguishers were serviced and the staff was given fire safety and fire-fighting instructions. When a small fire did break out, it was quickly extinguished by the person in the area at that time.

My husband and a few other adults were responsible for a dozen teenagers on a trip to Hawaii several years ago. When we went to the beach it was our policy to post one of the men as a lifeguard. One day I had a feeling that one of the children would drown. I told my husband, so he posted an additional guard and they moved closer to the surf and refrained from conversation. Sure enough, an hour later, one of the teenagers, Joe, got caught in a serious undertow, but because his predicament was noted early, the guards were able to give him instructions and help him to safety.

—Joanne Mied, Novato, CA

Precognitive experiences, whether in dreams or in our waking states, can spur us on to action if we pay attention to them. The main problem of acting on the information can be illustrated by the next dream, which is similar, in that a warning may have prevented a terrible accident from occuring.

In high school, at age 17, I had a friend named Dana. She had relatives in Nevada whom she visited several times a year. I had a dream one night that she was driving to Reno and had a terrible accident and died.

The next day I asked her if she had any plans to go to Reno soon. She looked at me strangely and said, yes, she was going that weekend. I told her about my dream, and another friend there turned white and said she'd had the same dream. Neither of us, who are still friends, are pranksters.

Dana told us we had vivid imaginations and that she was still going. However, she later decided not to go and is still with us.

That dream was like no other I've ever had. I really believe she's alive today because she did not go.

—D. Carmichael, CA

This is a situation where the future, had it really been that Dana was to die if she went to Reno, is impossible to judge. Dana decided, for whatever reason, not to go to Reno. Whether that had anything to do with the dream warnings of the other two girls or not is impossible to say. Whether Dana was correct in saying that they had vivid imaginations is also impossible to say. Since she didn't go, there was not accident or death.

Was this a precognitive dream experience? Since we don't really know what would have happened (nor can we ever know) if Dana had gone to Reno, that question cannot be answered (well, maybe in a parallel universe . . .).

A friend of mine had broken his leg; he was in a cast for five weeks. I was absent from our class the sixth week. I dreamed he had no cast in choir class and that I walked up to him and said "I knew you had your cast off." Two days later, everything went right into place and I saw he had no cast. I went to him, repeated the words I had said in my dream, adding that I had dreamed this would happen. He moved away from me like I had some sort of plague.

—C.M., Bridgeton, NJ

In the events that followed this dream, it would appear that C.M. purposely followed up on the dream with the same words uttered in that dream. The reaction? Typical . . . the friend though C.M. was weird or "had some sort of plague." This is, unfortunately, the reaction of many people when friends relate psychic experiences. Rather than accepting the experiences for what they are, or even trying to look for alternate experiences, most of us react from either fear or the idea that such experiences are not "normal."

In fact, subjective paranormal experiences like this one are quite normal, and would undoubtedly be considered such if everyone came out publicly with their experiences, rather than keeping them inside due to the assumption (though often correct) that people will think they're nuts.

Of course, there is an alternate explanation for C.M.'s dream: C.M., knowing that the cast would inevitably come off, and that choir class was inevitable with the friend, simply had a dream about that anticipated class. It is logical, even down to a point of C.M. possibly anticipating in the dream that the friend would react negatively if approached with "psychic" experience.

My dream states are not quite clear and are usually danger signals about someone not present. The unusual thing is that the person closest to the one endangered appears, rather than the person involved. For example, my uncle appeared to me in July warning of my aunt's heart attack in September, even giving the month. I contacted my mother about it.

Then I saw Bob Hope appear three months before Bing Crosby's death.

—A.M., San Diego, CA

Here we have a fairly common problem with psychic dreams. A.M., like many others, has dreams of future events in which there are symbolic representations of individuals affected, in this case the perceived "person closest to the one endangered." In the dreams of others, symbols may represent people or even specifics of the situations. It is interesting that the dreamer comes to recognize the symbol as such and can decipher what that symbol represents.

In various forms of dream work, the psychiatrist/psychologist/dream worker may help people come to terms with their own internal symbology and mythology, rather than having the dreamer become dependent on someone else's symbology (as with most of those dream interpretation books out there).

In A.M.'s dreams, there appears to be a conscious recognition of the symbols, in advance of the actual events occurring. In my experience, I hear from many who have had various psychic experiences, including psychic dreams. One such recent report came from a San Francisco Bay area woman who felt she was having precognitive dreams. She'd had a dream of a black milk truck, which was followed (after some days) by a relative killed in collision with a truck. Was the dream truck representative of the actual event? That's hard to say, since there was little in advance of the relative's death to tie that dream symbol to anyone's death in particular. It is possible that the dream was representative of something else. Without a better look at the woman's dreams in general, a connection between that event and the symbol which happened after the event, is a tenuous one; and even then it wasn't very clear.

The woman's question, however, was not whether that had been a psychic experience (for she accepted it as such), but what she could do about future events if she continues to have such dreams.

I'll deal a bit more with that in a while, but suffice it to say for the moment that unless you recognize the dream as providing information about a future event, and unless you can decipher what the symbols represent, there's not a whole lot you can do with that information. It's too incomplete, and not even something you are going to consciously associate with a future event. How can you do something about a situation if you have no information other than "something bad happened in my dream"? You can't, and you can't feel guilty that you "should have done something" when, after the fact, you connect a dream to an event.

Sometimes, there is not even so much as a memory that you had a dream about a future event, until the event happens, as with this next experience.

> The first time visiting a friend in Chicago, I had an experience. We were taking a short cut and were about to enter a newly constructed building. Before entering, I hesitated and began to describe the yet-to-be-completed inside. I had dreamed of this place and now it was before me.

—S.W., Woodstock, GA

As mentioned earlier in this book, one of the more common experiences connected with psi is the feeling you'd been in a situation before, déjà vu. One of the over forty explanations for particular déjà vu experiences is that the reason you have that sense of familiarity is that you had, at one point in the past, a dream very similar to (or perhaps exactly like) a situation you're entering into. Rather than remembering a dream at that point, you simply get a strong, but vague, sense of familiarity, of having lived it before.

In my own life, I've had many déjà vu experiences, most of which are simply a strong sense of familiarity. Sometimes I do get the sense that the situation was something I had dreamed about, though I recognize that the dream was only similar to the situation, and I really can't consider that a psychic experience.

On the other hand, as with S.W.'s letter, I have on occasion had the memory of a dream rushing back into my mind as a physical experience is happening. I have an absolute "knowledge" (or sensation) that the information rushing in was from a dream (and I can sometimes even remember when I had the dream), rather that something psychic happening right then and there. It doesn't seem like some sort of "vision," rather it's a definite "memory." In some instances, I've known not only that I had a dream of the events, but also what was coming next. In fact, on a couple of occasions I recall "freaking out" the people I was with because I knew (and vocalized) what was happening (and being said) next.

The real problem with precognitive dreams and their value is actually multiple problems.

First of all, you have to remember the dream. If there is partial recall of the events/information from the dream, you may disregard it, or simply not have any information of any use. Of course, as detailed elsewhere in this book, just about anybody can learn to remember their dreams, even in the rich detail you might need for utilizing information you peg as "psychic."

Secondly, even if you remember the dream in full detail, you must consider the form of the information and whether there's even enough to use. Psychic information is notoriously partial in nature. As with the dream of the airline disaster mentioned earlier, partial and incomplete information may be basically useless.

If you know a family member will be in a car accident, but the car you see is that person's car, which he or she drives every day along the same route you see in your dream, and there is very little other detail (other than, say, that the accident occurs with a blue van), all you can really say to that person is "be wary of blue vans." Remember, though, that you don't want to breed paranoia—such a warning taken too seriously can cause that person to effectively panic at the first sign of a blue van, which in turn could actually cause the accident that you foresaw.

Along with this is the idea that the information may occur in very symbolic form. Without being aware that seeing a giant blue beetle chewing on your car is symbolic of a car accident between your car and a blue, Volkswagen "bug" or "beetle" means there's no way to interpret and apply that dream information. Of course, that also could merely be a dream brought on by watching one too many Japanese monster movies, bearing no symbolic connection to any future event at all.

If you truly wish to work with dreams to determine what your personal symbology is, then read on for what is presented in the chapter in this book on "Dream Work." The interviews with dream workers such as Dr. Montague Ullman shed quite a bit of light on this.

Another basic problem of utilizing precognitive information is the actual recognition by the dreamer that the dream is important, that it says something about the present or future. You can have lots of dreams that seem to come true after the fact, and those may or may not have been precognitive, depending on how much you read into the symbols of those dreams, and how often you have dreams that don't come true.

If you have learned to remember most of your dreams, to determine if a particular dream is precognitive or not, you really must look at the importance you place on that dream. Most people say that their psychic experiences generally feel different than other experiences. It would almost be as though there is some flashing light or asterisk attached to that experience or dream that says "Hey, listen up . . . this is psychic stuff here . . . pay attention!" The dream must be recognized and weighted with some sense of it being important before you'd even pay enough attention to it to consider it psychic.

Then, after viewing it as important, there's the issue of acceptance. You have to accept not only that it is potentially psychic and telling you something, but that what it says may not be complete or may be symbolic of something. You'd then have to either consciously analyze what the information might pertain to or go with a "gut feeling" or sensation that what you can get out of it relates to "X" situation or event or individual.

Furthermore, if you plan to do something with the information, you have to decide just how to apply it. Should you tell the person it might affect (if it affects someone other than yourself)? Will assuming the information is future stuff and accepting it as such make that person (or you) paranoid about that predicted event? Could having knowledge of that event actually cause it to happen? And of course, there is the issue of whether that other person you told would accept the precognitive experience you had, or would see you as "crazy" or having a wild imagination or cause him or her to avoid you like you had "some sort of plague."

Finally, there is the question I've brought up many times before: Now that you have the information, can anything be done with it?

When we're talking about precognitive experiences, in dreams or in conscious experience, we're back to the idea and problem of just what the future is. If you have a view of a predetermined future, what good is the information? The answer may simply be that such information can psychologically prepare you for the inevitable. Of course, I think most of us would be uncomfortable with that. I and many others I know are more comfortable with some sense of empowerment in our lives, that we have some say in the way our futures shape up, some free will in choosing our destiny.

People often see psychics and fortune-tellers in order to learn their future. Many such seers do not put enough (or even any) emphasis on the control and responsibility we have for our own lives and choices. One of the marks of a good, ethical, "psychic" is a proviso with any "prediction" that the future is ultimately yours to make. Psychic information seems to best be utilized if you see it as pointing to probabilities, to events likely to happen, where you as a participant have some power to cause the event to happen or not happen.

In studies of precognitive experiences reported to places like The Central Premonitions Registry run for years in New York City, the majority of reported precognitive experiences (including dreams) were of events which could have alternate outcomes depending on human intervention. While it would be impossible to stop an earthquake from happening, if your dream related when and where and how strong it was to be, that information (if accurate and taken seriously) could save lives once people were warned to get out of the area.

In other words, even seemingly inevitable or unstoppable events and circumstances (such as natural disasters) can have different outcomes depending on whether the precognitive information relating to the people to be affected by the disaster took heed of your warning.

Once again, I must impress upon you that taking the information too seriously can have drastic negative effects as well. Just as a psychic telling you something like "You are about to find a sum of money" might cause you to scan the environment until you find that dollar lying on the sidewalk or all that change in your sofa, a "warning" of danger could have you checking out your surroundings so cautiously that you actually panic at the first sign of anything resembling that dream, placing you *into* the danger you had hoped to avoid . . . a self-fulfilling prophecy.

I also need to take a moment here to further discuss the role of coincidence in all of these experiences.

People have common experiences; fact is stranger than fiction. Both of these cliched expressions are accurate to an extent. I've lived out experiences I had seen occur in television shows (even some happening on soap operas, and I'm not talking about *Dark Shadows*). People have common experiences to a great degree, in a given society. Just because I suddenly recognize a situation I'm in as being "just like" the one I saw on *Cheers* or *One Life to Live*, doesn't mean I should suspect that the writers of those shows "tuned in" to my future (or past or present, for that matter).

Fiction is generally based on, at least partially, real, human experience. While the television show *Alien Nation* is not fact-based (in that there is not a colony of over 200,000 extraterrestrials living in Los Angeles), it *is* based on people's real experiences of prejudice, bigotry, racism, sexism, religion, and the integration of "outsiders" into another culture. Many episodes of *Star Trek: The Next Generation* are parallels to situations such as those in Northern Ireland, returning Vietnam vets, and drug use.

Dreams are often similar reflections of common human experience. Coincidentally, a dream you have relates to a real experience. Events *do* occur by coincidence. This is to be expected.

Skeptics point out that to place value on the precognitive

content of a person's dreams, you have to take into account the number of dreams that don't come true or that occur mainly by coincidence. You may be able to judge that a given dream was not likely a precognitive one as it stands alone among all those other dreams that didn't come true, making it statistically insignificant. It also could simply be a coincidence that you dreamed the situation in advance.

What's the answer to this? Is it coincidence or not and how do you know? Was it a common-experience-type dream or psychic?

If you are looking back after the event, realizing that you had a dream about the event before it happened, whether that was a precognitive dream really can't be determined unless there was a lot of detail recorded before the event, and that detail was specific enough to that event to say it was unique. Of course, to you, the dream may feel different, and that may be what makes it different than something considered purely coincidence.

So, what if you have the dream and realize before the event that this is about the future?

Well, if the other problems, from partial information to recognition of importance to acceptance of the information are overcome, and you can make use of the information, it doesn't matter if we're speaking of a true knowledge of a future event or simply the mind making an educated guess based on what you already know that something is likely to happen soon. *Use the information*.

For some reason, there seems to be this perception that psychic information may be more "knowing" of the future than any sort of conscious, rational, logical prediction based on hard information. The answer to this dilemma is perhaps dependent on whether there is a "knowable" future (or even a probable future for us to "read") and if so, whether it is truly possible for information to come from that future to our present.

Without more knowledge of the workings of time itself, it's probably a question best left for sometime in the future. Ultimately, it doesn't matter. If the information is useful, whether based in a "psychic knowing" of the future or on logical, intuitive, emotional, or illogical "guesswork", then use it. Take responsibility for creating your own future, and the possibilities may become clearer to you, psychic or not, in your dreams or awake. Make that future your own.

CHAPTER 12

PSI, Psychic Dreams, and Some Theories

Okay, so we all have some degree of psychic ability, or so you're told. What causes a psychic experience? What is in certain individuals that appears to make them more psychic than others? How could we actually get information from a distance or through time? Let's explore a few ideas about the way psi works and the theories behind it.

Belief in the possibility of psychic ability seems to be an extremely important factor in whether a person has or recognized psychic experiences. In studies of the "Sheep-Goat Effect," the term and methodology coined by parapsychologist and psychologist Dr. Gertrude Schmeidler, there is often a significant difference in the experimental results of participants in psi experiments between those who believe in (at least) the possibility of psychic functioning ("sheep") and those who don't (skeptics, disbelievers, or "goats"). This correlation of scoring on ESP tasks, with sheep typically scoring above chance and goats typically at or below chance, has been seen in many experimental series.

We do know that belief may be tied to a performance issue. One who believes in psi may simply have the tendency to perform in psi experiments, in much the same way an athlete or musician has a better chance of a successful performance if he or she has confidence in his or her performance. Doubt is the performance "killer" it seems, in a variety of tasks human beings perform. It is also possible that the "Sheep-

Goat Effect,'' where it occurs outside the lab linking believers to a higher incidence of psychic experiences, may have more to do with believers (or at least folks who don't discount the existence of psi) being more likely to recognize or categorize an experience as psychic than a disbeliever (or someone simply likely to need to pigeon-hole an unusual experience in categories that ''make sense'' in terms of what is culturally and/or scientifically accepted today.

Such predisposition toward one thing or away from another, or ideas that shape the way an experience may be perceived, can affect the results people have in a psi task. One may believe in psi but not particularly enjoy a particular kind of experimental task, or may simply not have enough personal confidence in doing well in that task. Think of it this way: this may be similar to an athlete doubting his or her own performance. A pole vaulter who knows someone can break the record may not have enough confidence to do it himself, even though he's physically capable of it. We all set limits on ourselves in what we can do and how well we can do it. Belief is important in many areas, though we may have a deep-seated sense of what we think we can do, and what things we can excel (or fail) at.

While it appears that belief and preferences, or biases, can influence whether psi shows up or in what direction it is aimed (positive or negative, depending on how you look at which is positive and which is negative), there are two influences that don't appear to affect ones psychic abilities.

First, let's take distance limitations. From the long distance testing that has gone on (the furthest being the distance from Earth to the moon—Edgar Mitchell conducted unofficial ESP tests while aboard Apollo 14), it seems that distance poses no problems for either strength or direction of the psi signal. This is in contradiction to the weakening of other forms of energy over distance. There has, however, been some suggestion that there may be some slight change in signal strength over vast distances. Future testings will take a look at this.

Secondly, lets take a look at time. Psi does not appear to be limited by any time restrictions. Precognition and retrocognition indicate that information can come from the future or the past. At present, we are still considering the exact nature of time, so it maybe that what we perceive as a straight time line from past to future may be all wrong.

Since psi is not limited by time or space, we can suppose that there may not be any known physical barriers to psi influences. Unlike the capability that lead has in stopping Superman's X-ray vision, psi testing done with various screening techniques has resulted in the apparent lack of being able to block either ESP or PK. However, experiments at the Mind Science Foundation in Texas have indicated that psi may be blocked by *mentally* created ''screens.''

Everyone has psi, but the frequency and strength of psi experiences vary quite a bit, and appear to depend on many factors, such as the aforementioned belief and preference variables. It appears that some have a greater degree of control (as much as one can control such an elusive faculty) than others. It may also be that due to our education process, which in our culture seems to ignore or deny such experiences, we may be interacting with the environment constantly on a psychic level and simply not recognizing it. Just as dependency on vision and hearing may cause us to not notice other sensory input as much as we could, our learning to depend on our senses and deny other ''unusual'' signals may cause our attention to stray away from psychically derived input and output, except, apparently, where there is a need for us to notice, or a goal to be reached through focused attention on psi.

Remember, having psi experiences is a normal thing. If everyone has these abilities, as studies seem to imply, and if we get reported experiences from people of all ages, nationality, culture, religion, and physical condition, then to have a psychic experience is to be within that range of human behavior we call ''normal.'' Not ''crazy'' or ''weird'' or ''bizarre,'' merely normal. People who reported lucid dreams used to get similar reactions. That, with appropriate evidence, has changed. Hopefully the acceptance of psychic experiences will change someday soon as well.

In too many families in western culture, children are told that they ''can't know something is about to happen'' or "can't make something move without touching it" or "can't know what Uncle Harry's thinking." One certainly "can't" see a real ghost. Such denial of experience, whether because a parent thinks the claims are the result of fantasy or whether the "can'ts" come because the parent doesn't believe in the possibility of such things, cause a person to grow up ignoring psychic interactions (since they really "can't" happen), or even to develop a completely closed mind to such things. In either case, both imagination and psi should be fostered and nurtured. We so often tend to set mental limits on what we can do that any process that helps us deny the limits helps us go past them.

In a family with a history of psychic experience, there is naturally going to be an open-minded attitude towards psi. It is therefore difficult to pin down whether a higher number of experiences or a greater control of such abilities is related to heredity or to instilling the abilities into someone (rather than out of them) or a bit of both. So do the abilities run in a family? Probably, though this could simply be due to a higher degree of acceptance and therefore recognition of psychic experience in a particular family.

The impressions one receives through whatever the psychic "channel" is are often unreasonable or illogical. A hunch to do something unusual (which later benefits you) is often not in keeping with what one logically sees about a situation. A person who is of an extremely logical nature, who analyzes situations without allowing for solutions from out of left field, may ignore any unusual input (psychic or simply from the subconscious). On the other hand, in looking over the variety of spontaneous cases of psi, its been seen that there is often an emotional content to well-perceived information. In any case, *thinking* about what may be psychic information, which is so often unreasonable or incomplete, causes that old problem of trying to fit the information into what we already know, while that information may simply not fit.

This may be why people of a more creative or artistic nature are seen as more psychic than non-creative people. Dr. Thelma Moss did a study in the late sixties looking at psi abilities of artists versus non-artistic folks. Of course, given what I said above, you can guess that there was a significant difference between the two groups, and that the artists scored above chance. A follow-up poll a couple of years later by another researcher showed a higher percentage of believers among artists than among non-artists. Other studies since then have also indicated that creativity and psi are linked, that creative people are better able to let the psychic information or interaction simply happen, without trying to "fit" it into one's picture of the way things must work.

The human personality also has its effects on psychic functioning. For example, extroversion has been tested quite a bit in relation to psi. There is an overall tendency for extroverts (outgoing people) to score above chance. Introverts, who may close themselves off, have the opposite tendency, with chance or below chance scoring more likely, so it appears that there is a better chance for a person to be psychic if he or she is outgoing, creative, and a believer in psi in both general situations and experimental conditions. If that person also grew up in a culture or family environment where belief in psi was in the open and not denied, there is even a greater chance of psi being evident in his or her life.

These variables, extroversion, belief, creativity, attitude, education, and also mood (the mood one is in while doing the psi task) may influence the entire range of psi. In dealing with emotional states, or moods, there doesn't seem to be any one kind of mood that's best for everyone. Some people have psychic experiences while in what might be considered negative moods (sad, depressed, bored, etc.) while others may be more psychic when they are "up" (happy, energetic, etc.), but the main functioning of psi points to some kind of goal-directed process.

What we know about psychic functioning indicates a few things. First of all, psi seems to be tied to a variety of psychological factors, from personality variables to emotional moods to belief factors. As a phenomenon so directly related to psychological variables, which are themselves inconsistent, it's no wonder that there is a difficulty in getting an individual to be psychic on demand. We (human beings in general) tend to set our own limitations where psi functioning is concerned. Our culture sets up belief system boundaries around the occurrence and even possibility of psi (remember that science and scientific thought are part of a culture's belief system).

We educate our children out of being psychic. We actually learn, within a cultural context, how to perceive the world around us. As infants and children in a learning context, we are taught to recognize certain shapes, colors, processes, sounds, smells, tastes, textures, and other physical factors. We are told that there are physical "laws," that objects and events behave in certain ways and don't behave in others. That shapes our own perceptions, and sets up certain expectations of how things around us should be and how they should behave. This fact, this perceptual expectancy, is a principle magicians make use of all the time with sleight-of-hand effects and illusions.

Other internal factors affect our recognition of and reaction to psychic experience. We each develop some form of internal logic that lets us, as individuals, make sense of the world around us and the behavior of others. We react to observations and experiences by thinking through, categorizing, and cataloging the experience as our logic dictates. We are also feeling creatures, and our emotional reactions to experience can either help us recognize and react to psychic experience or cause us to ignore or even fear them.

So, while psychic ability is distributed throughout the entire population, some people are likely to be more psychic than others due to the various factors that are related to psi's appearance. It's a normal process (since everyone has it), yet conscious psychic experiences, while not as uncommon as many think, are not as frequent as other kinds of "normal" experiences.

Yet psi is likely to be happening all the time, just as our other senses are operating at some level almost all the time (although there is no real visual input if you close your eyes), yet what we consciously perceive is not always everything we think we receive through our senses. Psychologists have spoken of a "cocktail party effect" in conjunction with the sense of hearing. Everyone seems to experience this at some time, whether at a cocktail party or not.

Think of psi the same way, always operating, but needful of your center of attention. Unfortunately, since we are taught so well by people and our physical environment to use just our "normal" senses, it may take something with a bit of an emotional punch to become part of your conscious attention, whether that intense signal tells you to stay away from a certain intersection to avoid an accident or it simply gives you the feeling that something happened to your Uncle Harry. If that signal can't get your attention with just the bit of information, maybe your subconscious gives it more of a punch by letting you "see" Uncle Harry.

What appears to be happening is that your psychic abilities, tied so well into your unconscious thought processes, are scanning the environment, looking for information that is useful or interesting and often something that will divert your attention from what's coming in through "regular" perceptual channels. That psi signal may fulfill an emotional, intellectual, or physical need or goal. The whole process may be unconscious, as some part of you, ever vigilant to find information important to you existence or state of mind, continuously scans the environment. The experience of receiving and recognizing that information may happen when there is a bit of information received that meets a need you have (aware of the need or not) or can direct you toward some goal or other. You may be consciously aware of the information piece or not, as you can be unconsciously directed to initiating a particular course of action (such as getting out of the way of a falling piano, even though you never once looked up). Your response may even be an unconscious psychic one, where the reaction is carried out through the use of psychokinetic ability.

Rex Stanford came up with a theoretical construct to cover this idea of scanning the environment, which is, in parapsychological terms, called a Psi Mediated Instrumental Response, or PMIR. You may be aware of all this happening (the entire process, from detection of the need-related info to the action that is taken), or it may all be handled, from start to finish, with unconscious psi processes. A response could be an nagging feeling not to drive your car down a certain street (to avoid a nasty accident), or simply causing a momentary lapse in memory that causes you to go elsewhere (not remembering where you're going), or even a simple mistake you make almost without awareness (like making a wrong turn). In other situations, the PMIR may be psychic in nature, causing you to see an apparition or to have a psychokinetic outburst (as in a poltergeist situation).

There are negatives to this kind of situation as well. While it sounds great that we are constantly scanning for things that will help us out in life, and hopefully responding to fill the needs, there are also opposite possibilities. Not everything we do is positive. If a person holds a negative self-image, it is possible that things will not work out for the better, since a person in that frame of mind may not expect them to. The need that is served may be to perpetuate the conscious image one holds, so one's psi may scan for and lead one into events that would strengthen that image. If the image is negative, the result could conceivably be something like a streak of bad "luck." In our dreams, those negative images may appear as nightmares or "evil" figures in otherwise sedate dreams. Facing up to such images and asking questions of them serves the purpose of working through any lasting effects of the information that could adversely affect you.

So, it would seem that we are scanning the environment, that we are intimately connected with it in and out of our dreams. But how might this connection work? What have we really learned about how psi functions?

Unfortunately, parapsychology currently has no central theory to explain psi. We do have ideas, and some partial theoretical constructs, but no overall explanation of how it all comes together. This may be partly a result of the somewhat artificial categories we have for psi, of the distinctions we make between, say, precognition and PK, or between clairvoyance and retrocognition. The words we use to describe these phenomena are merely constructs, labels, that may in and of themselves be inaccurate, and may be leading us past the real questions we need to ask.

For example, there can be much conceptual confusion between psychokinesis and precognition. Not really understanding how time works or how the future is constructed, we are not really sure if information can come from the future, especially if the future is indefinite (and since it hasn't happened yet). Do we really get information from the future, are we making a guess based on what we know or what we can find out through clairvoyance, or are we using PK to make that predicted event more likely to happen?

Part of the reason no central theory has been provided is that there is still confusion in not only what we describe as our conceptual terms describing psychic phenomena, but also in the description of how space and time operate. It may be that we will have to wait until the picture of the "known laws of the physical universe" change or are expanded a bit before we have the right information to compose such a theory. In addition, there is a need for greater sophistication of technology in order to conduct experiments that might once and for all pinpoint a psi effect in a physical way.

There are some ideas about psi and its functioning, such as Stanford's PMIR model. At present there are a variety of conceptual "theories" that may explain some or most of the way psi functions, but unfortunately, because of still unknown angles to this difficult question of "what is psi and how does it operate?" no one can really say which of these is correct. Because of this apparent lack of information, or perhaps as a failing of the limits of our laboratory techniques, we simply don't have a definitive answer to that question. However, one might look at the issue of psi from the standpoint of not having the right questions, rather than looking for answers. In general, all the answers to scientific questions are out there. Unfortunately, science in general (in fact, life in general) is like a game of "Jeopardy!"—we have the answers and they'd probably make sense provided we can come up with the right questions.

One proposed idea is that somehow the mind must be able

to tap into some universal pool of "free" energy and information. The energy needed for a psychokinetic act, moving or affecting an object with the mind could come from outside our own physical bodies from such a source. Information existing in a universal "library" is an old idea, called the Akashic Record by various folks in New Age and spiritual belief systems, and may be compared with Jung's idea of a collective unconscious. Physicists today are still trying to complete Einstein's last work, the idea of a unified field, that all matter and energy in this universe is intricately interconnected. It has been suggested that our minds can somehow tap into this unified field and utilize the connections between everything to affect physical objects and processes or to simply send or receive information at a distance or through time (sounds remarkably like the "Force" in *Star Wars*, doesn't it?). Of course, this means that there is an as-yet-unknown energy process going on.

Which leads us to a next point, that the energy being used either in PK, ESP, or even by minds-without-bodies (our "ghosts," if you will) is very possibly in unknown form to current physics. This energy could be part of that unified field, ready for tapping into, or could simply be part of our own minds, which some believe are energy fields themselves. Or it could be something altogether "new" (to human science, anyway).

William Roll, one of the busiest spontaneous case investigators (especially poltergeist phenomena), postulated a "psi field" that every object has, whether living or dead. It is the psi field that interacts with other psi fields, enabling information to be copied to and from these fields, or to allow energy transmission to or from the fields for psychokinetic interactions. It is such a psi field that we gain information from in the case of hauntings or psychometry. Again, we are dealing with an unknown energy form, unless the psi field or psi energy is a new use of a known force.

Among the "known" areas that may relate to psi are electromagnetism, gravity, and quantum (subatomic) particles. One of the oldest explanations for telepathy is the idea of "mental radio." This relates to some kind of structure in the brain that acts similar to a radio transmitter/receiver, with psi information being carried by some kind of electromagnetic wave, similar to radio waves. Unfortunately, as far as we know today, there aren't any structures in the brain which could be capable of this.

I should mention that I know of someone working on a new device that can pick up and amplify certain brain wave frequencies from a distance, without the use of the typical electrode-involved EEG scan. What this amounts to is a method of detecting brain wave "signals" at some short distance away from the body, which may lead to further development of a theory of "signal transmission" from the brain which could be applicable (or not) to parapsychological research. Of course, sending signals from one mind to another doesn't exactly explain how clairvoyance works or how PK might work (since they are instances of mind interacting with objects and events, as opposed to mind to mind), and I know of no one with a radio that can receive a signal from the future. In addition, there has been psi testing while the "receiver" was enclosed in a Faraday cage, a set-up that screens out most of the electromagnetic spectrum, yet subjects still seem able to perform well in that psi task. It would seem, therefore, that either some electromagnetic waves not screened out are responsible, or there was some other process altogether.

Electromagnetism might still be useful in describing psi functioning. It may yet be found that some part of the electromagnetic spectrum is used in the psi process, perhaps in combination with some other physical energy system. Magnetic fields, such as the geomagnetic field of the earth, are now looking better and better as having a connection to psi, as I'll describe shortly.

Physicists have spoken of a "particle" of gravity, called a graviton. Gravity which would be linked with other forms of energy by a completed unified field theory, could be manipulated to produce a variety of PK effects or even somehow to carry information or allow information to be passed through space and time. There is simply the problem of how one might actually tap into and be able to manipulate such particles as gravitons. Currently, we have no way to directly detect such particles, so any theory connecting them with psi functioning is still pending.

A few physicists, especially those interested in whether the mind (or consciousness) is some kind of energy field generated by the brain and body (and possibly separable from the body), have expressed interest in looking at psi processes. Some have even expressed the idea that such processes take place at the quantum level of interaction, and that there may even be a "new" particle responsible. Physicists today often think of the world as less material than most of us do. After all, matter is composed of particles with relatively vast amounts of space between particles. The book you hold, for example, is solid only at our level of physical size. In the sub-atomic world of the quark, particles are often quite distant from one another. While processes in our world seem to follow fairly rigid physical "laws," interactions at the sub-atomic, or quantum, level are probabilistic—predictions made as to how things will interact are in the form of probabilities.

At the quantum level, it is apparent that physical "laws" may break down, and some, such as the "inverse-square law" (relating to a "signal" weakening over distance), may fall apart in the case of some particles. In addition, one theoretical particle that may be related, the tachyon, may be breaking a speed law, as it moves faster than the speed of light (in fact, it can never move slower), and may even be capable of traveling backward in time. Such a particle, if it can somehow carry information, might solve the problem of how precognitive information comes from the future (but may not necessarily settle the question of whether there is a *definite* future). With the tachyon, though, we have one definite problem: If this particle only travels faster than the speed of light, how do we, as beings that only travel slower than that speed, gain information from that speeding particle?

One other point made by the "new" physics deals with the very nature of reality. The Heisenberg Uncertainty Principle deals with the uncertain physical state of everything until it is actually observed or measured. In other words, there are only probable states of existence for an electron until it is measured, and its state at the time of measurement is defined by the observer. Whether a tree makes a sound when it falls in the woods may really depend on the presence of someone (or something, such as a tape recorder or an animal or insect) being around to hear it. Taking this a bit further, it may be that our minds, our consciousnesses, somehow affect the states of all physical processes, of reality itself. Many eastern religions speak of a shaping of reality with our minds, and psi may be a visible sign of our ability to do this.

There has been speculation in a related area, that I would like to mention. Some parapsychologists and physicists have also been looking at actual manipulations of space and time when discussing how psi may work, especially without limitations of distance or time set on how it interacts with the world. This may end up sounding like a bit of science fiction, but it has really been discussed, and is certainly no more bizarre than what is discussed by physicists and astronomers when they discuss the physics of a black hole.

Space and time (or space-time) are often spoken of in terms of a "fabric" that can theoretically be warped and perhaps even torn. Einstein showed us that the presence of intense gravitational fields (such as created by bodies composed of enormous mass) can actually bend or warp space itself (which is why light cannot escape from a black hole—the gravity is so intense it has an effect on photons of light, and warps the space around it completely). Light has been shown to bend around massive bodies, following the curve of the warped space. Imagine a straight piece of optical fiber, like what is being used for phone lines today, through which light travels. Even though light travels in a straight line, the line is defined by the fiber (the space) itself. Bend the fiber and the light still goes through. Bend the space light travels through, and the light is still going "straight." The more extensive the gravitational force, the more space warps. It has been suggested that in a black hole, space may warp enough to develop a "tear."

At the sub-atomic level, we have forces even stronger than the gravity of a mass that will warp space—we have those that hold the mass together. It has been suggested that at the quantum level, the forces are so strong that there is continual tearing of space-time. Physicists call the area beyond the "tear" in space-time "super-space," which transcends our ideas and measurements of space and time, a "place" from which any point in our own space-time continuum can be reached from any other. If this sounds familiar, it may be because this has been called both "sub-space" and "hyper-space" by science fiction writers.

The idea is that whatever the mechanism is that carries information in the psi process may work at the quantum level, carrying information through super-space to and from any point in space and time, thereby alleviating the limits of distance and time. It also means that there could be an electromagnetic process, as psychic information can travel through any shielding by taking a shortcut through super-space and, in effect, go around the shielding. However, another idea has been suggested in this process, that not only can you reach all points in our universe, but also points in other universes. Science fiction writers have for years played with the idea of parallel worlds, universes in another space-time that may be anything from extremely similar to our own to vastly different. Today, some physicists are getting around to the same idea. In the light of such a, perhaps, bizarre notion, when psi information goes wrong, it may be that the information is being received from a present or future world just the slightest bit different from our own, with similar situations and different outcomes.

An idea that works with that of super-space is one proposed by David Ryback. He and others have suggested that we work with a holographic model of the universe, rather than an analytic one, where the past affects the present which affects the future. Any particular location in the whole of the universe is a "piece" of the larger "hologram" that contains all the information from the whole universe, past, present, and future. We can somehow tap a piece of this hologram and gain access to all the information we need, any time we need it (if our psi is working, of course).

You may have figured out that I wasn't kidding about there being no central theory. If there is to be one, several things need to happen. First of all, psi may be elusive enough that only with extensive research with the some of the newest technology can we get any sort of laboratory results. Unfortunately, parapsychology is in a sorry financial state, and there is little enough money for salaries and lab space, let alone equipment. In addition, it may just be that the nature of psi is such that we haven't developed the technology capable of "finding" it.

Secondly, psi tends to happen in "real life," rather than in the lab, so studies of psychic experiences may need to shift back to looking at the experiences as they occur to "normal" people in "real life." In addition, there is evidence that our physical environment may affect the incidence and form of psychic experience, as it affects other workings of the human body and mind. Dream studies may yield a good compromise, as unlike other mental states that may or may not be necessary for psychic functioning, dreams do occur on a regular basis, even in a laboratory. Lucid dreaming techniques may allow for an exploration of psi through a control of dreams that would seek out the dreamers psychic ability or deliberately program the dream for a psychic experience.

That central theory we're looking for may come from increased efforts to see psi as it operates in everyday human life, rather than from proving its existence. Laboratory studies should change to allow for our "spontaneous psi" to happen, rather than to look to exclude all other problems, all "normal" explanations, if the patterns of psi's processes are to be found. Psychic dream studies may be an open avenue with lots of room for information about psi to be uncovered. Looking at that connection between our own psi and ourselves, and looking beyond ourselves to other environmental "forces" or cues that can affect psi may yield the best leads on what's happening.

Over the past few years, there has been more and more interest on the affect that electromagnetic and magnetic fields have on us, both from the standpoint of physical health and that of psychological behavior. We hear a lot today about electromagnetic "pollution," that the electrical fields of appliances such as heating blankets have caused detrimental physical effects. On the other hand, there has been some indication that some frequencies of magnetic fields (as in magnets) may help in the physical healing process. The kind of effect may have to do with whether the field is electromagnetic or magnetic in nature, and what the frequencies and field strengths are.

Neuroscientist Michael Persinger of Laurentian University in Ontario has been, for a number of years, interested in physical correlations to psychic functioning. Studies of the magnetic field of the earth (geomagnetic field) in connection to human behavior and to psi in particular by Persinger and others have brought forth some interesting correlations (and therefore more questions) of environmental influences on psychic functioning. Measurements of the fluctuations of the geomagnetic field are taken at a number of sensing stations around the globe. Such a field is quite different from both the basic background magnetic field, which doesn't vary much, and the kinds of electromagnetic fields produced by appliances, electric mass-transit systems, and other items of technology (like computers). The geomagnetic field does vary, as it is affected by solar activity, weather patterns (storms, particularly), and even movements of the earth.

Low and ultra-low frequencies of magnetic fields do affect biological systems, though not necessarily in negative ways. Behavior of animals and humans can also be affected by fluctuations in magnetic fields. The studies of Persinger and others have used indicators of geomagnetic field frequency and strength to look for correlations to both laboratory results of parapsychological experiments, and at spontaneous reports of psychic experience (both of which include, of course, psychic dreams). What has been learned? While the work is still in progress to correlate a variety of effects of the geomagnetic field on human behavior (including psi, in particular), the findings indicate a couple of trends.

Telepathy and clairvoyance experiences (in and out of laboratory experiments) tend to occur more frequently on days of "quiet" geomagnetic activity, in essence when the activity of the field is lower than the average, and where it's quieter than the activity on the days before or after. On the other hand, this relationship to "quiet" times doesn't hold for precognitive experiences or for sightings of post-mortem apparitions (apparitions that appear up to three days of the death of the individual being seen).

There has been some discrepancy in the findings, as when studies were made of the record of results at a couple of East coast laboratories, there was no such correlation. Yet in looking over the data from a variety of sources, the connection between telepathic and clairvoyant experiences to low geomagnetic activity seems to hold. Why the differences in the results of the precognition and post-mortem experiences, and between the lab studies?

The sensing stations are few and far between, and unfortunately cannot provide localized readings of the geomagnetic field. Local storms or earth movements can apparently affect the geomagnetic field fluctuations in a given area (such as the general area of a lab site), and without such local data, it is difficult to isolate why there are a few exceptions to the general findings. Another factor that may come into play is the idea that local electromagnetic fields (from technological devices) may interfere with whatever the process is that allows someone to be apparently more psychic during "quiet" times in the field.

As to precognition, it is possible that there is a connection between the geomagnetic activity on the day of the experience, with the field strength and activity of the day of the predicted event. As telepathy and clairvoyance are, by definition, real-time, the time factor may not create a problem as it might with precognitive experiences. Precognition may occur through a similarity of the geomagnetic field activity at the two times (time of experience and time of event). Parapsychologist and writer D. Scott Rogo, in his book *Psychic Breakthroughs Today*, mentioned another possibility: ". . . there is good evidence that cases of real-time ESP are more vivid and carry with them more of a sense of conviction than precognition experiences. Geophysical factors might enhance the *sense of conviction* cases of real-time ESP bring with them, a factor to which precognitive experiences may be immune." (page 79).

In the July 1990 issue of *Omni* magazine ("Magnetic Ghosts," *Omni*, page 74), Paul McCarthy wrote that Persinger has linked post-mortem apparitions to the geomagnetic field. Apparently, the experiences often take place when the geomagnetic activity is high, not quiet. Other studies have suggested a connection between such "highs" in field activity and poltergeist activity (psychokinesis).

Persinger and others have proposed a couple of possibilities with regard to the psi-geomagnetic connection. The first is that the geomagnetic field affects the incidence of psychic experience (and therefore some mechanism in the brain) allowing it, or even causing it, to happen. The other is that psi is always working within us, but the geomagnetic field affects the brain and its receptivity to the "signals." So, according to this, we are always being psychic, it's just that only under certain environmental conditions can we consciously receive, process, or even remember the psychic information. It is also possible that whatever influences psi, regardless of how it's influencing it, is some other environmental variable that changes along with the fluctuations of the geomagnetic field.

Whatever the effect on us, there is some connection now seen between the geomagnetic field and our psi experiences. According to Persinger and Stanley Kripper, the sudden quiet periods of activity may "facilitate telepathy by: (a) producing environmental conditions that promote exchange of information between the agent and the percipient, (b) allowing normal 'telepathic factors' already in the environment to be amplified between the agent and the percipient, and (c) evoking transient alterations in brain function such that normal telepathic factors (that do not change with geomagnetic activity) can affect the percipient's sensitized temporal lobes" (from "Dream ESP Experiments and Geomagnetic Activity," *Journal of the American Society For Psychical Research*, April 1989, page 101).

"Temporal lobes" refer to part of the brain in which much interest has evolved over the past several years. Studies by Dr. Vernon Neppe have linked activity in the temporal lobes to subjective paranormal experiences. The temporal lobes play a vital role in memory, hearing, and some hallucinatory experiences. Minor dysfunctions in the temporal lobes have been suggested to cause mystical experiences, experiences of déjà vu, and other psychic experiences. Studies of the temporal lobes show them open to environmental factors such as geomagnetic field activity. The temporal lobes are apparently more open to such factors during REM sleep, which may suggest a connection between dream content and the environment. Persinger and others have been looking to the temporal lobes as being connected to some, if not all, psychic experiences, although there is the unanswered question of whether the temporal lobes merely help process information retrieved psychically or whether the "psi center" of the brain is actually in the temporal lobes (that is, if psi is actually a function of the brain or the mind, which some say is independent of the biological brain).

Serena Roney-Dougal, a British parapsychologist, has been looking into activity in the brain and connection to geomagnetic and other environmental variables. Her particular interest has been in the biochemical melatonin, produced in the pineal gland (the gland called "the third eye" or something similar by several mystical traditions and cultural belief systems). The pineal gland, still not fully understood, seems to help govern our biological clock, as well as interacting with a wide range of other functions of the body.

According to Roney-Dougal and Persinger, a sudden change in the geomagnetic field, in either direction, may affect the temporal lobes and inhibit the production of melatonin. A drop in melatonin may cause small seizure-like behavior in the brain and dredge up visual imagery. Small electrical charges directed at the temporal lobes can also cause this drop in melatonin production. It may be situations like this, where the inhibition of melatonin may cause visual hallucinations, that get related to sightings of post-mortem apparitions, according to Persinger. His correlations to the fluctuation of the geomagnetic field indicated an increase in the field as necessary to such experiences. This could either lead one to the conclusion that such apparitional sightings are truly just hallucinations, or that the only chance a ghost gets to say goodbye to a loved one is during highs in the geomagnetic activity.

On the other hand, Roney-Dougal, in a paper to the Parapsychological Association in 1989, proposed that it is the sudden change in the geomagnetic field, not the direction, that causes the chain of events to begin. Although it does appear that a change has a connection to having some sort of psychic experience, it remains to be seen whether the direction of the change is unimportant to particular kinds of psychic experience.

But do such fluctuations make us psychic or do they simply increase our receptivity to something already there? In other words, are we radios needing to be turned on before getting a signal, or are we already on, just waiting to be tuned into the right station?

We don't know this as yet, but there is a great deal of interest in such environmental factors having direct impact on the human system, whether related to psi or not. Dreams may be affected as our bodies, and therefore brains are affected, by physical factors in the environment, whether natural or artificial. The effect of such variables on dreams is unknown at present. Psychic experience and performance does appear to be affected by changes in the geomagnetic environment, although it may be that the same things that affect geomagnetic activity (from solar flares to thunderstorms) affect our psi abilities or the receptivity and recognition of psychically derived information.

In dreams, as in waking experience, this holds true. One added factor supporting psi in dreams, however, is that the production of melatonin, the suppression of which is now being looked at as related to experiences we deem psychic, is also inhibited during a normal night's sleep.

Where does that leave us? Just with the sense that there are lots of ideas and theories out there, not just around psychic functioning, but also around dreams. In fact, we know quite a bit about how the brain works, but in comparison to how much we *should* know, we know next to nothing. When the answers in front of us start to make sense so that we can frame our questions correctly, we may finally understand the workings of the brain, the mind, dreams, and psi. In the meantime, we can work with the dreams and knowledge we've got.

CHAPTER 13

Dream Work
and Dreamweavers

As you've figured out by now, there are a number of reasons to want to work with your own dreams. The authors of the book *Dream Telepathy* sum it up succinctly with the following:

> There are three intrinsic properties of dreams that make them objects of special interest to those engaged in psychotherapy, but which apply equally well for anyone seeking greater self-knowledge.
> 1. Dreams are concerned with unfinished emotional business, known psychiatrically as areas of unresolved conflict. An incidental event, hardly attended to at all during the day, may open up a particular area of conflict which later, as if on a slow fuse, becomes the subject matter of a dream. The triggering incident itself is often identifiable in the dream and is known as the day residue.
> 2. Dreamers are very active in relation to the conflict that intrudes itself into their awareness. One of the things they do is take a backward glance over their own lives, scanning them for incidents historically related to the conflict that besets them. Long forgotten childhood episodes are woven into the dream if they can shed any light on the origins of their immediate focus of concern. It is as if the

dreamer, finding oneself in a state of partial arousal in the course of the sleep cycle, asks the critical question 'What is happening to me?' with the answer coming in the form of the insistently intrusive feelings triggered by the day residue.

The dreamer asks and answers a second question: "What are the historical origins of this disquieting threat to my equanimity?"

3. Having identified the emotionally intrinsic event, and its linkage to selective aspects of his past personal history, the individual now lets the dream explore the full implications of the threatening event and his or her capacity to deal with it. Then there ensues an interplay between character defenses (hang-ups) and resources leading either to a resolution of the feelings mobilized by the conflict, or failing in that, leading to awakening.

The opening scene in the dream is the setting and expresses the mood, feeling, or idea triggered by the day residue. Then follows a middle portion which further develops the theme now projected. It is enriched by past, as well as additional present, experiences linked to it at the feeling level. Finally, there is a terminal period of resolution which, when successful, results in the continuation of the normal sleep cycle and when unsuccessful, leads to awakening.

—From *Dream Telepathy*, by Montague Ullman and Stanley Krippner with Alan Vaughan (2d ed. McFarland & Company, 1989, page 175).

So how *do* therapists work with dreams, and how can *we* work with our own dreams?

For just about anyone willing to look in a book, dream interpretation has been a "simple" matter of recalling any images from a dream and looking up such symbols in a book of dream symbols and meanings. The book would tell you, often with an air of definite authority, just what that artichoke you ate in your dream meant. Of course, if you check the same symbol in five or six such books, you might easily get five or six "definite" meaning of the symbol. So who can you believe? What do your dreams mean?

I don't presume to make this chapter encyclopedic with regards to the many kinds of therapeutic approaches to dream work. Freudian psychologists use one way, having to do with Freud's own views of the purpose of dreams, while Jungian therapists work with Jung's concepts of dreams and their functions. Therapists from other schools of psychological thought use the models appropriate to their own approaches to therapy in general. To learn more about specific psycho-therapeutic approaches to the place of dreams in therapy and psychoanalysis, I suggest you read more in such areas or contact a therapist who specializes in Jungian, Freudian, Gestalt, or other forms of therapy. Ultimately, it would appear that to really deal with a dream, the interpreter, the therapist, the diviner needs to be you, the dreamer.

In addition, though the bulk of what I will be covering in the first part of this chapter has to do with non-psychic dreams, it's important to consider that, in terms of dream work, the non-psychic dream and the psychic dream really differ very little. The major difference is the content, rather than the mode of dreaming. Both kinds of dreams have information in them. A "normal" non-psychic dream has information content from our memory and sensory experience. A psychic or paranormal dream has information from those same sources, yet also draws on psi processes to supply information. Making use of, analyzing, or working with our dreams can be very much the same, whether the dream is psychic or not. It's the identification of the information as psychic and therefore applicable in other ways that makes the psychic dream one that has "added" value (such as application of the information in business, criminal investigation, daily relationships with others, connections to the environment and to other people, or foreknowledge of some impending event, good or bad).

To quote Dr. Loma Flowers of the Delaney & Flowers Professional Dream and Consultation Center in San Francisco:

All methods of dream analysis rely on the assumption that dreams have meaning of psychological relevance to the dreamer, but differ in the way that meaning is extracted. The traditional methods of dream interpretation evolved in the context of psychoanalysis and are consequently directed toward analysis of the transference, of the psychodynamic origins of the neurotic conflicts, and toward the collective unconscious. The contemporary eclectic methods are evolving in the context of individual growth—with or without therapy—and are directed more toward insight which can be more immediately applied to daily living. These differences produce variations in interpretation of the same dream. As in psychiatric treatment in general, the goal one is seeking from dream interpretation influences one's approach to the problem and choice of technique. It is therefore important to step back and choose a technique of dream interpretation in light of the results one is seeking and appropriate to the style of therapy being used.
—from "The Morning After: A Pragmatist's Approach to Dreams," by Loma K. Flowers, M.D., *Psychiatric Journal of the University of Ottawa*, vol. 13, no. 2, 1988, page 70.

Montague Ullman, who is interviewed following this chapter, has been a pioneer of the idea that working with dreams does not have to take place only in therapy, that one doesn't necessarily even need a trained therapist in working with dreams. Ullman and others advocate placing dreams in a social context, in sharing dreams with others in a group format so as to really deal with the dreams, rather than to place dreams in a larger context of counseling or therapy.

In formal therapy, which is typically a one-to-one (patient and therapist) relationship, there are certain controls the patient gives up to the therapist. The therapist, as the "expert" being consulted by the patient, is in control of any number of things, from the direction the therapist may want to pursue in exploring the patient's psychological make-up to the suggestion of how long therapy may take until it's over and the work is done. This is not to say that a therapist may not ask the patient "What do you want to work on today?" Therapists do that, of course, but always from a place of control of the session and the therapy in general. The roles of therapist and patient are unequal.

Unless the therapy session (and series of sessions) is/are specifically designed to work with the patient's dreams as source material, rather than all the waking experiences of the patient's past, a dream and its meaning can be lost in the greater context of the overall therapy, and the patient's history with the therapist. If you are in therapy to deal with emotional problems caused by relationships with the opposite sex, the therapist will generally be pulling from the entire scope of your past and present to consider any number of influences on relationships you've had. A dream in such a context becomes simply another source of clues, rather than a means to reveal the problem and deal with it. The dream is only a small part of the work being done by patient and therapist.

In group dream work, such as Ullman's format, the dreams of the group members are the central focus of the work to be done by the individuals. The individual dreamers in the group are in control of what they say and how much they reveal to the group. Even the group leader, who acts more as a facilitator of the process rather than as the "expert" in the group, has an equal role with all others with respect to dealing with the dreams themselves. There is respect by the group members for individual privacy of the group members, for the ultimate authority the individual has over his or her own dreams, and for the uniqueness of the individual that each dream addresses. This does not mean that the group should not be lead by a therapist, just that a therapist is not a necessity.

I recently interviewed a therapist from Marin County, California, who has worked with clients' dreams for a number of years, in both individual therapy settings and group settings. Pat Kampmeier is also a student of parapsychology, a topic she has taught in courses to the general public over the years.

LA: How long have you been working as a therapist using dreams as a tool?

PK: I started leading groups and working in private practice about the mid seventies.

LA: Did you start the dream groups from a therapist's standpoint, or was that simply because you were interested in dreams?

PK: I was a teacher at the time, and I taught adults because I was asked to lead some workshops, but I had started doing some private practice work about two years before that. I came at it from a therapeutic point of view, as well as that of a teacher. I was working with normal people that were curious about their dreams and wanted to know what to do with them.

LA: Were your dream groups based on any particular strategy?

PK: I had a background in Jungian work, and a background in the Edgar Cayce type of work. I'd been keeping my own dream journal since the early sixties and had tried different models of working with dreams. I had tried Ann Faraday's methods first, which are of course very well known and basic, but I've read extensively—I probably have eighty or a hundred books on dreams—so I've taken techniques from each of them and applied them as they seem to work for me or for someone in my group. That varies somewhat with the dream and the personality of the dreamer.

LA: Is curiosity the main reason people would come to see you about their dreams, or are you working with people's dreams as they come to you for therapy?

PK: Some people do dreams every now and then as part of their therapy and some people come with the predominant thing they want to do is dream work each time they come. That may be one time or it may be ten times, it might be once every few months, it might be three or four years [before they come back]. It varies considerably.

LA: Do you find that there is a benefit in working with a dream work group over individual work?

PK: They're different. It depends on the kind of material that you're willing to expose in front of others. It depends somewhat on the personality of the dreamer, too.

When I'm working with a group, the material that one person presents in their dream, as we talk about it, triggers recall in the other people in the group that have some symbols in their dreams that are similar to that of the person I'm working with. That's kind of a yeast effect. It means I can look at pieces of a number dreams and talk about a symbol that several of them have in common. That's interesting to do. It's a little bit different than the work you have to do with an individual. And there are certain things I probably would limit as to how much I let a person open up in front of a group. Most of my groups have been long-term, though, so people get to know each other, know what their issues are, and their places of pain, and where they're growing, and symbols that have come up over time. That's one of the great things about a group, because you get to look at dream series, rather than single dreams.

LA: Is a key for those working with you to sit down and keep that dream journal?

PK: I think so. There are occasionally people coming in that don't have any written record, but that's unusual. Most people I work with have kept dream journals or want to be taught how to do that. But I would say that most of the people I've had in my dream groups have done this, have kept a journal of some kind or another, have kept track of their dreams. I do teach how to do it, not only a written journal but a tape recording collection, too, if people are hesitant to write things down or don't want to come out of sleep that much [to be able to write dreams down].

LA: How does one put the dream journal together?

PK: The format I use is pretty standard and works whether you are putting it on tape or writing. You log in your date. I usually log in the day of the week, as that gives me some clue as to whether I was working the day before or not. I usually log in and teach people to log in whether it's a middle-of-the-night dream, a morning dream, or a late-afternoon-nap dream, because I think the quality of material is different.

I usually teach people to log the day residue, which would be the area with which we were most preoccupied or concerned with during the day. For some people, they may be very active out there in the world, but may have a lot going on inside. They may be puzzling over a relationship or fighting something out with their mother or spouse or one of their kids, or working on feelings that they have about themselves. If so, if they've been deeply preoccupied, then that's the really crucial day residue.

For other people it's actually what they did during the day, because their energy is free to be with their activity. Those things in which they were most involved would be the day residue for them. That gives us some kinds of clues as to what the dream's about. We often dream, of course, of what we were doing the day before.

I just tell them to write the body of the dream. I talk to them about the various elements of a dream. It does structure your writing a little bit; that is the scenes, the locations, the characters, the animals, the major objects that occur in the dream, major colors if they seem to be particularly noticeable, the mood of each little section.

LA: Do you find people remembering their dreams more and more as they get into the process of keeping a dream journal?

PK: Very much so, unless they get material that is too painful. The very first person that I worked with, interestingly enough, in 1971, had a dream in which her pilot husband went down in a flight. It really happened within a day or two, I don't remember the exact timing, but it frightened her so much she blocked her dream recall for about fifteen years, so we had to work with that.

It scared her. I don't believe she believed in precognition at that time, so it was very frightening to her that she would know ahead of time.

LA: Do you find that most of the folks in your dream groups tend to have occasional dreams that they would consider psychic?

PK: Sure, but I think in the short-term groups, where you just get together for an afternoon or part of a day or a full day, rather than one that stretches over time, where I only see people one time, I often have people come in who will have had something really startling happen.

I remember a woman who had a very unusual incident. In a dream, she was driving in the car behind her husband. He was in one car in front of her with one of their children and she was one car right behind him. They pulled up to a stop light in a bad neighborhood in Chester, Pennsylvania, and while she watched, two young guys who were standing on the corner ran around, dragged her husband out, and threw him on the ground—she thought he was killed—and drove off in the car with her child. I believe her husband was in fact killed in the actual incident.

It was very startling to have this exact incident later happen in her life, very frightening and very upsetting.

LA: At the time she had the dream, did she "know" it was something other than a nightmare, a sign of things to come?

PK: I don't know that she did. I think she just thought it was a really bad dream, and quite unusual. She came to the class because this unusual thing had happened to her. That's a different kind of person than those who come to my long-term group. They tend to be into a journey of working with themselves, with their own issues.

LA: Are those people in the long-term group able to come up with a qualitative difference for those dreams they might consider psychic?

PK: Sometimes they know. Sometimes the elements of the dream don't quite fit. The psychic elements overlay over the others in the dream. In fact, I've had people talk about having two or three levels going on at one time, where they have the dream, and they have a mentation level—a thinking level—and then a third level which seems to be a psychic overlay which comes in on top of their normal dream, which is kind of unusual.

LA: I've asked the question "How do you know it's a psychic dream?" of other people. The answer seems to be "you just 'know'."

PK: Sometimes. I don't think there's always that feeling of conviction. You just have to watch the dreams and see what happens in your life, too. I've had a number of people say to me that they went out with their spouse, or met them and went out with them one time, then dreamed they were going to marry and they did. They seemed to know, somewhere deep inside themselves, that this was their partner for life. I just love those kinds of dreams. I don't know that it's love at first sight, but it may be recognition.

LA: Why should people work with their dreams?

PK: I always tell people that the experience of the dream itself is worth something, even if you do no work with it at all. It opens up a dimension in yourself that helps you feel full and complete. It has characters and feelings and happenings that are not necessarily like your daily life. It's an enrichment. Just experiencing the dream, being willing to lie in bed and go over the feelings and feel them deeply, to really just be there with it, changes us.

But of course there's some work we can do with our feelings and with our mind by going through a process, by underlining key words [in the journal], key activities or peoples names and then doing some association work with it. It depends on the school of thought. Gayle Delaney says to "pretend I'm from Mars and describe this particular thing to me," that's the way she goes about it. She doesn't want anybody else's input or mythical input. Jung says you ought to look things up in various kinds of handbooks that have to do with myths and legends and pull in all the historical and archetypal kinds of things. I think there's something to be said for that, too. Freud lets you associate far afield from the dream, wherever you go with it. Jung wants you to stick with the material of the dream, while some people feel that it's all symbolic.

The Edgar Cayce people [the Association for Research and Enlightenment] feel there's often a real-life level with the dream. You need to check out this "me" that's interacting with a part of "myself," that's one level. Another level is this "me" that's interacting with people that I know in real life, should I look at the dynamics here, and what I feel about that other person. A third level is that kind of psychic, precognitive or telepathic, overlay. I think the Cayce people always encourage you to look at that possibility with dreams.

There are people, of course, that don't ever look at that. There are people for whom it's always the internal dynamics, that it has nothing to do with normal life. In the sense of the dream material, they say it's all symbolic. I think that a lot of it is very practical, daily life [material] that we don't need to take to the symbolic level.

Before getting directly to psychic dreams, let's examine more closely some fundamentals of dream work.

One of the most important points to keep in mind is that to work with dreams you have to remember your dreams. While it may work in some situations to rely on spontaneous flashes of what you recently dreamed, to really get into dream work, keeping a running record, a journal of your dreams, is extremely important, according to most of the dream work experts out there.

First of all, you need to learn to recall, to remember your dreams after you wake up, more frequently, more easily, and hopefully in greater detail. People can learn to recall their dreams, even to the point of recalling at least one a night. Techniques used by dream researchers and therapists, and subsequent surveys and studies indicate that just about anyone can learn some degree of dream recall. Some people are naturally good at recalling their dreams, others can barely remember getting out of bed to check on the kids during the night, let alone any dream imagery.

There may be some degree of difference in the activity of the brain of those who can and can't recall dreams, although such brain activity may change as an individual becomes one who can regularly recall his or her dreams. Dr. Roseanne Armitage and Tom Fitch at Carleton University in Ottowa, Canada, conducted a study of such differences between those who have a high degree of dream recall and those who have low recall. With the low dream recallers, there appears to be a large shift in electrical activity between the two hemispheres of the brain when awakened from REM sleep, as though the hemisphers are knocked off balance. For those people, sleep and wakefulness are two very different states. For the high recallers, there is very little electrical disruption between the hemispheres when awakened, with what appears to be a greater continuity in brain processes as the sleep transitions from sleep to waking consciousness.

How do you learn to remember your dreams? As with lucid dreaming, psychic experience, or other forms of psychologically related experiences, intention and motivation seem to play a large role. In fact, just the act of getting *interested* in working with your own dreams may have an effect. On starting the research for this book, I started spontaneously recalling more dreams than any other time in my life (except during college when I seemed to be having a number of spontaneous lucid dreams). If you tell yourself over and over, especially before falling asleep, that you will remember your dreams, and that you *want* to remember your dreams, you have a much better chance of that happening.

To fix the intention in your head, it is important that you provide yourself with something to record the dreams you recall. Most people tend to keep a written journal of their dreams, and have a notebook and pen or pencil by their bed. On the other hand, some people like to go the electronic route, keeping a tape recorder handy, as it's easier for them to speak into the recorder rather than expending the energy of writing something down on awakening. It might be best to have both forms of recording (writing implements and tape recorder) simply because you will then have the option of one or the other (or both) on awakening with some dream imagery in your mind. You might also keep a flashlight or small, not-so-bright lamp handy in case you wake up during the dark of the night with a dream.

If you do go the tape recorder route, I would suggest going back over the tape when fully awake and transcribing the information from the tape to paper, adding any additional imagery that may be recalled while doing that. Some people are now transcribing all dream images and other related information into a word-processor or database so as to be able to scan quickly for patterns and relationships between dream content and what's happening in their waking lives.

Remember that to really look at your dreams and their place in your life, you also need to be recording information from your awake and conscious states. You probably should choose another time during the day or evening to record such information, so as not to be confusing it with your dream content, but such information will tend to help understand where the dreams are ''coming from.'' So record the happenings of the day that may relate to any dreams you might have, the events, issues, and emotions that may stay with you. Keep note of that day residue. You might also note any recent events in the news that were of particular interest or upset you, as societal issues on our minds may also play out in our dreams.

Some dream workers suggest carrying a notebook (or mini-cassette recorder) during the day to take note of any other dream images that may be spontaneously remembered, and to keep track of the things during the day that may fall into your dreams later.

The journal process is, as you can tell, something that may require a bit of commitment of time and mental and physical energy. However, if you truly wish to work with your dreams, such a commitment is necessary. It is not imperative that you can recall even one dream a night, as many will tell you that even a dream a week, recorded appropriately with day residue and other information, will be beneficial to work with. However, as Pat Kampmeier and just about all others who work with dreams report, the process of keeping that journal will tend to increase your dream recall, as you recall more and more, your motivation and interest and intention will increase, thereby reinforcing the whole process.

Okay, so you record the day's events and feelings, have your journal-keeping devices by your bed, and you're ready to go to sleep. Again, it seems to be extremely helpful to have running through your mind the idea that you *will* remember your dreams. I've spoken with a couple of people who work with their own dreams who repeat that order within their minds every once in a while during all waking hours, to further program themselves for dream recall, though the intention at bedtime alone seems to work.

There are three points of awakening that might arise within a regimen of keeping the dream journal. Upon awakening just after a dream (or as a result of one), stay relaxed and allow your thoughts to collect themselves, the images to arise. As you have just been through REM sleep, there is a better chance you'll remember the whole dream, rather than just fragments of it. You may ask yourself "What was I dreaming?" as suggested by Stephen LaBerge, and allow the images to come forth. It may take only a second or two, or a few minutes, and you may recollect the whole dream or just parts of it. As the dream takes form or fragments of the dream come up, focus on them for a moment. Do not try to analyze, identify, or categorize the images, rather just take note of them and allow them to bring out other pieces. Then record the recollections, from the fragmentary or whole dream images to feelings, colors, or anything else that may come to you. You might want to try drawing anything you can, in addition to jotting down or recording the words. When you fall back to sleep, repeat the intent to remember more dreams that night (keep in mind we go in and out of REM sleep a few times during the night).

You may awaken naturally in the morning, though not necessarily after a REM stage, with some dream content floating around in your head. Again, relax and let your mind wander. Keeping your eyes closed appears to help in this process. Even if you don't recollect a dream at all the moment you wake up, the process of asking yourself about your dreams and allowing any images to collect may help recall. Record any images or feelings you get. If you plan on going back to sleep, repeat the recall intention.

Finally, you may awaken because of an alarm of some kind, whether for work or something specific to do during the morning. If you get caught in the middle of REM sleep with that alarm, you could be set to record some rich detail about your dreams. Relax, recollect the images, and record them. If you recall nothing, relax a moment and let your mind wander, and ask yourself what you could have been dreaming. Record whatever you get. Gackenbach and Bosveld (*Control*

Your Dreams) suggest that you might set your alarm for a different time, perhaps a half-hour earlier, if you don't recall any dreams, since those thirty minutes may place you in a REM sleep stage.

It is important to remember a couple of things about the journal process. Record *all* dreams, *all* fragments of dreams, and any other feelings or images that may come to you as a result of the recall process. You must be committed to recording everything and every dream if you want to really work with them.

You should record all images, however, fragmentary. The imperfect memory we seem to have of our own dreams parallels the incomplete information transfer that often accompanies psychic experiences. You might recall an important shape or feeling or color from a dream that can still be related to your waking life without identifying or categorizing that information (in other words, without labeling it "the Eiffel Tower" as opposed to simply recording a dream of a tall, steel-lattice shape which might be part of the power station down the street).

With experiments in ESP such as those with remote viewing or the Ganzfeld work, parapsychologists have learned that analyzing, labeling, or identifying the imagery or other information "received" often causes our minds to "flesh out" the actual psychic information with other images that are unrelated to the actual target. In remembering dreams, we might get an incomplete image that we "fill in the blanks" for, effectively mis-identifying what the dream was about simply because we tend to be frustrated by incomplete pictures. However fragmentary the images are, they typically can relate to a waking event or issue, regardless of whether they've been identified as "such and such" a person or object or not.

Don't worry about keeping items remembered in any sort of "correct" time sequence. The order of occurrence of events and images in a dream may be difficult to get straight while conscious, unless of course the whole dream is remembered. With regard to time, it is important to jot down the date and time of the dream or recall, as well as such time information for any waking events recorded, so as to best make use of the journal later.

Regardless of the method of initial recording of the recalled information, whether in written or taped form, the act of copying or transcribing it into a more permanent notebook or onto a computer tends to bring up more imagery and scenes from the dreams, as well as memories of items needful of recording from waking, conscious time. If you've done any drawings, keep those with the permanent dream journal as well. Some dream workers suggest titling the dreams, as you would a short story.

A review process of the journal is also helpful in reinforcing dream recall. As you go back over previously recorded dreams, you may have new imagery show up, or new feelings arising. Record this information as well, as it often enlightening in the process of interpreting your dreams, and does reinforce the motivation and intention of the whole procedure.

In terms of interpretation, remember that you are the best interpreter of your own dreams. The issue of how you work with your dreams is one you may want to look at. As you've read, there are more than a few ways to work with or interpret dreams, whether by yourself, in a one-to-one setting with a therapist or friend, or in a group setting. There are some advantages to each type of setting, as well as differing views on which is more successful. (There are a number of books out there, some already mentioned, that address in-depth the relative effectiveness of each format. Check the bibliography for such titles.)

Montague Ullman and others have advocated bringing dreamwork to the people, so to speak. Working with a therapist may be necessary for some people who need to look deeper into themselves than what their dreams may tell them, and I've already discussed the issue of control in dream work settings with a therapist. The one-to-one situation may work well for you if you simply work with a friend or relative who also is working with his or her own dreams, more or less working as a mini dream group. Bouncing the dreams off someone you already trust may alleviate some of the concerns many people have around sharing their innermost "secrets" with a group of people you must learn to trust. Gayle Delaney suggests telling the dream to the therapist (or other individual or group) as though the listener is an extraterrestrial, perhaps a Martian who knows absolutely nothing about our world, not even what a piece of paper or a banana is, or who Elvis Presley was (or still is, depending on whom you talk to or which tabloid you read). This allows for rich detail without labeling to occur.

If you are working with the journal on your own, you may consider Delaney's advice. If I had to describe images from the perspective of including a lot of information that could allow for someone totally unfamiliar with the "thing" in my image, I could easily avoid identifying that image which in turn would allow for more open (and perhaps easier) connections to my waking life. The Eiffel Tower may mean nothing to me, but the general shape and construction of such a dream image may reveal my unvoiced concern about that electric power structure near my home.

The group setting is one that does seem to work well for many people, because of the commitment involved (in both recording the dreams and participating in the group process) and in the very format which allows the dreamer to stay in control. Ullman's group process involves four stages of discussion of the dream which I'd like to summarize and comment on. Check out Ullman's books for a full explanation.

In Stage I of the group process, the dreamer "volunteers" a dream, allowing the group to ask questions for clarification so as to grasp the content of the dream as clearly as possible. There is no absolute expectancy that each member of the group has to have had a very recent dream to share, so there is a safety net for those who may not wish to share a dream at a particular session. In addition, the act of relating the dream to a group (or even to an individual) often allows for insight, especially if others ask questions for clarification.

In Stage II, the dreamer sits back and listens as the group discusses the dream and any imagery or feelings or ideas it conjures up for them. The group takes the dream as their own for a time, allowing for free association that may spur on other members of the group with ideas, or jog the dreamer's own insight and memory of other dreams or real events. Intuition may play a big role as the group members speak out their own perceptions and discuss the metaphors which the image may bring to them. The dreamer, now simply an observer, may feel safe in that position as a non-participant, able to accept, deny, or ignore anything heard without offending or affecting anyone else in the group. At the same time, the dreamer is working on his or her perceptions of the dream that have now evolved as part of the group's discussion of the dream.

Stage III returns the game to the dreamer, who responds to the group discussion with how his/her understanding and perception of the dream has been affected, evolved, changed, or grown. The control of the dream and discussion of it is back with the dreamer, who may elicit further discussion and dialogue directly from the group. The group may prompt the dreamer with further questions for clarification or suggestions of connections, but it is the dreamer who may share, hold back, or accept whatever it is from his/her waking life that can now be related to the dream. The dreamer has the right of control, the right to respond, ignore, accept, deny, or ask for further comments and questions from the group.

Stage IV involves a review of the dream by the dreamer alone sometime between that group meeting and the next. During that time, the dreamer should revisit the dream in light of everything that came out during the last group meeting and discussion of the dream, noting any further ideas or interpretation of the dream. This allows the dreamer a greater freedom of working with the dream (as he/she is not constrained by the format of the group meeting) with a richer, more detailed information base to draw on (the dream's content plus whatever came up during the working of the dream by and with the group).

The group process does require a commitment and an investment of regular time, as any process of therapy may involve (although if you look at a therapist-less dream group as therapy, it is self-controlled therapy). Later you'll read some of Montague Ullman's comments on the dream group process.

If you want to work alone you are among many others of similar intent. While any dream work does require commitment and some amount of time, working alone does so without the rigid schedule a group or one-to-one format may require. Once you have that dream journal going, and you are recalling and recording dream imagery on a regular basis, you can begin to review the journal for patterns and suggestions of connections and relationships to your conscious life. Let me reiterate that it is important to not only record the dreams (or dream fragments) themselves, but also whatever strikes you from your waking day. Also, as you copy over your brief notes to a more permanent journal or computer record, jot down any associations you may get from the dream characters, objects, or events.

Ask yourself questions as you review your dreams, such as "Now why did I dream that?" in order to bring up associations to waking life, and jot them down. Gayle Delaney, in her book *Living Your Dreams*, suggests that we look at dreams as we would a theatrical or film production, where you are the producer, director, writer, special effects person, and actor(s). You might ask yourself questions like "Why did I write this scene this way? Why did I write it at all?" or "Why did I direct the characters to act this way?" or "What's my motivation or emotion for this scene?" or "Where does this scene (dream) fit in to the overall plot of my life?"

In interpreting dreams, whether from a series or singly, you need to remember that dreams are often metaphors of situations or concerns from our waking lives. Look at how the actions, events, characters, and objects may have different meanings for you and try to collect a series of symbolic meanings for yourself. In other words, you might learn from reviewing your dreams that certain things appear more than once in your dreams and represent specific things to you each time they appear. Our dreams typically concern us directly, with the exception of some psychic dreams which may reach beyond an immediate impact on us. Often the imagery in our dreams does concern situations of immediate concern (same day) and can be easily "read" from the dream. Other imagery may reappear in dreams because it points to a continuing concern or problem or interest. What's important is to remember that the dreams have their "fit" in your own life and should be looked at as both literal representations as well as symbolic ones.

Have I given you any easy answers or methods for working with your dreams? Well, the answer is yes and no. Dream experts say that the methods of both dream recall and interpretation are fairly easy to learn, and appear to work for just about anyone. On the other hand, the commitment to keeping a journal (very regularly) and the continual time expenditure in the recall, recording, and reviewing process is difficult for some people. You, the dreamer, need to decide if you really want to do it, if you're motivated to do it. Remember that such intent and motivation seem to be a necessity to any dream recall or interpretation process.

You may not only be able to program yourself to remember your dreams, but also to wake up each time you have a dream, which should in turn increase recall. Some people are able to do this with a simple addition to the statement of intent (to recall dreams) you go through at bedtime. Repeating to yourself "I will remember my dream as soon as I wake up, and I will wake up as soon as I finish a dream" may push the program along. In any event, the process of programming yourself is not a fast one, and may take many weeks, rather than a few days. But it does seem to work for just about anyone, so don't be discouraged. You can do it if you believe you can.

So, what you need to balance against the "downside" (the commitment of time and energy) is the potential "payoff" of working with your dreams. Dreams appear to help us learn and may aid in memory formation. They can help us to approach and work through traumatic events in our lives. They can relate to our past history or to very immediate events in our lives. They are providers of what is often the most honest information we offer to ourselves. They can help us understand ourselves more thoroughly, from our fears and anxieties to our hopes and "dreams" (no pun intended). They enlighten us to our own connectedness to others and to the world around us. They can provide us with in-depth information on how we really feel about events in our society. They can be utilized for stress reduction. They may provide creative insights or solutions to problems that are bugging us. They can be means of escape and entertainment. In general, they are a natural resource for all people.

Besides the idea of working with dreams to find out more about ourselves, there is the application of using dreams for decision making and problem solving. As business and management training is now including some emphasis on intuitive and creative problem solving, techniques of dream work are being included in instruction. "Sleeping on it" is not a far-fetched method of coming to a decision, and some, notably Gayle Delaney, have written on the incubation of a dream in order to look for solutions to specific problems.

This technique, according to Delaney, is fairly simple but requires commitment, as with other techniques of dream work. Keeping the dream journal is an integral part of the incubation of a dream, as review of the journal is essential. You must choose a good time, a good night to work on a specific problem, and it should be one when you are not too tired and have not been drinking alcoholic beverages or taken drugs which could affect your sleep. You want to review your dream journal before going to sleep, taking note of the day's happenings and feelings. You need to have an internal discussion of the problem to be solved, thinking it through from any number of angles so as to decide what needs to be addressed and what kind of information would provide a working answer. Bring up and note any feelings that may be associated with the problem.

Next, you need to come up with an "incubation phrase," a one line question or request that provides a succinct description of the problem, showing a clear and deep understanding of the situation to be addressed. This should be your final decision of what to incubate, what the dream will address.

Focus on that incubation phrase as you go to bed (and to sleep), leaving that uppermost in your mind (along with, of course, the intent to remember the dream). On awakening, go through the recall and recording process, reviewing the information provided by the night's dream(s) for possible solutions to the problems.

Many people have had a good deal of success with using their dreams to solve problems, whether through the purposeful method of dream incubation, or simply through the process of keeping and reviewing the journal. Often the solutions and information provided seem to be from some source outside the experience of the dreamer. While some of that may be intuitive solutions pulled together by the subconscious from seemingly unrelated memories, some of it seems to be from outside ourselves, as though the part of us that was dreaming was truly able to get information from outside sources. That, of course, leads us back to psychic dreams.

In the "normal" process of working with dreams, paranormal or psychic dreams may appear. Some of these may be problem-solving dreams that include information we could not possibly have known from outside sources. Some may be dreams of events that we don't connect with at the time, later learning that the dream predicted that later event. The dreams may be of events from the past, present, or future, and may be about events or people directly connected to us or far removed from our lown lives.

Once again, working with psychic dreams is often the same process as working with any other kind of dream. Why have I covered so much on the different ways of working with non-psychic ("normal") dreams? Well, as I mentioned at the beginning of this chapter, psychic dreams are just plain dreams, though with extra-added-value—more information from sources outside your sensory experience. One can work with psychic dreams in the same way one works with the non-psychic variety. Dream incubation, for example, is a valid technique when applied to any kind of dream. In fact, the idea of incubating a particular question or problem, even if you don't think you have the answer to it, coupled with a willingness to accept (or even to seek out) information through some psi channel, can yield wonderful results. What's important about working with your dreams is not strictly whether it contains psychic information or not, but whether the information can be used in a way that is pertinent or applicable to your life.

Of course, one difference between the content of the psychic and non-psychic dream is that for many people, psychic dreams contain information that is not directly applicable to the dreamer. If I dream about a murder or disaster in some other location (and nowhere near me), that information, if truly psychic, may have no value in my life. However, if that dream of disaster was not psychic, if the information came up from my subconscious, it may be a representation, a metaphor for something in my own life.

This leads to the all-pervasive question: How do you know a dream is psychic or not? There are many answers to that question, and many viewpoints. To gain a better understanding of such viewpoints, I'd like to present three interviews to you. The first is with psychic practitioner Joanne Mied, the second with psychotherapist/psychic counselor Beth Hedva, and the third with psychiatrist and dream expert Montague Ullman. The three interviews cover a continuum of experience of working with dreams, psychic and otherwise.

Working with dreams may work for you in a group setting, or a one-to-one relationship, or simply through working on your dreams yourself. The viewpoints expressed by the following people do lean towards the group setting, as that allows for the dreamer to bounce ideas off others and to get their own input, which may be intuitive or even psychic. However, working on your own is very possible, and may be the best route for many to take. The common procedures, however, need to be followed, no matter how you plan to work on your dreams.

Keep a journal or log of your dreams. Use that and conscious intent to learn to remember more of your dreams. Keep track of the waking events in your life in the same journal. Note if any of the dreams seems unusual or more ''important'' or more ''real'' or maybe even ''psychic.'' Review the journal regularly for patterns you may not have noticed as you jot down the dreams. And always consider that content of the dreams may relate to how you are running your life (or to the outside world, if they appear to be so connected, as psychic dreams often are).

In Appendix A of this book, you will find some "experiments" you might try with your dreams, specifically aimed at psychic information and experience as it comes through them.

CHAPTER 14

Interviews With Three Dream Workers

In deciding on what would make my book different from others having to do with dreams in general, and the very few that deal with psychic dreams at all, I thought it would be interesting for readers to see the perspective of different types of dream workers. This interview is with a psychic practitioner who has worked a bit with dreams. Those that follow bridge the jumps, which are admittedly very small, from psychic dream worker to therapist dream worker.

Please note that any words/comments in brackets ([]) have been added by me for clarification.

AN INTERVIEW WITH JOANNE MIED

Joanne Mied of Novato, California, works with what she calls "psychogenic research" in applying her own psychic abilities. To quote her own description of the process: "Many life problems, both bodily and emotional problems, are simply what they appear to be and they require the help of specialists . . . social workers, medical doctors, and psychologists. However, some of these problems are not simply what they appear to be; they are psychogenic. That is, they have their origin (genesis) in the human mind, spirit, or soul (psyche). Psychogenic research is a benign method by which the underlying origins of these problems are revealed and released.

"Psychogenic research discovers the origin of bodily, emotional, mental, and other life problems through dowsing. Dowsing is an ancient art of information gathering used to discover the location of something valuable that is not visually accessible. For example, dowsing is used to find pure drinking water, to discover oil, or find deposits of gold or other precious minerals. As a healing tool, dowsing is a means of discovering what lies under the surface of an individual, a relationship, or an event. In psychogenic research, the psyche is dowsed to unearth the subtle causes of an individual's problem. It is not scientifically known how dowsing works, but it appears to have three components: the mind of the operator, the dowsing wire, and the spirit (or psychic component) of the operator. Although the mechanism of dowsing is not fully understood, the accuracy and effectiveness of it has been proven repeatedly."

Joanne has been working with her own psi abilities for years, including work with her own dreams and the dreams of others.

LA: What are the categories you use in labeling your psychic dreams?

JM: I use different categories than you: an astral dream is what you're calling an astral projection dream.

LA: Out of body experiences in dreams.

JM: Those are real easy. After a couple of them you can figure out what they are easily because they're very clear, they're always in color. If someone's telling you a dream they'll say something like "It was exactly like it happened, except I could fly. The grass was really green—it was just a beautiful sunny day. Just real. Really real." Those are the kinds of things they say. They can fly.

LA: In those dreams do they realize they are dreaming, as with lucid dreams?

JM: You mean are they conscious? Not necessarily. Suppose you have a dream about your friend who lives in Italy. If you call him, and you have information that you got in that dream, he'll always verify the information. In other words, you learn things in those dreams that are actually true because you actually went there.

The second one's the initiatory dream. That's a dream where you have some kind of experience with a teacher or you have a profound insight. The way that you can tell those dreams is that the following morning you have a bodily reaction. It stays with you bodily, like you'll notice that you're happy for the whole day. It's almost physical. You're in a heightened energy state for at least twenty-four hours; sometimes it will last three days.

The next category is junk release, garbage [dreams]. Last night I had a dream and I was trying to take a shower and get my towel together. Basically, I was supposed to be waking up, so that's junk.

Premonitory dreams have a particular quality too, but they're harder to describe. If you keep a dream diary, and you follow up on your dreams, there's a certain flavor to them. It's really hard to describe, but you come to know it.

LA: That makes sense given the precognitive dreams that most people tend to have. They know that this is something that is probably going to come true and that's what makes the dream different for them in their own minds.

JM: And they [the dreams], again, are very clear, and you'll see details and colors.

The last category is dreams about dead people, dreams where you have conversations and encounters with people that you're related to who are already dead.

LA: What about your psychic dreams?

JM: I'm obsessed with premonitions, and I have tons of them. I wrote down nine just off the top of my head, which was interesting for me to see because some of them were dramatic.

For example, I had a dream of this couple getting into an accident on this windy road up to Mt. St. Helena, and they did. I never told them [about the dream] and the following weekend they did get into an accident, and their car was totaled. But they were unscathed, which was exactly what I dreamed: that their car was totaled but they were unscathed.

LA: Do you feel that if you had told them about the dream that you might have placed them in more danger because they would have been worried about the dream prediction? Would that have made them overly cautious and altogether not gone there at all, but been less cautious in other ways?

JM: Well, it's funny, this dream in particular was a turning point for me because I was pretty close with this guy. He scolded me for not telling him about it [the dream]. I have had a lot of premonitions over the years through dreams and when you tell people it never makes any difference. I've rarely seen anything that anyone ever changed.

LA: I think that's a dilemma that a lot of psychics face when they pick up things that might even be just starting right "now." You can pick up a kind of pathway of what's going to happen down the road, and revealing that information could even actually cause a situation, or just simply allow it to come to the surface a little bit quicker. Perhaps you're saving them a bit of grief if it comes to the surface quickly in such a situation. A good counselor can see that, of course, in a counseling session with a couple. Later, one member of that couple might even say the same thing to the counselor, that it was his or her fault.

Perhaps the counselor advanced the situation by letting somebody say "Well, there's something going on here," but that's an observation, not a cause of a situation.

JM: Being psychic is really a double-edged sword. Having people being responsive to it and being able to help people with it has really, for me, lessened a lot of the pain of it in the last couple of years. I was thinking today how I didn't really know that everyone didn't have the ability.

LA: So you, like many other folks, see others as people like you, but realize that many are blind to their abilities, not realizing they can "see" in the same way.

JM: Right. And I thought, I would see things in people that they couldn't see in themselves, so I would say something about it and they would deny it. I thought they were just lying. It took me a long time to understand that they really didn't know that. There was a disconnection in there. That's the only way I can see it now. It seems like people honestly don't see it, but it took me a long time to understand that. I just thought people were lying.

LA: So obviously you've been psychic pretty much all your life.

JM: Yes. When I was a young child, my brother died. I had a full premonition of his death before it occurred, and I told my friend. If I had any doubts that I had that experience, they certainly didn't.

LA: When your brother did die, was their reaction very negative, or did they feel that you were maybe a bit "spooky?"

JM: No, it wasn't negative in their feeling. In my feeling it was. You know how children are. Everything's your fault when your're a kid, and I felt that. It took me a long time to release that. My dad also trained me, interestingly enough. He was an engineer, of all things. He trained me to be psychic. We would play card games and then at the end of every card game he would flip cards and have me first guess black or red. You know, "What am I looking at?" When I got that down then it was "Which suit is it?" I got really good, and of course he knew enough about probability to be able to tell when I was doing well and when I wasn't. Every time we'd play cards, that's what we did. I can't remember which came first, whether this was before my brother died or after.

LA: How did you come to be working professionally with psychic abilities?

JM: Well, for years I had no control over it. When you start meditating you have even more experiences. About twenty years ago when I started meditating, it got more exaggerated, but I still had no control. I couldn't really focus on anything or come up with a yes or no. My husband has had a bad back. Three or four years ago he went to this psychic. This guy used a wire and helped him a lot. So I went to him for allergies and he worked on me. I thought, well this is great. I could learn that.

So I learned to use the wire and that, really, you can do anything with that. I still get information. Sometimes I just blatantly get information, and other times I have actual pictures, and other times it's just a feeling, but then I can always use the wire to focus in.

LA: When you say "use the wire" you're talking about what?

JM: You know what dowsing is? Basically, the one [wire] I have is a sophisticated version of the old coat hanger. It's a great tool for me.

I can scan somebody's body for anything you can name —muscle tension. I can tell whether they're left-handed or right-handed, usually, by the amount of tension in their arms. It's whatever you put your attention on that you can scan for.

LA: You've told me that you did some dream work with children?

JM: Yes, I've worked with teaching children, talking to them about dreams. It was at a boarding school where I worked as a math teacher. I taught math and computer science, but it was a pretty open school, and I also taught a religious studies class they had. It was a very broad religious studies class, and so for six weeks we studied shamanism. That's how we got into dreaming.

LA: Were there ways you helped the kids with their dreams?

JM: One was meditation. Another is having the intention of remembering your dreams when you go to sleep. Keeping a dream diary. Discussing the dreams at breakfast, lunch, and dinner.

It was a boarding school, so that was part of the meal conversation. If you didn't have a dream, we basically created a peer pressure to dream.

LA: What else?

JM: You have to make the transition out of your sleeping state into your waking state without a jar, so that you're not shifting into the left brain so intensely that you lose your contact with the right brain, so we didn't have alarm clocks. I'd go around and wake them up and say "Good morning. Time to get up. Remember your dreams." They would right away have that cue when woken up.

If you can't remember them in the morning, intend to remember them during the day, and you will. Usually there will be a moment during the day where you'll see something that will remind you of the dream, and that will let you remember it. Or, if you have another meditation during the day, like in the afternoon, when you're going in or coming out [of the dream state], lots of times you'll remember them then.

LA: I've certainly had the experience of remembering a dream from seeing something or experiencing something during the day. Often very clearly where the entire dream comes back to me because of that little stimulus.

Did you do anything with helping them program their dreams, with intentional dreaming?

JM: About six girls and two adults took on the project of trying to visit a specific building at 2:00 A.M. in their dreams. The outcome was interesting. Each morning, before talking to one another, the girls and the women would record their experiences in their dream diaries. And then at breakfast, we would compare them. After four nights no one had succeeded in reaching the destination. On the fifth morning, Megan, Sarah, and Laura reported success. They each had succeeded in going to the building. They described the darkened building. They each described seeing the other two people and none of the other dreamers.

The other thing was for the kids to once a month go back and reread their diaries. One example was this boy Ian. He had this dream that he went to the ski lodge. The school was on a ski mountain. The kids skied for free because a month before ski season they went up and served at the ski lodge and helped them clean up. Ian and one of the teachers went up to the ski lodge to find out when the kids could come and what they were going to do that year. When he went in he saw that the ski lodge was being remodeled. This one guy was standing there with a saw in his hand. The stairwell had been changed.

Well, it turned out that he had actually dreamed that a long time before, but he didn't remember that he'd dreamed it, even though he'd written it in his diary.

One thing about premonitory dreams is that people don't tend to remember their dreams. In Marin [County, California], there was a fire [one New Year's day]. Two old people died in this fire. I happened to know a woman whose parents they were. Three months before that, she told me one morning that she had a dream that both of her parents died. But after her parents died, she didn't remember that she'd had that dream.

LA: She didn't remember telling you?

JM: She didn't remember. About three weeks later, all of the sudden *I* remembered that she'd had that dream. I told her, and then she remembered. I think people have even more [dreams] than they think because I've seen so many cases where people do have premonitory dreams and they don't even remember them.

LA: I've actually remembered a couple myself as the dreamed-about events are happening or just after the events. A lot of the dream imagery rushes back into my head. I know a number of people who have that experience. In fact, sometimes it seems to be an explanation for the déjà vu experience; that you didn't really have the experience before. The sensation of familiarity is because you had a dream of the experience. So in some respects you are living it a second time, you were there before, though in a dream.

Tell me a bit about a couple of these premonitory dreams.

JM: There was Ian's dream about the ski lodge. One of the other children, Megan, had this dream that Jennifer's bird died. Within three days, the cat got in and killed the bird.

I dreamed about going to an art sale and seeing these Disney postcards. My husband and I were looking at these Disney postcards and this teacher came in and said "Here we have the religious art of the world on display for you and you're looking at Disney postcards." He was making a joke, but he was also being critical.

The Disney postcard was framed. You know how the Indians have this special way of framing pictures so that they use them for worship? This Disney postcard was framed like an object of worship. And I said to him "Isn't this funny? That a Disney card would be an object of worship?" He said "For you, this is an object of worship," meaning, this is an example of what your life should be, if your life were worship.

The card was a picture of two cartoon cows dancing. The thing about it was that the male cow was playing, and the female was dancing to his music. She had this particularly ecstatic look on her face, a mindless look of just complete surrender.

I had that dream during the week and on the weekend I did go to an art sale. There was all this religious art but there was one Disney postcard for sale, which was the one from my dream. I was of course stunned, just stunned. I was saying to my husband "This is the card. This was in the dream." He was not as impressed as I was.

So I went up to the person who was in charge and said "Hey, in my dream there were more cards. There were a half dozen cards." And she said "Well, look, I'm just taking over for lunch. You'll have to wait until Mary comes back."

When "Mary" came back she said "Oh yeah, we had a bunch of them, but so-and-so bought all of the others. This is the only one we have left."

It [the card] was exactly like in the dream. And it was for me.

My husband and I had just gotten married and it really was an issue that I was dealing with in my life, about what it is to be in a relationship to a man in a spiritual way, beyond just being married in a conventional sense, basically like the card was, to dance to his music ecstatically. What is that and what does it mean? It was a pretty far out incident.

LA: Working with the kids and their dreams, did they ask you questions? What did you tell them about whether things were going to come true or not from their dreams, and if they had any control over that? Or did you at all?

JM: The children didn't look to us for help, in a way. They had such a strength. They would have visions in meditation that they would tell me about that would just blow me out of the water.

LA: And they took them pretty much in stride?

JM: Yes. It wasn't that big of a deal. In fact, their exam for the shamanism class was to answer five questions giving examples of extra-sensory perception. In other words, one extra-sensory smell, touch, taste, and almost every kid could answer all five questions. It was mind-boggling. The kids were from about thirteen to eighteen, the full range of high school. It was extraordinary.

It wasn't extraordinary to them. I think the most extraordinary thing was when they actually took it upon themselves to pray for a new kitchen. The kitchen in the school needed remodeling. The project they took on the last couple of weeks of class was to pray and visualize the kitchen being remodeled. And when the kitchen was remodeled that really brought it home for them.

Joanne has discussed working with her own abilities and applying them to working with others. While many consider such people (who call themselves psychics or intuitives or whatever you want to call them) "phonies," or "charlatans" or even "crazy" because there is hesitation or disbelief in accepting psi functioning, extended perceptions, as real, there appears to be an insight that people such as Joanne have to offer that goes beyond "normal." As there is no gizmo or test we can apply at this time to verify that a "psychic" is truly more psychic than anyone else, what you may simply consider is that people with such professed abilities, real or imagined, may have something to offer.

As a magician/parapsychologist combination myself, I have run into out-and-out phonies, and I know the "tricks of the trade" so to speak. But what I find interesting is often the intentions of psychics, even some who realize that they may not be more psychic than anyone else. An intent and desire to help people come to resolution in their lives, combined with a bit of ethical behavior, goes a long way. It may be that many who are "psychic" are simply good observers of human behavior, and are capable of helping others simply with their observations.

Joanne seems to be one of those people whose insights into experience and behaviors, especially with dreams, is extremely helpful. Working from her own experiences, which under the labels of psychic experience and parapsychological concepts do appear "psychic," Joanne is able to help people work through their own experiences, their own dreams.

Combined with a good background in human psychology, such insights could, perhaps, be even more powerful, or simply better accepted by folks who have "problems" with accepting the psychic side of things. My next interviewee embodies such a combination.

INTERVIEW WITH BETH HEDVA, Ph.D.

Beth Hedva, Ph.D., writes, teaches, and counsels people to use their psychic and intuitive resources to heal the past, and to find and fulfill their unique life's purpose. An expert in the field, she has taught at John F. Kennedy University and was core faculty in the department of clinical psychology at Antioch University. Founder of the Psychic Hotline, offering information and referrals nationwide to people in psychic distress, Dr. Hedva's skills as a clinician and hypnotherapist combine with her twenty-two years of experience with psychic and intuitive realities. One of her areas of interest and expertise lies in working with dreams.

As someone who often gets calls from people who have experienced fear or other problems with having psychic experiences, I have felt very comfortable and assured that referring people to Dr. Hedva means that they get the counseling or further referrals they need.

LA: A lot of people who are psychic talk about having and psychic experiences since they were very young, thinking this was perfectly normal, and only later discovering that other people didn't. Was this your experience?

BH: That was definitely true for me, especially with dreams. My first awareness of psychic reality was from dreams. I had the same dream as a girlfriend of mine, which actually I discovered after she came back from Christmas vacation with a broken leg.

During Christmas vacation, I had had a dream about her where we had been on a skating rink and she had broken her ankle skating. Indeed, she had broken her leg skiing while we were on break [vacation]. I was talking with her about that during recess one time in school, and I discovered that we had had the same dream previously about a dragon burning cars as they were going down the street.

I had precognitive experiences in childhood dreams, too. It didn't hit me until I was seventeen years old, actually, that

I was having experiences other people weren't having. I thought all along that everybody saw the world as I did, but then I realized other people were not tuned into such subtleties.

LA: Did something happen that confronted you with that fact?

BH: Yes. I was in a foreign country on a trip with a group of kids my age; our counselors were also on the bus. One of the girls broke out in hives while everybody else was out hiking, and I was on the bus with her. I was sick that day and was doing some hypnosis with her. Not that I was trained in hypnosis at that time, but I was doing guided meditation and telling her to relax, and taking her on this little inner journey. I could see her getting agitated, not that there was that much going on on the outside. I said something very directly to her like "You don't need to do this in order to get attention. You can just relax and heal" or something like that. I saw my counselors look at each other as though I was crazy—like, where was I getting this information, where was I getting this interpretation—I must really be off the wall.

All of the sudden, I realized that they weren't seeing that level, that they weren't seeing the level of intention that was behind her actions. It never occurred to me that everybody couldn't see that until that point.

LA: And how did you feel at that point?

BH: I felt a twisting inside and pretty alone. I felt mainly invisible, like they thought I was on an ego trip, or like I was trying to be something I wasn't. It was a hard awakening, a rude awakening.

LA: When I met you years ago, you'd already gotten your MFCC (Marriage, Family, and Child Counselor) licensing to work as a therapist. Were you also working as a psychic counselor?

BH: Yes. I actually began doing readings and teaching right out of high school. I taught my first class on the psychic and intuitive sciences at sixteen when I graduated school. For me, the psychic and intuitive arts, whether they were using tarot, astrology, palmistry, whatever, were a pathway to help people learn to read the subtleties, to perceive the deeper levels.

LA: And the counseling end of that?

BH: Counseling was a natural offshoot. I remember when I was seventeen, I made a choice that I wanted to make a career out of my hobby, and at the time, I thought that that was to study ESP and become a parapsychologist and all that. After exploring research at the Institute for Parapsychology in Durham, North Carolina, I realized that I wasn't getting enough people contact with that.

That was when I decided I would go more toward clinical counseling modalities in psychology rather than research or experimental psychology.

LA: And you feel that your psychic abilities help you with that quite a bit, as well as the counseling mode helping you as a psychic?

BH: Oh, absolutely. There's a level of insight and also a modeling of self-trust that I think is really important to my clients. In order for us to trust our intuition, we have to trust ourselves, and self-trust is the basis for self-esteem. In any clinical work, I'm always helping people to develop their intuition under the guise of self-esteem mastery, autonomy, these kind of issues.

LA: How do dreams tie into this?

BH: Dreams are a source of information. Frequently, our conscious mind is cluttered with conflicting notions of what we ought to do, other people's opinions and attitudes balanced against cultural pulls and personal wishes and needs. A dream will frequently cut to the core of what's really going on with a very powerful symbol or image that can then guide the person.

LA: Recently there have been more physiological theories with regard to dreaming, such as Crick and Mitchison's. What's your view on dreams?

BH: Well, I think that there are a lot of different points of view about dreams, but I see dreams as a multidimensional expression of consciousness. They work on lots of different levels. One level might be the idea that it's [the dream's] a random firing of neurons and you get a lot of discordant images and pictures; it's a way of bringing the body back to equilibrium. There's that possibility. But I think more than anything there is also the possibility that there is meaning in the dream stage, if we can learn to speak the language of expanded states of consciousness. It seems that symbol and metaphor is the key to understanding—the key to that language—the language of intuition.

LA: In reading a lot from the experts who write and talk about dreams, metaphor seems to be the one point that pops up. I believe it was Gayle Delaney here in San Francisco who said that dreams are like poetry, which uses much in the way of metaphors.

BH: Exactly. And puns. Puns are great in dreams.

LA: I've talked to people with some very humorous dreams.

BH: Yes, but puns, especially, because they contain more than one meaning, and so can slip by the conscious mind. Here you are telling your dream and then all of a sudden, it means something totally different.

LA: Do you think people have a hard time understanding that that's what's going on?

BH: Perhaps initially, but it's the kind of thing like when you read something versus when you speak it aloud. You get a different impression or interpretation. I think dreams are like that, too. We have the dream when we're in the dream experience. Then, in the telling of the dream, we get a new perspective. And then, in the hearing of the dream, for example as I reflect a dream back to a client, there's yet another point of view that comes forward. There are these different dimensions that open up.

LA: Do you try to work with people in terms of having them program their dreams to try and resolve conflict?

BH: Oh, sure. Also, I suggest to people that they can use dreams to make contact with people who they haven't had contact with if they're feeling out of contact or connection, or if they need to resolve certain issues, let's say with parents, partners, friends, or whoever. Or if somebody has died, I suggest they meet them in the dream state, in the world between worlds.

LA: When you give those type of suggestions, do people come back and ask you how much of that might be real?

BH: Frequently. And what I tell people is that there are different levels of reality, and what we're really looking at is "Does it have validity to the individual?", subjective validity. I'm pretty much a phenomenologist, when it comes right down to it, and if it has significance to the person who's having the experience, then that's what I'm looking for.

LA: So rather than saying you shouldn't concentrate or have to worry about whether it is a ghost or an out of body experience, you're saying "Let's look at what's there," the content.

BH: And then for some people who are a little more curious, I can say "Well, you can always call your friend [who was in your dream] and ask them" if they've been thinking about you or if they felt your presence, or whatever.

LA: Have people done that?

BH: Some. Actually, I have a friend who was living in Germany for a while. She and I used to have what seemed to be pretty consistent contact in the dream state. We would write each other and say "I just had a dream about you . . ." and our letters would pass each other's. We would find out that we had both been dreaming about each other. The content of the dream might not have been the same . . .

LA: But the two of you showed up in the dreams.

BH: Exactly. Which I think is significant.

LA: Have you worked with people and their precognitive dreams?

BH: I've had some people come to me specifically because they've had precognitive dreams that have been frightening, like a potential death, some see a car crash, that kind of thing. One of the main things in working with people who are dealing with precognitive experiences is helping them to understand the difference between probability and actuality. Also, whenever we're dealing with precognition or any kind of psychic event it seems to me that it's very important to bring it into alignment with an understanding of the spiritual dimension, that somehow this event is contained within a larger picture, and that the larger picture is being guided or managed by a higher power that is benign, first of all, and has more wisdom, overview, perspective, knowledge of everything than we do, just because our physical brains are limited. We can only know so much. I see that a lot of the psychic distress signals that we get are challenges to open spiritually, to come into a deeper sense of direct contact with a spiritual source.

LA: Or maybe just the spiritual side of ourselves.

BH: Exactly. When I say spiritual source, that's what I'm talking about. I'm talking about the self within, which we can trust, which has a deeper knowing that no matter what happens in life there's something within that I can count on. I can count on my self to handle it. For example, if someone dies, well, okay, I know that I did the best that I could do, whatever that might be. I know I can get through the grieving. I know that I can get on with my life, that kind of thing.

LA: When people come to you with psychic experiences, specifically in dreams but also just in general, are people mostly afraid or do you think there's more of a fascination on their part?

BH: I would say that there were more people afraid seven to ten years ago, and now what I'm finding is that people are calling mainly because they are, well, fascinated is a nice word, as is curious, and also they're already developing and wanting more. Already having experiences, not being afraid of them, and looking for more.

LA: Why do you think that is?

BH: I think that since there is more in the popular press about the phenomena, there is less fear about it. So, as people are having experiences, they're beginning to label them and recognize them. I think that wanting more is a natural function of the human psyche; the desire for more, the desire for growth is something that's intrinsic to us.

LA: You think it might also have something to do with the "repackaging" of some of the psychic experiences? Words like "intuition" instead of "psychic" being more acceptable?

BH: I'm sure that that's part of it. Today, people are much more interested in exploring what's possible and gaining more experience rather than being afraid of the experiences they have. That's the biggest shift. Around ten years ago people would have experiences and they would be afraid, they would think there was something wrong with them, or that there was something weird going on and they weren't sure how to control it. But there's been a major shift in the mass mind around psychic phenomena, particularly that psychic awareness has become linked to spiritual awareness.

In the past, psychic awareness has been very much associated with issues of power and control, mind control, mind over matter, trying to manipulate people mentally and physically. Now it's more along the lines of using affirmation to get in contact with one's higher self, making direct contact with higher power, creating instead of trying to "win friends and influence people."

In the last ten to fifteen years, there's been a whole development of a spiritual awareness, one of surrender, one of allowing, one of being aware that there's such a thing as a higher power which has a greater sense of wisdom, order, and purpose which we in our limited capacity are not, perhaps, in tune with. But through our psychic and intuitive ability we have the possibility of making a direct contact with this higher sense of order, and through a sense of surrender being able to feel more at peace with the events that are happening in our lives.

There is a spiritual shift that's happening right now, as we move from feeling as though we need to be afraid, in control, and dominate our environment in order to survive, to rather allow things to happen, and surrender to the possibility of life unfolding. It's just a whole different orientation to life.

LA: I think there have been misunderstandings or blocks for something that has come out of parapsychology directly. Parapsychologists, in their own way, have been saying that with these "abilities" the human mind has a direct connection with the environment and with other human minds. We may have to take an even greater responsibility for our actions and thoughts that previously thought.

BH: I think so. There is a unifying principle at work here. I think you're bringing up a really good point because the whole concept of taking responsibility is a notion that's been around in the human potential movement for some time and it's filtering over to the psychic world. The psychic and spiritual world, clearly, is about taking responsibility for our thinking as well as our actions. The whole concept of taking personal responsibility is another piece in the spiritual puzzle, a very important piece. As we each take more personal responsibility for our actions, and for our thoughts, then we are more aware of our impact and our effect on each other and on our environment.

It's wonderful that there is scientific validation for this, that there is proof that there is an interaction between thought and matter. The main thing is, if we accept that we are responsible, then we don't have to be afraid of people controlling us anymore, because after all, we're responsible for that as well. But if we are responsible, than we have to take responsibility for the idea that what we say, do, think, or feel matters not only to us, but to other people or our environment, to our system as a whole.

LA: As to dream connections and interactions, people often connect with their own pasts as well. Beyond that, when people talk to you about their dream experiences, have you gotten any dreams reported to you where people are viewing their dreams as experiences of past lives?

BH: Yes, definitely. I don't care so much if we can research it and find that the life existed because there's a newspaper clipping that this person, whomever they identify as the personality, existed. That, to me, is not as important as the subjective validity. In the work that I've done with people around past life material in particular, there seems to be a theme that emerges from the past life, either centered around the conflicts of that life, or the gifts and lessons of that life, or the comforts of that life. And either it's something that the person is longing for in this life or still struggling with in this life, so it then becomes a metaphor for what the person is dealing with now, and gives insight into another approach that they may or may not have considered right now. I think it's very valuable. I'll do some hypnotic regression, too.

LA: One of the big controversies around hypnotic regression is that the hypnotherapist may simply be stimulating the client to come up with, effectively, a dream or a recreation of a metaphor of their problems in the context of a past life.

BH: Right. And that's a possibility. It seems to me that whether it's a guided fantasy or an actual (what we're calling) "memory" of a physical event, the processing of the experience, the release of the energy, the emotional energy that is effective in a situation is what's essential. Through the regression work, a person is able to release the energy. So it doesn't matter to me as much, as I said before, about whether it actually happened or it didn't happen, if the person's able to relive the experience in their imagination in a way that does not bring the same terror and/or fear, passion, anxiety. The first time they talk about the experience of doing regression work is almost like a desensitization process. If they can do that, if they can come to talk about the experience from a place of detached awareness, then just that in itself is a very powerful process. They have learned that it is possible to have feelings and not be identified with their feelings.

LA: Some who work with dreams advocate a social context for sharing dreams, and other therapists/dream workers tend to like the one-on-one perspective. How about you?

BH: I have found that some of the most powerful work I have done with dreams has been in intuition support groups. What I'll do is have the group move through guided meditation into a very subtle state to begin with, a kind of semi-trance state. Then I'll have the dreamer tell the dream. At different points in the dream, I'll have the dreamer stop, and I'll suggest to the group that each person simply observe any thoughts they have, any feelings they have, any impressions they have, any colors or images. Is there a title or caption that they receive at this point? And then we'll go through the dream until it's completion, and when they come out [of the semi-trance state], I'll have the people share the different impressions, titles, captions, pictures, images that they received. It's phenomenal—the depth of information and the psychic level of information that gets transferred to the person who is telling the dream and trying to gain insight into what's going on.

For example, there was a woman in one of my groups who told a dream about this bird that kept falling down.

[The following example is taken from Beth Hedva's doc-

toral dissertation "A Community Model For the Uses of
Intuition in Clinical Practice," Columbia Pacific University,
August 1989, pp. 228–231]

I asked Sue to share her story again from this deep inner
state. At different points in her second telling I gently inter-
rupted, suggesting a metaphoric involvement of the senses,
to remind group members to shift from an outer listening to
Sue's story to an inner "hearing," "seeing," "feeling," or
"knowing." Each individual's own mysterious quest for understanding cast the reflected light onto different aspects of
the dream and dream symbols. Something of significance was
revealed to each woman, a treasure from within to be brought
out to the group.

Notice how much more succinct and coherent Sue's dream
is as told from this inner state; concise, clear, and to the
point. Communing with the source within leads to a new kind
of communication. No explanations, justifications, and
"opinions about." Also, as she spoke from this inner state,
a telepathic impression was communicated vibrationally. Her
words were soft, steady, and resonant. Colors came alive.
Inner images were more vibrant. Clairsentient women felt
Sue's experience as though it were their own. Communication
on all levels of consciousness was amplified.

"My hand is reaching out and it's cupping the
bird's breast. My hand is between the legs, and the
bird is beginning to sink down and feel heavier and
heavier in my hand. As it does that, I'm lifting the
bird back up. And with a powerful energy, I'm setting it on its feet. And I'm letting go. I'm in total
awe of the colors. The colors are just radiating now.

"As I turn—over to the left side of me and
down—I'm noticing some ugly-looking rubber
boots. And this man is sitting on his feet and legs
seem very relaxed. The green of his pants—it's just
distasteful! It's army green with some mustard-
yuckie-looking color in it. And yet I recognize those
feet and that color as a 'Rescuer,' and I am puzzled

by that. I can't take my eyes off of his feet and his legs.''

Sue's dream was held as a healing story from the source of being. Each woman went inside herself to make contact with her own core experience of the dream; and then offered these perceptions to Sue. Each perception, like a piece of a grand puzzle, revealed another aspect of the mystery-teaching hidden in Sue's dream. Each woman's ability to share her intuitive perception without explaining it, judging it, or justifying it allowed Sue to look at her dream from a new point of view. Like pieces of a puzzle, the deeper meaning in the dream took form.

LA: You go on in the next few pages of your dissertation to discuss some of the points shared by members of the group in the telling of that dream. For example, one member, you report, talked about some imagery revolving around "knees that were weak" and "spindly little legs" and received a "title" for the dream "Holding Up My Heart." Another received something about Sue's father, and a "title" of "How My Father Weeps."

You then go on to discuss her reaction, how she discussed that her father had died a couple of years before and that before he died, he'd been thin and had knees that needed support. You reported that Sue used the phrase "people used to tease my father that he wore his heart on his sleeve."

I found that interesting, especially since further discussion of that session in your dissertation brought out other elements that the group picked up on, leading to a recognition and understanding that the dream had to do with alcoholism, her father's and her own, and "standing on my own two legs about it . . . and it's kind of ugly, being an alcoholic—like the ugly green shoes."

BH: What happens in a group is that you're dealing with the collective energy. There's a chance to get to the depths that are not possible in one-to-one. In the group mind, one individual may have a piece which triggers an intuitive hunch from another member of the group, which takes a third member to yet an even deeper level, and that kind of interaction just isn't possible one-to-one.

LA: A similar methodology has been used in working with psychics where they have several psychics working on the same project. You tend to then get pieces that fit together as parts of a completed puzzle.

BH: Yes, it's like the majority vote [technique].

LA: How about nightmares?

BH: Nightmares are, as a communication from the deeper parts of the psyche, trying to bring something forward into consciousness, and that content can either be positive information or conflicting information.

For example, we don't usually think of a nightmare as something that could be positive, but this is a wonderful example. There was a woman who had a dream of having to confront this black wolf. This wolf was all-powerful, and she had this feeling that the wolf was evil. In doing some work with her, what we realized was that it was not so much that the wolf was evil, but that she was reacting to her conditioning which programmed her to believe that being a powerful woman was evil.

LA: Something she felt would not be socially acceptable.

BH: . . . and so that got projected onto the wolf. In doing deeper work, she had a chance to re-own her power.

Nightmares can also be an indication of areas of anxiety or areas where we are in conflict in our lives, either with people or circumstances or situations that are disturbing us.

LA: In terms of confronting them, lucid dreaming has been said to offer a very good opportunity.

BH: The concept is that, especially with nightmare work, what we do is we turn to confront the image and ask for information and observations. We turn to it and simply say "Who are you and why are you here? What do you want from me?" rather than running from it or avoiding it.

In doing dream re-entry work what I'll frequently do is have them [the dreamer] again in a meditative state, go in, rekindle the dream imagery, confront the dream image, and then observe what changes if they face the image. They also observe themselves—How are they feeling in their body?

How are they feeling emotionally? What thoughts do they have?—taking it step by step, communicating that information to the dream image, again noticing what changes, reaching out and touching the image, perhaps then becoming the image and looking at the world from that point of view.

In unifying with that which has been so terrifying, there's frequently a major shift in the imagery, first of all, and also in the experience, the subjective experience of the person who had the dream. Rather than being terrified, there's usually a reporting of feeling whole, of feeling comfort where once there was terror. So it's a really remarkable process.

LA: Children tend to have more nightmares than adults.

BH: Yes, and a lot of times what I do with children is I will draw in helpers. I first will take the child to a very safe inner world where they can make contact with a dream guardian for a guide, someone who is there to help them, whether it's in the form of an animal or a talking tree, or a friend, whatever the person might turn up as. One little girl I did some work with (this little girl was also dealing with ghosts) ended up having a guide who was a girl, just a few years older than herself. When we went back into the dream images or whenever she confronted the ghosts, it was actually her dream guardian who did the confronting for her.

LA: In the film *Dreamscape*, Dennis Quaid's character worked with a parapsychologist and technology that allowed him to enter and interact in the dreams of others. There was a great segment where he went into the nightmare of a boy who was afraid to even sleep, because of the nightmare snake-man that haunted his dreams. In this case, Quaid's character was trying to act as the guardian you speak of, although it wasn't him that actually rid the boy of the creature. He was about done for and as I recall it was the boy who ended up knocking off the snake-man. It was not the "guardian" who did the final act of overcoming the monster, but the boy himself.

It seemed to be a selfless act on the part of the boy, one that gave him the courage to stand up to his fears. He couldn't confront the creature by himself, so it seemed that having Quaid's helpless character there took the helplessness that the boy felt away from him. He no longer felt helpless to defend himself because he had somebody else to think about, to defend.

BH: Also, then, he had to get outside himself, to get bigger than his fear, which is really the point. Whenever we are drawn outside ourselves we find there is more to us than we imagined. We do come into contact with greater parts of ourselves.

LA: You've mentioned that you've had quite a few lucid dreams yourself.

BH: Right. One of the things I especially like about lucid dreams is they give me a chance to realize that I'm doing work on lots of different levels of consciousness, not just out in the outer world, but also in the inner world. In my lucid dreams, especially, I get lots of information. I feel as though I'm having a client consultation with people I'm getting information about, different workshops and classes that I do, different things that I'm supposed to do.

LA: In terms of death and dying, there seems to be the misconception that if you die in your dream, you die in real life. I know I've been through "death" in my dreams before, and am still here to deal with life.

BH: Right. That's definitely not true. I've died in my dreams before.

LA: And of course, there's that old tale that if you have a falling dream, you need to wake up before you hit or you'll die. I've had that kind of dream, although when I hit it seems to me that I just get up and brush myself off, like Wile E. Coyote in a Roadrunner cartoon.

BH: Right. The thing about dreams and working with dreams is that we're talking about lots of different levels. I look at dreams like Toontown in *Who Framed Roger Rabbit?*, because there's this feeling that energy follows thought. If you think it, it becomes true in your dream. So if you're anxious or scared—and I also tell people this when they're doing astral travel work or working "out of the body" or exploring their dreams in the beginning—it's very important to direct the attention of your thought. If you're afraid, all of the sudden you'll start fabricating images that become a manifestation of your anxiety or your fear, so it's important to direct your thought toward, let's say, where you want to go, the person you want to be with, the result you want to accomplish. You think it and it happens in the dream. That's the most important thing to be aware of.

LA: One of the major questions of my book has to do with action following thought and dreams—people have a problem in determining what is a psychic dream and what is not, or what is a psychic experience and what is not. How do you know it's a psychic dream?

BH: Dreams are multidimensional, and there's a level that I think also included the transpersonal and spiritual domain. Those dreams in particular contain a quality—it feels almost realer than real—the colors are brighter, the light is a little more refined, the conversations seem more fluent. You're able to remember specifics that in some way allow you to feel as though you've really contacted a person, or seen someone, as though you've been with them. The level of memory is more defined, the textures or smells or qualities.

Somehow when you wake up from a dream like that, there's a feeling that something has happened, something real has happened. It's something more than just a dream, and it doesn't just evaporate during the course of the day. Something remains about that dream, and I think that's a really good signal that there's something more happening for us.

Perspectives such as Dr. Beth Hedva's are quite interesting, since they combine a variety of traditions, backgrounds, and experiences. In this case, Beth has brought together her personal experience in psychic functioning with a background and education in psychotherapy. This, I believe, is an effective combination for a counselor or therapist, regardless of whether the counselor is utilizing psi to better understand the client or whether the education in therapy helps in understanding the psychic input.

Such a recognition of the excellence of the combination of psi and a counseling education has been spreading. I've spoken to more and more ''psychic practitioners'' who have gone on to education and licensing in counseling, as they realize that being psychic, whatever that really means, is not quite enough to truly understand and help one's clients.

There is obviously also the recognition on the part of Beth and Joanne Mied, as well as by others, that the dreams people have are excellent sources of psychic input, canvasses that can yield not only insight into the person having the dreams, but also into the many ways that person connects with the environment, whether on the purely physical level or on the ostensibly psychic level.

You probably noticed that Beth and Joanne had very similar answers with regard to how one knows whether a dream is psychic or not. This is, of course, what I've been telling you throughout this book, and that's no coincidence.

It's very difficult for me, when asked how one knows that a dream or other experience is a psychic one, to give a definitive answer. The person having the experience just notices something "different" about the experience. Our culture/society has created labels for those "different" experiences, those labels being "psychic" or "extended perception" (to use Keith Harary's term) or "paranormal." They are just labels, as of now, since we haven't come to a full understanding of what's really happening. But to the person having the experience there is a difference between a psychic dream and a "normal" one. It's simply that putting this difference into words is difficult, as it is when you try to tell someone how you feel emotionally. You use a label, such as "anger" or "fear," but they're just labels. Describing them to people who have not had the same emotional experiences is difficult, as is describing how a psychic experience feels different than any other, or as it would be for a sighted person to try to describe the color blue to a person blind from birth.

INTERVIEW WITH MONTAGUE ULLMAN, M.D.

Montague Ullman, M.D., is a psychiatrist and psychoanalyst who founded the Dream Laboratory at the Maimonides Medical Center in Brooklyn, New York. At that center, he and others worked extensively with studies of dreaming, and conducted research dealing with telepathic dreams. That research has been discussed in journal articles as well as in the book *Dream Telepathy: Studies in Nocturnal ESP*, co-authored by Dr. Stanley Krippner and Alan Vaughan. He has long been interested in dreams from a variety of perspectives, culminating in shaping a group dream work perspective both in this country and in Scandinavia. An excellent discussion of this group method can be found in his book *Working With Dreams*, co-authored by Nan Zimmerman. He is the author of a number of other articles and publications on the subject of dreams, and is co-editor (with Claire Limmer, M.S.) of *The Variety of Dream Experience*. He is currently Clinical Professor of Psychiatry Emeritus at Albert Einstein College of Medicine, a life Fellow of the American Psychiatric Association, and a life member of the society of Medical Psychoanalysts.

Dr. Ullman's professional history has been intimately entwined with the study of dreams, and provides much insight into what one looks for in working with dreams. His multifaceted interests in dreams, from the psychological to the physiological, the sociocultural to the paranormal, has done much to influence others who work with dreams.

LA: What got you interested in the particular area of dreams? You've been in this area for how long?

MU: Fifty years or so. It's hard to say what got me interested. I began my training as a psychiatrist in 1942 and I don't think I knew much about dreams at that point. When I returned from service overseas in World War II and started psychoanalytic training, then I really began to get a feeling for dreams and working with patients. I can't put my finger on anything specific except that they intrigued me, I liked working with them [dreams], and I found working with them extraordinarily helpful to the patients. Because I was approaching psychoanalysis not from a classical point of view, although that was part of my training, but from a cultural point of view, the point of view that I gravitated toward in those days, I never quite felt that Freud had the right answers about dreams.

He did call attention to certain basic features of dreams, namely that dreams were precipitated by residues of recent experience, that dreams contained significant references to the past, and that associations were an important therapeutic key. With those basics he certainly started us off on the path toward using dreams effectively in therapy, but his concepts of wish fulfillment, censorship and disguise never really took hold in the work that I felt most profitable with dreams.

LA: I think that when most people think of Freud and dreams they think of very sexual stereotypes.

MU: He did emphasize repressed sexual impulses in his theory of wish fulfillment.

Somehow dreams were a central focus of my years as an analyst. I wrote on the neurophysiology of dreaming, the active function of dreams, the therapeutic use of dreams, and the paranormal dream. My interest in psychic phenomena went back to my college days. As a practicing analyst, every now and then I'd encounter patients whose dreams included material about my life they had no business knowing about.

This was in the forties. Along with Jan Ehrenwald, Jule Eisenbud, Bob Laidlaw, and half a dozen others, we got together in a mutual protective society. We formed the medical section of the ASPR and shared our experiences with telepathic and precognitive dreams.

At any rate, it was a special area of interest to me. I gave up my practice in 1960 to become Director of Psychiatry at Maimonides Medical Center, because by that time I was interested in setting up a laboratory to explore the paranormal dream under experimental conditions. When I had started this before on a pilot basis with Karlis Osis and Douglas Dean while I was in practice, it was impossible for me to do both. So I had an opportunity to go full time, and I did. We established the laboratory and began the work on dream telepathy.

That, for me, ended in 1974 when I resigned. I went to Sweden to teach at Gothenberg. There I began to teach students about dreams experientially, and there evolved the group process that I have since developed. I've since spent three or four months a year there ever since teaching dream work. Here [New York] I've been teaching dreams through this group process both to the profession and to the laity. It's been a very exciting turn in my career to be able to devote myself to this.

LA: The whole idea of the group process is very interesting. You mentioned a cultural approach. Do you find that teaching in Europe there's a lot of diversity between not only the dreams themselves but in the ways people approach remembering their dreams?

MU: My experience is largely in Sweden and to a lesser extent other Scandanavian countries. There are differences in dream content that are culturally induced.

For example, the Swedes have a much more intense and much more deeply ingrained feeling about nature than I had growing up in New York City. It hardly ever occurs that you get a Swedish dream that doesn't have some reference to nature; a tree, a bush, a flower, a mountain, a stream, a lake, something green, or the snow.

LA: How are the folks that you've worked with in New York City? Are they rarely giving nature references?

MU: They are more apt to dream about traffic.

LA: Of course.

MU: In terms of issues, they are largely the same. I think that there are some issues that come out more blatantly over there [Sweden] in some ways. The idea of young people getting married and both people working, a situation that has developed over the last ten years or so here, began much earlier in Sweden. The state intervened much earlier in Sweden. In other words, the state made it possible for parents to keep getting their salary and stay home and take care of their infant for the first year or so, and made it possible for both parents to do that. They also created day centers for very young children, from a year-and-a-half or two years on.

Since the early seventies, when I first went there, I encountered many young Swedish mothers having trouble accepting the idea of sending a two-year-old to a day care center. That was one interesting thing.

The other is that Swedes, under their social-democratic system, have grown up in groups and are more comfortable in groups. There's a very strong work ethic built into their daily life, a very strong kind of selfless ethic. You have to be for others.

So, more than here, I encounter, for example, people waking up in their forties and fifties and asking themselves "What is there in life for Me? My whole life has been working for others and taking care of family, doing for others. . . ." They suddenly realize that they may be missing something.

There are also interesting cultural differences in the way I experience doing dream work with Swedes and Americans. Swedes have the reputation of being very reserved, and not showing their emotions on their sleeves, so to speak, but what I found in working with them is that they trusted me and they trusted the process I use. So when they did a dream, they went very deep into their own psyches in a genuine and honest way. It was almost as if I'd find myself in the middle of an Ingmar Bergman scenario.

Now Americans, and this is of course a generalization, are more open on the surface with their feelings and a little bit more guarded down below. That was another interesting cultural difference.

I've enjoyed working with them [Swedes]. It has been fifteen or sixteen years that I've been working over there, and now they come over here for training in leading groups. I've trained so many people over there that they've now organized a Swedish Society for the Advancement of Dream Work, which is designed to train competent leaders there now.

LA: There have been a number of dream centers popping up around the United States lately. Some take similar viewpoints to yours and many are back with the old dream interpretation idea of reading a handbook to see what the symbol represents. The general public can go into a book store and see many books on dream interpretation, on other forms of dream work, and on lots of theories about dreams. When you read some of these books, do you get a good feeling about what their point of view is, where they're coming from?

MU: I understand where they are coming from, but I disagree with so many of them because I feel that they lose sight of what I feel is a very important thing. I feel that they are oriented, and to some extent they are helpful, to helping the individual work with his or her dream. Some do it with more simplification than others. To that extent, they offer help.

But as far as I'm concerned, a dream, to be fully realized, is best worked out in a supportive group setting. There is something in the nature of the kind of emotional healing that takes place in a group. It's like emotional healing in any other circumstance; that is, it's a social event.

LA: That makes sense, since the content of dreams is often social within the context of the dream.

MU: But they begin as a private communication. For a person really to appreciate all that they've put into the imagery, I think they do need help, the help of other human beings. I think this goes even for very sophisticated dreamworkers. For example, I have been working with dreams for almost fifty years and I've developed some sophistication in working with my own dreams. Even as I'm dreaming them I'm figuring what they might mean. But I also know that when I have a chance of bringing a dream of mine to a group, I get a richer yield than if I work on it by myself.

LA: Is that because when you are discussing the dream with other people, they are asking you questions that might help you delve further into it?

MU: They are doing a number of things. They're providing a safe, non-intrusive, social support system that the dreamer finds and needs. It takes some courage to look at yourself awake as honestly as you did when you were asleep and dreaming. That requires the support of an interested social milieu that is stimulating without being invading or intrusive.

The whole point of the strategy that I've worked out in my groups emphasizes two things. The dreamers need, if they are going to get into dream work, to feel safe in a public, social situation; that is the safety factor. The second factor is the need to be stimulated to make discoveries about himself or herself that are difficult for them to make by themselves, and where that stimulation is not intrusive, and where the dreamer is the gatekeeper of their unconscious.

LA: And the process is not an instant one.

MU: It's work.

LA: In your dream groups do you find people coming forth with paranormal dreams?

MU: Not as often as one might expect, but maybe that's because our focus isn't on them. It does happen from time to time. I have written a number of papers on a small project that I've been involved in. I brought together a group that was interested in paranormal dreams. We met every week and shared dreams looking for paranormal connections, psi communication in a dream-sharing group. There, when the focus was on it [paranormal dreaming] we got it.

LA: The question comes up often of "How do you know when a dream might be a psychic one?" Has there been anything in your years of work that would enable you to answer this with something other than "Psychic dreams feel different?" I realize this is a tough question, and that it probably has many answers.

MU: There are people over the years who have written to me and said they have paranormal dreams and that they know when these occur. The only thing I can pick up from these various reports is that they feel these dreams are different from their ordinary dreams and that an image appears in those dreams that they have previously associated with paranormal and precognitive dreams, or just by the very feeling of urgency to share it or do something about it, the dream is paranormal, but there is no single, consistent one.

LA: I've noticed is that people tend to remember their dreams spontaneously more often when they consider the dreams paranormal, as though it's more important to remember.

MU: Well, yes and no. You may remember a dream merely just by accident. If you are awakened in the course of a dream you would remember it. Or you're in a place where you sleep longer than you usually do and you remember it simply because you've slept longer and gotten into the longest REM period. I don't think you can always say [you remember] it's because its the most important.

You can't judge a dream by waking standards, so we don't know how important a dream is until you work on it and make the connections to whatever is going on.

LA: For the people involved in your own dream groups, as to the issue of remembering their dreams, besides the qualitative issue [how much is remembered] is there a quantitative situation? Do people remember more dreams as part of the process?

MU: Dreams are recalled more readily when people find themselves in a social milieu where dreams are discussed. People come into my groups who are intellectually interested but who say "Well, I haven't remembered my dreams since I was a child." But they'll begin to remember dreams.

This happens in therapy. There are many therapists who have had the experience where patients come in who haven't remembered their dreams for a number of years. But if the therapist is interested in dreams then they begin to recall them.

LA: Going back to what the general public sees, we have a bunch of books on working with dreams. We have your book and so-and-so's dream interpretation book and, credentials of the author notwithstanding, we have a wide range of good and bad information. Do you feel there is a lack of good information going out to the general public on dreams?

MU: What information there is is not always reliable.

LA: There seem to be very few experts who are talking to the general public about dreams, even when it becomes temporarily of interest. There's Stephen LaBerge . . .

MU: Right. There are reliable professionals like Ann Faraday and Gayle Delaney, who know what they are talking about. She [Delaney] has her own point of view of how to work with a dream, and it's valid as far as it goes.

What I like about my point of view is that I'm able to share the skills I'm involved with. If the people can stay with it long enough and understand the principles, they can go off on their own. They're not relying on an expert.

LA: Because they're working with their own patterns in a socially supportive context.

MU: Right.

LA: Do you have just a word of advice for people who want to do something with their dreams, besides of course . . .

MU: Read my books!

LA: Of course, read your books.

MU: There are no quick cures. Change is not easy, and

dream work does involve helpers. I make the analogy with obstetrics. Childbirth is such a natural event that women probably gave birth to children before there were obstetricians. If you need an obstetrician, it's a good thing we've gotten to the point where you can have one. And if you need psychiatric help it's a good thing we have trained therapists. But a lot of women can do very well with a midwife just to help ease the child out to life. That's what the dreamer needs. Some dreamers need therapists, but most dreamers just need a midwife to bring the dream out into the open.

The three perspectives of the people you have just encountered, Mied, Hedva, and Ullman, psychic, psychic/therapist, and psychotherapist, yield a nice continuum of experiences with dreams and particularly with psychic/paranormal dreams. What I found most interesting in discussing the subject with these three and others is the idea of our own role in working with dreams, that we have the responsibility, ultimately, in not only looking at what the content in dreams may represent, but in the judgement of a particular dream as psychic or not.

Dr. Ullman put it most succinctly, I think, with his final line. "Most dreamers just need a midwife to bring the dream out into the open."

Perhaps what is most needed in the processing of the information from psychic dreams is a "midwife," another person to bounce the information off of, who can help us frame our own questions of "What does this particular image mean with regard to reality?" Discussing such dreams with others seems to aid in recalling further specifics from dreams and in increasing remembrance of dreams. With psychic dreams, discussions of the dreams may be the final deciding factor in recognizing the dream as a perception of a real event, past, present, or future.

If you don't tell the person you dreamed about that you had that dream, how will you ever learn if that person shared the dream? If you don't verify, in some way, the information you think came from a real current or past event, how will you ever know if the perception in the dream was correct?

And if you don't either record the dream or discuss it with someone else, how can you be sure you dreamed the event before it actually happened? It might have been faulty memory.

With dreams, social context in which to discuss them seems to be beneficial to the integration of the information, themes, lessons, and even garbage your mind is attempting to process. Setting up a dream group with others in which you can discuss such things will make them easier to deal with, as you will find yourselves acting as "midwives" for each other in giving "birth" to what you really need to learn from those dreams.

CHAPTER 15

Working with Psychic Dreams and Experience

In working with psychic dreams or experiences, there is an implicit assumption that we can easily separate a psychic experience from any other experience at the time the experience is happening. While that may be true for some forms of psychic experience, where you somehow "know" that the experience is "different" from so-called normal ones, we've learned that dreams can be a bit tricky.

In general, our dreams reflect a connection to our inner selves, even if the dream is of an international-scope event that may not touch us directly. Seeing or hearing about the event in the news can often affect our dreams and reflect our reactions to it. Psychic experiences in general and psychic dreams in particular may be psychic perceptions of what is important to us personally, information sought out by some part of us to incorporate into our lives, or of events that we personally see as important to our views of the world. They may also be psychic perceptions of highly emotional events that have nothing to do with us or what we are interested in.

There appear to be two things happening within our psychic experiences. On the one hand, we seem to be scanning the environment for information that will somehow be of interest to us, to our lives in general or to the solving of some problem we are connected to. On the other hand, we seem to also pick up other random signals. An analogy might be to radio scanners, where a radio operator is scanning for a signal from the local police or fire department. The operator might scan until hearing a snatch of conversation that indicates the source is the one desired. There may, however, be another source transmitting very powerfully yet with no particular target in mind (like a call for help from a disabled vehicle or aircraft in trouble). The signal may be strong enough for the scanner to zero in on, even though the intent to pick it up was not in the radio operator's mind.

Our dreams, as random as they appear to be, do have their patterns, which are often discernible by looking through a series of dreams in a journal. With psychic dreams, random signals from the outside appear to drop in, whether we are looking for patterns or not. These random signals, having nothing to do with our own lives (though potentially important to others), may cause a person working with his or her own dreams to pause and puzzle over it, trying to make the item fit in with other imagery in dreams.

So, if you accept the idea of psychic information and that we may occasionally get random signals, you have to allow for some items appearing in your dream journal to be "glitches" that you may have to leave out of the interpretation process. Such psychic glitches may be later connected to real events in the world, or you may never find out about the event to which the information belonged. Otherwise, much of the information from dreams you "know" are psychic can be connected to your own life or knowledge base and can therefore be learned from as easily (or as hard) as other dreams.

Looking for psychic information in dreams really is an extension of recalling, recording, and reviewing your dreams using a dream journal. When jotting down imagery and feelings from dreams, if one of those feelings is that you are sure there is something "different" or "psychic" about the dream, make a special note of it. Over a period of time, you might note specific patterns of emotions, issues, or images in both your waking state and your dreams at the time of the psychic dream.

People who report psychic dreams on some kind of regular basis are usually able to note the differences between a paranormal and a "normal" dream in their journals. They have learned through their own experience that the dream is of a particular form, that it may carry something "extra." Unfortunately, there is no single method or concept I can now relate to you that would enable you to immediately categorize your dreams as psychic or not. Keeping the journal and reviewing it and your experience with particular dreams will lead you to find your own way of "knowing" that the dream is something out of the ordinary, perhaps carrying psychic information.

As you work through any dreams you consider psychic, also look at the type of psychic dream it was. Are your psychic dreams mainly precognitive or telepathic? Are they perceptions of real-time events or past situations? Are they happening during the lucid dream state or when you feel you may be having an OBE-type dream? Which type is more frequent? Are there particular events, issues, or emotions connected with each type of psychic dream you have? Do you feel a character in your dreams was really some contact by another person, living or dead? Are you having apparitional encounters in your dreams? Hopefully, the information I've offered you in this book, along with the various examples of psychic dreams and comments by others has helped you in understanding what you might consider a psychic dream or experience, and what forms it may take.

Simply, it all boils down to looking for patterns in your dream experiences. This pattern recognition is also important if you are trying to work on psychic abilities while awake. Keeping a journal of unusual waking experiences, especially ones that might be psychic, and looking for patterns in them seems to allow people to recognize that they have been having psychic experiences of one sort or another all along. However, as with dream journals where you're noting all perceptions remembered from the dreams, working on psychic ability while awake requires some degree of observation of the physical world around you. It is only after you can really, consciously be aware of your "normal" perceptions (though the "normal" senses), that you can start to recognize the "extra" information that may be coming in to your head.

So, you might try simply exercising your powers of observation on a regular basis. Notice sights, sounds, smells, and other sensations, and notice your own mental and emotional states throughout the day. Look at the relationship of things and people around you to your moods and physical feelings. If you are having psychic experiences, keep track of how you are feeling physically, mentally, and emotionally, before, during, and after the experience. Note what you've eaten, and if there are any unusual situations going on in your life, any concerns, stresses, or other interpersonal reactions. Transfer it all to a journal, as with a dream journal (and you may even want to keep both journals going, to get a full understanding of both waking and sleeping consciousness in your life).

By observing your personal circumstances and feelings while having psychic experiences, you can look for patterns that may lead to or cause the experiences. You may then be able to narrow down what motivates you to be "psychic," and devise some exercise to repeat the experiences. The more you learn about why you have your experiences, the more you may be able to control their appearance and direct the abilities. If you are not having such experiences, this exercise may not only help your powers of observation, it may also allow you to notice experiences that you had not considered as "psychic" before. However, don't go overboard in labeling things as "paranormal," since you may end up misleading yourself about how truly "psychic" you are, which can cause some problems.

There's also the flip side here that the above exercise is a good way to actually get rid of unwanted psychic experience. By seeing the patterns in your life that may cause the experiences, you can learn what you need to do to avoid them.

As a final note, you might also try programming yourself for psychic dreams, or incubating a dream with the intent to seek out information that may not be within your own experience or memory. Repeat to yourself that there is a target or location you'd like to dream about, and what that target is; or incubate a dream for information about a future event, or one in the distant past and see what comes up; or ask for a solution to a problem even though you have no direct physical access to the information that may provide the solution; or ask for a message or contact from a friend or loved one who has recently died. Remember to try to verify, as best you can, any information that comes through in such dreams, for if you don't relate the information to the real world, you cannot be sure you made the psychic connection.

Some have reported a good deal of success with such "psychic programming" of their dreams, though it would appear that no one can be psychic in this way (or any other way) on a very reliable basis. We are still ignorant about how psychic functioning might work and how to make it work on a more regular, repeatable, reliable basis, both in our conscious waking state or in the dream state.

Maybe if we all incubate our dreams for solutions to that problem. . . .

CHAPTER 16

Dream a Little Dream
of Conclusions

Throughout this book, we've talked about dreams, sleep, psychic experience and ability, and the nexus of all of these: psychic dreams. Hopefully, I've presented answers to questions you've had in all of these areas as well as raised some questions in your mind. The questions you now have may, in fact, outnumber the answers. That is as it should be.

In my own studies of paranormal experiences and parapsychology, I've learned a great deal from the literature of the field, experimental reports, attending parapsychological conferences, conversing with others in the field, from skeptics and critics of the field, and from the few psychic experiences I've been lucky enough to have myself. As someone in the field of parapsychology who has sought out publicity and the use of the mass media in order to provide accurate information about the paranormal to the general public, I have been contacted by hundreds of people each year with some question about psychic experience, or some report they wish to make about their own experiences. So, most of all, I've learned from the experiences of people like you, the reader of this book.

Parapsychology, as a science still trying to stand on its own two feet, has taken on a group of human experiences that appear to be indications that the human mind/consciousness/soul/spirit is capable of vastly more than what we consider within the range of "normal" experience. Parapsychology looks at experiences that suggest that the mind has information and communication processes that extend beyond the "walls" of the human skull, experiences that indicate some form of interaction between the mind and the physical environment around it, and experiences that seem to signify that the mind/consciousness/soul/spirit is capable of some separate existence from the brain that spawned it. As I've indicated, there is an enormous amount of information that is still necessary before we figure out what these experiences are.

Studies of dreams, psychic and otherwise, indicate that there is an extensive information and/or memory process happening in the brain and mind during a different state of physical being from the conscious one, that being sleep. I've discussed what we apparently know or assume about the workings of the brain with regard to dreaming, as well as various ideas and theories that try to explain how dreaming happens, what effect it has on us, and how it "works" within our own psychological set-up. Of course, given the conflict between some of these ideas, you can easily get the idea that there is much we still need to know about the place of dreams in our lives.

So what's it all mean? What should you have gotten from this book? Two things.

First of all, I hope that leaving you with the understanding that the process of science, whether physical or social science, is a process that never stands still. Hopefully (but not realistically) scientists are people who are in a constant state of learning more in order to better understand the universe around us, and humans specifically. There is much we still need to know about the workings of the human brain before we can make more sense of how the mind works (even what it is) and how the brain/mind combination affects both our physical and psychological makeup. Science is a search for questions that hopefully make sense of the answers provided by the world around us and within us.

A next step in that line of thinking leads me (and hopefully you) to realize that parapsychology, dealing with the human mind (which we know so little about) and certain aspects of physics and biology which we are still learning about, is not at a stage where extensive explanations can be given about subjective paranormal experiences. Parapsychology is studying experiences which need much in the way of expansion of our understanding of the mind/body connection and in the understanding of the physical world before an understanding of them may be complete in any way. After over 100 years of psychical research (but much less time in studying psi experimentally) what is really clear is that we may not be "there" yet in approaching an understanding of the workings of psychic experience, just as we're not "there" yet in understanding the human brain and/or mind. As the knowledge base of science grows and more is there for parapsychologists to draw on, we will undoubtedly come closer to that understanding of what psi is or is not.

The second, and more important lesson I hope you've learned is that while there is much we do *not* know about dreams and psychic experience, there is much we *do* know about how we can integrate such experiences and mental states into our own lives. Regardless of what psychic experience is (or is not), there is something to be learned from such experience. Whether dreams are a byproduct of neuron firings in the brain (as Hobson theorizes) or are a deliberate means of the brain/mind to process and integrate information, we can learn from them and what they tell us about ourselves. People *are* working with their dreams right now. People *are* able to program themselves to recall and record their dreams. People *are* able to incubate dreams to address particular issues and problems in their lives in order to provide themselves with solutions. People *are* able to "wake up" in their dreams, to become lucid/conscious in this non-conscious state. And people *are* able to use their dreams as a vehicle for connecting with other minds and with the world around them, past, present, and apparently future.

Whether you decide to use the information from this book to look at whatever dreams you might spontaneously remember or whether you decide to pursue the process of working with your dreams, psychic or otherwise, remember that we are all psychic to some degree, which means that some of the myriad dreams will provide information from beyond your own experience and range of "normal" perceptions. Even if you keep no journal, you might want to ask yourself (at bedtime) to remember your dreams in the morning, and to seek out information and answers that might help you in your daily, waking life. While it's "neat" (to some) or "scary" (to others) to think we can get such information psychically, what's most important is that dreams can give us ways to help us understand ourselves and others around us.

Maybe if all the leaders of the world shared the same dream one night . . . now *that* would be a great dream.

Through understanding and acceptance of our own experiences we become fuller human beings. As humans we can always learn from our own experiences, no matter how silly or how painful they may be. What we call psychic experiences are no exceptions, and given that dreams are a "free" avenue for the mind to play at being psychic without the restraints (belief and otherwise) our conscious minds often place on such experiences, psychic dreams are extremely fertile ground for us to be psychic.

So tell yourself "it's okay to dream" and "it's okay to be psychic" and that it's certainly "okay to be psychic and dream at the same time."

Dream on and learn. . . .

APPENDIX A

What Can You Do (Next)?

After reading this book, you might gather that I agree with a number of experts that the dream group method of working with dreams is possibly the best. In many respects, I do, although I don't feel that the only way to work with your own dreams is in a group context. First of all, a group is not always easy to get together. Secondly, it's hard to say just how many people might make a good group. In addition, the methods of controlling your own dreams, whether incubating on a problem or initiating a lucid dream session is pretty much a solitary practice. The dream group (or even one other person with whom you are discussing your dreams on a regular basis) can help work through the dreams, understand the patterns or specifics they may present, but without you, the dreamer and your own dreams, the group process falls flat.

So, let me say that you can work with your own dreams, and you can try to notice psychically-derived information or even prompt the dreams to go in such directions.

Throughout the book, I've given you pointers to remember and work with your dreams. So, if you decide to work with dreams to initiate psychic experience, you must do a few things first.

1) Keep a dream journal or log. Get into the habit of recording your dreams on a regular basis. Remember that the

intent to do this is often necessary to increase dream recall, just as such intent or motivation to be psychic is often necessary to have repeated psychic experiences. Keep note of anything out of the ordinary, how well (or poorly) you slept, how tired you were when you went to bed, what you ate, how you woke up, what your mood was when you went to sleep, any issues on your mind, and how much (or how little) sleep you had. If a dream was particularly striking (or seemed "different," lucid, or even "psychic") make a special note.

2) Make the *intent* to dream and *remember* your dreams become a part of the daily routine. The more you remember and record in your journal, the more you will remember your dreams.

3) Review the dream journal on a regular basis. Look for patterns in the dreams, both in the content of the dreams as well as how striking or unusual any of the dreams might have been. Look for connections between certain dream images (or how they "felt") and the physical factors (how tired, what you ate, how much sleep, etc.) and psychological factors (mood, intent, issues on your mind, etc.). If you begin to see patterns, make special note of them in your journal.

4) If there are patterns noted, you might try to see if you can repeat the pattern-related dream purposefully. If, for example, you've noticed the same images in dreams popping up (or dreams of flying/out of body experiences) when you are in a particular physical or emotional state, you might try recreating this state to see if the same kind of dream recurs. However, be cautious with this. I don't condone or suggest including the use of any drugs, illegal or otherwise, prescribed or not, in this sort of "experiment." In addition, be very careful how you "play" with your physical and emotional state. If the pattern you're noticing includes a physical state of less than a healthy amount of sleep or not eating properly, you need to consider if the end result (the dream) is worth the price (ill health). I don't believe it is.

5) If you are already having dreams you consider psychic, whether telepathic, clairvoyant, or precognitive, look carefully at the patterns, not only when the dreams happen (and

your physical and emotional states) but also the kinds of psychic information (telepathic, etc.), the people/events being connected to, or the general themes of the experiences (disasters, illness, good happenings, friends, relatives, strangers, famous people, etc.).

6) If you have a dream you believe is psychic, check it out against existing information. If you have a telepathic dream, check the information with that person. If you have a clairvoyant dream of an event or location, try to match the information with the reality. If you have a dream of the future, keep an eye on the news to see if it comes true, or, if it is a situation you can reasonably interact with, use the information to help or hinder the predicted outcome.

Caution: Always remember that there may be nothing you can do to change the outcome of a predicted event. By this, I don't mean that the future can't be changed, just that we can't always be in a position to change it regardless of how much we know. For example, if I know (from a dream) that a political figure is to be assassinated, there may be nothing I can personally do to change that (unless I had very specific information I could relay to that person's security personnel). *I cannot allow myself to either take responsibility for the event or feel guilty that I couldn't alter the outcome.*

7) Tell yourself repeatedly (along with "I will remember my dreams) that you will have a psychic dream ("I will have a dream dealing with the big meeting I have next week" or "I will connect, telepathically, with my friend Chris" or "I will go out of my body in my dreams and visit Moscow"). Incubate an issue for which you may have no information stored in your memory and connect it to being psychic to find the answer.

PSYCHIC DREAMING EXPERIMENTS FROM HOME

Experiments with dreams can only be conducted after you begin the process of remembering and recording your dreams. Otherwise, you may have a momentary satisfaction that the process to have a psychic experience while dreaming worked, but no real remembrance of what it was about. The following exercises naturally follow after you have begun the recall and recording of your dreams.

1) Clairvoyance/remote viewing in your dreams: Where the "target" locations or events are current to the time of the dream.

a) Select a location somewhere in your geographic vicinity where you've never been. Do not go to that location until after the experiment. Incubate/think about visiting this location in your dreams. Record dreams over a period of time (say a week) and pick out any content you think might be related to that location. Copy that down separately.

Take that copy as well as the journal entries of the experiment-week to the target location. Compare the information you identified as being related to the actual physical location. Then look through the journal entries for any other descriptions that may be related.

Consider how well you did, including why you thought some content you picked out as related wasn't, and why some descriptions you didn't pick out were related.

Try this with more distant locations (which you may have to find photos or descriptions of or someone who is from there, or who lives there currently to learn if your dreams were accurate).

b) Select an event that will occur somewhere in the world during the time you'll be asleep. Go to bed with the intent that you will observe the event in your dreams. Record the information/content of the dreams upon awakening, then through the media or witnesses who may have been there, compare the content of the dreams to the actual events.

Keep in mind that simply dreaming of the outcome of a sporting event or battle that occurs while you are asleep does not necessarily mean you had a psychic experience. It's also possible that your dreaming mind made a good guess. Look more closely at the descriptive content of the dreams (it's not who wins or loses, but descriptions of how the game was played).

Try this on several nights to see what kind of "hit" rate you get.

c) Arrange with a friend (who is anywhere but at your location) who will be awake and doing something (preferably not something which could later cause embarrassment) while you are asleep to take note of what s/he is doing during that time period.

Record your dream content and compare it with notes taken by your friend. How well did you pick up on your friend's activities?

2) Telepathy in your dreams: The "target" is a living person and what s/he dreams or has in his or her mind.

a) Have a friend select a number of pictures or illustrations from books or magazines, trying to make them as different from each other as possible. Do not have your friend show them to you.

On specific nights, have your friend select one of these pictures and concentrate on it, during the time you are to be asleep. On the same nights, "program" yourself to dream of what your friend is looking at.

Upon awakening, take down as much information as possible. Then get together with your friend and see how much of your dream, if anything, corresponds with the actual target picture.

b) As a variation of the above experiment, have your friend study the picture before going to sleep. Both you and your friend should record your dreams for that night, then compare them both to the target picture and to each other's dreams.

You may find a correspondence to either the picture or to a dream your friend had that had nothing to do with the picture.

c) Make a conscious agreement between yourself and a friend/lover/relative who can also recall his or her dreams (at least to some degree) that you will share a dream. One of you, without telling the other, should then program yourself to dream of a certain topic or event or issue.

On awakening, both of you should record your dreams and

compare notes. Besides the contents of the dream, did you each dream of the other? Did you both show up in the dream?

d) Make a conscious agreement between yourself and a friend/lover/relative who can also recall his or her dreams (at least to some degree) that you will share a dream.

"Program" yourselves, not with an issue to dream, but simply with the idea that whatever the dream(s) you will share it/them.

On awakening, both of you should record your dreams and compare notes. Did you have the same dream? Did you both show up in the dream?

3) Precognitive dreams: Here you'll work with "targets" selected *after* the dreams are recorded.

a) "Program" yourself to dream of a friend visiting a location he or she has never been to before (preferably a local one). Spend a week with this "program," recording your dreams each day. Select the content or descriptions you think may relate to your friend.

Have your friend go to a location in your vicinity he or she has never been to (you might have the friend make the selection from a map just before going to the target location). Accompany your friend to the just-selected location and compare your dream-notes to the actual location.

b) As a twist on the above experiment, dream of a location you will visit on an upcoming business trip or vacation (again, one which you'd never been to before). Record your dreams up until the time of the visit and compare with the actual location.

c) Have a friend select a fairly large (say twenty-five) number of pictures or illustrations from books or magazines, trying to make them as different from each other as possible. Do not have your friend show them to you.

On specific nights, "program" yourself to dream of the next day's target. Record the dreams you have that night and have your friend select a target picture from the group. Then get together with your friend and see how much of your dream, if anything, corresponds with the actual target picture.

d) As a variation, your friend could select the pictures and seal them in opaque (preferably very thick) envelopes. After waking up and recording your dreams, select a target from among the envelopes, open it, and compare to your dream journal.

e) Select a "topic" or "issue" that will have some activity in the immediate future or a particular personality to focus on who will be doing something (whatever it is) in the immediate future. This should be something you can either check out in person or through the news media, such as the activity of a celebrity (which has not been announced or decided upon at the time you go to sleep), or where the next earthquake or tornado will occur somewhere in the world, or what the next event is that will occur in the Middle East, or even what will occur in the life of a friend over the course of the next few days.

Focus on the selection and "program" yourself to dream about it/he/she/them.

Record your dreams on awakening, and continue the process over a few days. Each day, you should compare what you've recorded with whatever you can find out about the selected target.

f) As a variation, make your own life the target. Keep track of how your dreams correspond (or don't correspond) to actual events in your life. This will probably work best if you designate specific time periods (say "next Thursday") as the target.

What use are the above exercises? If you begin to find connections between your dreams and outside experience and events, especially experiences and events for which information you have could not have come through your own sensory experience, memory, or logical inference, you may actually begin having more vivid psychic experiences in your dreams (and likely in your waking life) without having to "program" for them.

It would appear that for people who accept psychic experience into their lives, who welcome it and are not afraid of it, the more experiences you notice, the more experiences you'll have.

And of course, the more you begin to recall and record your dreams, the more dreams you'll recall and be able to record.

Don't be discouraged if the above exercises don't work right away. For many of us, no matter how much we want to have a psychic experience, it appears that we still have our deep-seated "blocks" and fears of them, due to the way we were all raised and educated in a society that typically downplays, ignores, disregards, or ridicules such experiences. As you try more and more to have such experiences, as you begin to take note of what is "normal" experience, you will begin to notice the "extras" that peek through, both in your dreams and in waking reality.

Keep on dreaming. Psychic or not, the lessons to be learned through our dreams can help us through our own lives and in connecting with the lives of others and the world around us.

Dreams can pick up on two realities, it seems: the reality that is our own experience, awareness, personality, and subconscious view of the world around us, and the reality that is how we connect to other people and to the world around us, the psychic connection to reality of the world.

Try these exercises for a while. Then let me know how you did.

APPENDIX B

Who Can You Call?

FOR MORE ON DREAMS

There are a number of universities and hospitals around the United States and in other countries that do research in the areas of sleep and dreaming. Rather than list them all, I would suggest contacting the Association for the Study of Dreams, below:

The Association for the Study of Dreams
P.O. Box 1600
Vienna, Va 22183
An international organization providing for an interdisciplinary study of dreams and sleep. Publishes a newsletter and sponsors annual conferences.

Other sources:

The Association for Research and Enlightenment
P.O. Box 595
67th and Atlantic
Virginia Beach, VA 23451
(804) 428-3588

The Better Sleep Council
1270 Avenue of the Americas

New York, NY 10020
(212) 265-0303

The Delaney and Flowers Center for the Study of Dreams
337 Spruce Street
San Francisco, CA 94118
(415) 587-3424

The Lucidity Association/Lucidity Letter
8703 109th Street
Edmonton, Alberta, Canada T6G2L5

The Lucidity Project
P.O. Box 2364
Stanford, CA 94305

The Pacific Northwest Center for Dream Studies
219 First Avenue South
Seattle, WA 98104

Stanford University Sleep Disorders Center
Hoover Pavilion
N2A 211 Quarry Road
Stanford, CA 94395-5573

ON PARAPSYCHOLOGY

One of the basic problems for people who have experiences
such as the ones detailed in this book is that they rarely know
who they can talk to about those experiences. In addition,
when they may need help with getting through an experience,
or in having any psychic disturbances halted, they don't really
know where they can find parapsychologists to help them, to
investigate, to counsel them, or just to refer them to appropriate sources of information or counseling.

Along with the problem of not knowing who to call is the
issue of who and what organizations are both reputable and
effective in helping people deal with psi experiences. To date,
there is no psychic hotline for people to call, though para-

psychologists in a few places hope to get one (or more) started, provided the proper funding becomes available. People may hear of parapsychologists and parapsychological organizations through media accounts of parapsychology, but such accounts often misrepresent phenomena, the "experts," and the organizations.

People can call themselves parapsychologists without any licensing or credentials, given that none are really available. You, as the person needing the help or information that a real parapsychologist can give, must be careful about who you do call for aid or information, since there are many more people claiming to be parapsychologists than there are full or associated members of the Parapsychological Association.

When encountering or seeking out a "parapsychologist," make sure you ask him/her questions like the following:

1) How do you define parapsychology? Make sure that the answer(s) are more or less in agreement with what you've learned through this book, and that the person's definition of parapsychology doesn't encompass things like crystals, vampires, or demons. While there are areas of experience (such as UFO encounters or studies of creatures like Bigfoot) that are more than worthy of study, a parapsychologist does not study such things as part of parapsychology. I am personally interested in a number of areas, experiences, and reported phenomena outside of the psychic arena, but such things are not technically part of parapsychology.

2) Why do you call yourself a parapsychologist? Answers like "I'm a practicing psychic" or "I've been chasing ghosts for years" or "I'm a practicing witch/astrologer/numerologist . . ." or "I've been interested in the field for years" are not acceptable. A person claiming to be a parapsychologist simply because he or she is psychic would be like a person claiming to be a psychologist simply because he or she has a mind. We are all biological organisms, but that doesn't make us biologists. If the person mentions doing research, inquire as to what that research is, and how it stacks up against scientific research into the paranormal.

3) Are you affiliated with any research or academic

organization? Most people actually in the field of parapsychology are at least associated members of the Parapsychological Association, and many work in accredited universities or colleges. Simply being a member of organizations like the American Society for Psychical Research does not, however, automatically make one a "parapsychologist."

4) What is your educational or professional background? The *only* accredited degree program in parapsychology in the country (in fact, in the western hemisphere) was at John F. Kennedy University. Anyone with "certificates" in parapsychology could have easily gotten their "certificate" or "degree" from a psychic development school or mail order parapsychology course (most of which are not scientifically and/or parapsychologically oriented). There are exceptions, the major one being Jeffrey Mishlove, who has the only Ph.D. in parapsychology in the United States (a special program at University of California at Berkeley). Most parapsychologists have their educational background in "mainstream" fields like psychology, anthropology, physics, etc. Other accredited universities may have allowed certain people to gain advanced degrees in the field by essentially creating their own degree program. In such cases, it's still important to check out their views and experience within parapsychology.

This is not to say, by the way, that some select people who are not parapsychologists by strict definition cannot be of help. There are several people out there who are not necessarily members of the Parapsychological Association who are knowledgeable, competent, and ethical. You should, however, make contact with a reputable organization or university to check such a person out before working with them.

Keep in mind that there are many people out there claiming to be parapsychologists, most of whom may charge money to come investigate or bust your ghost, or handle your psychic problem. At present, those of us who do charge for investigations are placing a value on the time we spend with you, as there is simply not enough knowledge of how psi operates to guarantee anything. And, some parapsychologists do not charge at all. Understand, however, that because of this, you may have to be patient when requesting help, given that the funding for parapsychology is limited, and the personnel even more so. If you contact a professional counselor for help, also keep in mind that such a person, who makes his or her living counseling or offering therapy to people, may very well charge for his/her services.

Just don't run out and hire a "ghostbuster" or "exorcist" without really checking to see that they are truly what they say they are, and without really understanding what your other options are. All too often I have heard that such people come in and immediately find the ghost (or demon, sometimes), then charge an arm and a leg (or thousands of dollars for "expenses" without any detailing of what those expenses are) to get "rid of it," never having really explored if there are other explanations or psychological causes for the events.

The following is a list of organizations and research centers you might contact for information and/or referrals. If there is no organization in your neck of the woods, one of these will undoubtedly be able to suggest someone local for you to contact, given that members of the Parapsychological Association are spread out over the U.S. and Europe (and even in Japan, South Africa, the USSR, South America, and Australia). These organizations may be membership societies, and many of them publish journals, newsletters, and even books. This list is followed by one which gives counseling help or referrals to people having psychic experiences. For any further contacts, you may call the Office of Paranormal Investigations, where I am co-director.

If you do contact individuals, please keep in mind that they will attempt to help you as best they can, but that a referral to another party may be appropriate for your needs and their schedules. In addition, you might speed your reply a bit if you include a self-addressed stamped envelope. If you want to contact me, you may do so either at the Office of Paranormal Investigations, or through my publishers (and please enclose that self-addressed stamped envelope, or I cannot guarantee a reply).

Academy of Religion and Psychical Research
P.O. Box 614
Bloomfield, CT 06002

American Society for Psychical Research
5 West 73rd Street
New York, NY 10023
(212) 799-5050
Membership society, which has an excellent library, sponsors public lectures, publishes a journal and newsletter, and has other publications available, such as a list of courses in parapsychology offered around the world. Investigations are conducted out of the ASPR.

Association for Research and Enlightenment
P.O. Box 595
67th and Atlantic
Virginia Beach, VA 23451
(804) 428-3588
See note in the next part of this list.

Bay Area Skeptics
4030 Moraga
San Francisco, CA 94122
Publishes a newsletter, "Basis"; presents monthly lectures.

California Society For Psychical Study, Inc.
Box 844
Berkeley, CA 94704
(415) 843-0307
Monthly lectures and occasional seminars/workshops; publishes a newsletter, "Iridis."

Center for Scientific Anomalies Research (CSAR)
P.O. Box 1052
Ann Arbor, MI 48103
Publishes a journal, *Zetetic Scholar*, and a newsletter.

Central Premonitions Registry
P.O. Box 482
Times Square Station
New York, NY 10036

Central Psi Research Institute
4800 N. Milwaukee Avenue, Suite 210
Chicago, IL 60630

Committee for the Scientific Investigations of Claims of the
Paranormal
P.O. Box 229
Buffalo, NY 14215-0229
Organization of skeptics, critics, and debunkers. Publishes a
journal, *The Skeptical Inquirer*.

Foundation for Research on the Nature of Man, Institute for
Parapsychology
P.O. Box 6847
College Station
Durham, NC 27708
Conducts research both in the laboratory and field investi-
gations. This is the organization started by J.B. and Louisa
Rhine, and conducts a summer study program in parapsy-
chological research. Publishes the *Journal of Parapsychol-
ogy*.

IANDS: The International Association of Near Death Studies
Box U-20
University of Connecticut
Storrs, CT 06268
This organization conducts research on near death experi-
ences, including interviewing people who have had such ex-
periences. Publishes a journal, *Anabiosis*, and has several
local chapters around the country.

Institute Fur Grenzgebiete
D-7800 Freiburg 1. Br.

Eichhalde 12, West Germany
Dr. Hans Bender, director

Institute of Noetic Sciences
475 Five Gate Road, Suite 300
P.O. Box 909
Sausalito, CA 94965

Mind Science Foundation
8301 Broadway, Suite 100
San Antonio, TX 78209

Mobius Society
4801 Wilshire Blvd., Suite 320
Los Angeles, CA 90010

The Office of Paranormal Investigations (OPI)
(and Psionics Consultants/Research and Investigation of Anomalies and the Paranormal)
P.O. Box 875
Orinda, CA 94563-0875
(415) 553-2588
Established in 1989, the Office of Paranormal Investigations provides a number of services to the general public, the scientific community, and the media. Investigations of apparitions, poltergeists, and ostensible hauntings are conducted, as well as explorations of other psychic and anomalous experiences and phenomena. Consulting and information services are available to researchers (in and outside of parapsychology) interested in expertise in magic and illusion to aid in experimental set-up and guard against fraud; to the business and legal communities and law enforcement with regards to the use of psychics; to media interested in learning more about psychic phenomena or seeking experts for interview or appearances on radio and television; to the entertainment industry interested in technical or scientific advisors for films or television programs; and to the general public interested in learning more about psychic experience, research, and investigation. OPI also conducts classes and sem-

inars, and will be publishing a newsletter and other information pieces in the future. Fees are charged for investigations and consulting services. OPI may be contacted at the above number, though out of area calls will generally be returned collect. Co-directors of OPI are Loyd Auerbach and Christopher Chacon.

Parapsychological Association, Inc.
P.O. Box 12236
Research Triangle Park, NC 27709

Parapsychology Foundation
228 East 71st Street
New York, NY 10021
(212) 628-1550
Supports research in parapsychology, has an excellent library, offers research and student grants, and publishes proceedings of annual conferences.

Parapsychology Research Group
3101 Washington Street
San Francisco, CA 94115

PSI Center (Parapsychology Sources of Information Center)
Two Plane Tree Lane
Dix Hills, NY 11746
Rhea White, director.
Offers services aimed at pulling together information for researchers and laypersons. Publishes *Parapsychology Abstracts International*.

Psychical Research Foundation
c/o William G. Roll
Psychology Department
West Georgia College
Carrollton, GA 30118
William G. Roll, director.
Interested in the issue of survival of bodily death. Conducts

investigations all over the country, though mainly poltergeist cases. Publishes a journal, *Theta*.

Saybrook Institute
1772 Vallejo Street
San Francisco, CA 90004

Society for Psychical Research
One Adam and Eve Mewes
Kensington, England W8 6UG
Oldest psychical research organization in the world. Conducts lectures and research. Publishes a journal, proceedings, and a newsletter.

Society for Scientific Exploration
c/o Dr. Peter Sturrock
ERL 306
Stanford University
Stanford, CA 94305-4055
An organization of scientists formed for the study of scientific anomalies, including psychic phenomena, UFOs, and cryptozoology. Publishes a newsletter and the *Journal of Scientific Exploration*.

Spiritual Emergence Network
California Institute of Transpersonal Psychology
250 Oak Grove Avenue
Menlo Park, CA 94025
(415) 327-2776
See below.

Spiritual Frontiers Fellowship
Executive Plaza
10715 Winner Road
Independence, MO 64052
See below.

Survival Research Foundation
P.O. Box 8565
Pembroke Pines, FL 33024-0565

Division of Parapsychology
Department of Behavioral Medicine and Psychiatry
Box 152
University of Virginia Medical Center
Charlottesville, VA 22908
Ian Stevenson, director.
The division of parapsychology is primarily interested in cases of potential reincarnation and in near death experiences.

Department of Psychology
University of Edinburgh
Seven George Square
Edinburgh, Scotland EH8 9JZ
This department of the University of Edinburgh is the home of the Koestler Chair of Parapsychology, currently held by Dr. Robert Morris.

Counseling organizations, or places to call for referral to appropriate counselors who can help you deal with psychically derived problems or with psychic experiences:

Association for Research and Enlightenment (ARE)
P.O. Box 595
Virginia Beach, VA 23451
(804) 428-3558
This nonprofit, open-membership organization was founded to preserve, make accessible, and disseminate the Edgar Cayce readings. Today, the ARE is on the leading edge in holistic health care, meditation instruction, reincarnation studies, and spiritual healing. Its programs are open to its membership and the general public, and are held throughout the U.S. and Canada, as well as its national headquarters in Virginia Beach, Virginia. They offer correspondence courses in spiritual and personal development and have a comprehensive selection of books and tapes.

Spiritual Advisory Council
2500 East Curry Road
Orlando, FL 32806

(305) 898-2500
This organization was founded in 1974 by a group of business people dedicated to interpreting spiritual and psychic practices in practical applications. Particular emphasis is on spiritual healing and mediumship. Formerly headquarters in the Chicago area, it now maintains a large center in Orlando, Florida, and has various groups in the east and midwest.

Spiritual Emergence Network (SEN)
California Institute of Transpersonal Psychology
250 Oak Grove Avenue
Menlo Park, CA 94025
(415) 327-2776
This international organization is located within an educational setting. It is a referral network which is dedicated to an understanding of the spiritual emergence, the promotion of public awareness, and the dissemination of relevant information for individuals, health care professionals, and interested organizations. Its newsletter is a chief educational feature.

Spiritual Frontiers Fellowship (SFF)
Executive Plaza
10715 Winner Road
Independence, MO 64052
(816) 254-8585
This organization was founded in 1956 as an interfaith, nonprofit fellowship by a group of religious leaders and writers who had deep concern for the rising interest in mystical and paranormal experiences. The goal of SFF is the development of new dimensions of spiritual experience. Local chapters and study groups, a bookstore and lending library, Project Blind Awareness, a reading list and study materials, a quarterly journal, and a monthly newsletter help round out program opportunities for members.

Spiritual Science Fellowship
P.O. Box 1445 Station H

Montreal, Quebec H3G 2N3
Canada
(514) 937-8359

This organization was founded in Montreal by a well-known educator, Marilyn Rossner. It is dedicated to psychic/spiritual traditions, mind-body movement disciplines such as yoga, and transformational psychology. It has a large center in Montreal offering a wide variety of courses in both English and French. It operates affiliate branches across Canada, and is affiliated with the Spiritual Advisory Council.

EDUCATION IN PARAPSYCHOLOGY

I and many others in the field of parapsychology have often been asked a couple of questions pertinent to the material in this book. First of all, where can one take courses in parapsychology, and secondly, where can one earn a degree in parapsychology so as to enter the field? Both questions are a bit limited in the way they can be answered, since the resources and support of this relatively new field of science are severely limited.

The American Society for Psychical Research publishes *Courses and Other Study Opportunities in Parapsychology* which lists a wide variety of courses offered for credit in and out of the United States. In addition, it offers some suggestion for graduate work in parapsychology, which I'll get to in a moment. It also lists a few non-credit courses offered at schools around the country.

The course list is by no means complete, in that it is limited by those courses the folks at the ASPR (mainly Patrice Keane and Donna McCormick) hear of, either from the instructors or some second-hand source. In addition, the updates were further limited by who responds to queries (of whether the courses were still being offered). There are just over fifty colleges and universities listed which offer courses for credit in the U.S., though undoubtedly there are many more. Other schools offer extension or continuing education courses, and there are many local adult education programs running courses in parapsychology. The Office of Paranormal Investigations is looking into offering a non-credit certificate program, taught by a few of us who have been teaching accredited parapsychology courses at John F. Kennedy University (and other colleges).

My suggestion to you if you want to take a course locally is to check with the local university or college, both the registrar's office and any office of continuing education. In addition, you should check all the adult education programs in your immediate vicinity. The only problem with extension and adult ed. classes may lie with who is teaching the class. I know of many psychics and others teaching parapsychology courses, which often incorporate all those things which I said were *not* parapsychology. In addition, some of those psychics (whom I often have doubts about as both teachers and psychics) are mainly teaching some form of psychic development or occult practice, and not parapsychology *per se*. So, be discriminating when signing up for a course, unless you're mainly interested in a bit of "entertainment," in which case it may not matter who is teaching the course. If the course is offered for credit or has been screened carefully by a faculty department in the university or college through which it is being offered, there is a better chance that the course may be a bit more related to parapsychology as it really is (though here, again, I have seen outlines of credit courses which made my blood turn a bit green).

One excellent course you can take is the summer study program at the Institute for Parapsychology, Foundation for Research on the Nature of Man, in Durham, North Carolina. This eight-week, intensive study program goes over methods of research and investigation in parapsychology, and is taught by some of the foremost researchers in the field. See the above address for information.

In addition, there are a number of places that offer correspondence courses, but I really think you may be a bit better off doing the reading on your own, starting with some of the suggested titles I have included in Appendix C.

In terms of actual study for a degree in parapsychology, as I mentioned in my previous book (and as you may read in other sources), John F. Kennedy University is the only accredited university or college that has offered degrees with the word "parapsychology" in them as part of a degree program. In actuality, nearly all the parapsychologists in the world do not have a degree in parapsychology and may have backgrounds in almost any science you can think of (though a good number of them have degrees in psychology). A number of schools offer degrees in psychology, anthropology, or other fields allowing you to do your work with a parapsychological concentration, often under the guidance of a parapsychologist affiliated/on the faculty of the university. Such schools include the University of Virginia, West Georgia College, Antioch University, Saybrook Institute, and Edinburgh University in Scotland, where the Koestler Chair of Parapsychology has been established.

If you want to get into the field of parapsychology, then go to a good, strong, undergraduate university, whether there is a course in parapsychology or not. Get a background in psychology, anthropology, physics, or some other physical or social science, but also take introductory courses in some other fields (especially psychology, physics, and anthropology) so you are familiar with concepts that might have a direct bearing on parapsychological research. Learn the ways of science (maybe a philosophy or history of science course), since we have noticed that people get disappointed when entering a course in parapsychology that it is as scientifically oriented as it is (and not just looking at auras or learning to develop one's own psi). A course or two in statistics and psychological research methods couldn't hurt, either.

Then, when looking for a graduate school, you might attempt to work up a master's program that will allow you to do research or investigation in parapsychological topics. If you have no one at your university to guide you (no parapsychologist, that is), contact one of the research organizations for suggestions. As to the fate of the degrees offered at John F. Kennedy University, they are, I'm afraid, no more, for a number of reasons, most notably that the degree programs at John F. Kennedy University were mainly funded by student tuition; there are no longer degrees directly in parapsychology or even specializing in the field. The Graduate School for the Study of Human Consciousness at JFKU has therefore cut back severely on the number of parapsychology courses offered at the university. Courses in the field may continue to be offered there, on an irregular basis, but I'm afraid that with the shut-down of the degree program, there no longer is any accredited university offering such degrees in the United States.

As far as the job market in the field goes, realize that it is, as of this writing, a bit limited. There are few research laboratories around, and fewer places that offer funding for field investigations. So, you may have to use that background of yours in whatever other field you've gotten it in to get a post in a university which might be open to your offering courses in parapsychology, and to your being able to do research in this area. Or, you might try writing as a source of income (something I'm obviously moving into), or lecturing, or running workshops. Applied psi is another potential source of income, as some parapsychologists are moving toward this area and working with businesses. This is one area I'm sure is going to open up in the very near future, and it is the aim of the organization I've started with Christopher Chacon to take all such potential services and place them under one "roof."

PARAPSYCHOLOGY: A FIELD IN FLUX

Parapsychology, as a field of scientific endeavor, is currently in a state of great flux and change, mainly due to the lessening of funding and the subsequent closing of some laboratory sites. So what could be wrong with the field of parapsychology that could cause such a fall in funding during a time when interest in psychic experience and New Age thinking is on the rise?

One problem has been the view that such topics, from a mainstream science and business perspective, are taboo. While covering a booth for the Parapsychological Association at the 1989 Convention of the American Association for the Advancement of Science (AAAS), with which the Parapsychological Association is affiliated, it was interesting, amusing, and sometimes thought-provoking to watch scientists visibly avoid our booth (by walking faster past it or giving it a wide berth). Some scientists who stopped by (after carefully looking around for signs of their colleagues) mentioned that they had to be careful, because even though they were interested in parapsychology and psychic phenomena, such interest could create problems for them within their own fields or jobs.

I recently had a conversation with my good friend, Keith Harary, president and research director of the Institute for Advanced Psychology in San Francisco. Keith who has a Ph.D., has had an intimate involvement with the field of parapsychology. As a research participant and researcher in many studies from out of body experiences to remote viewing, Keith has been on all sides of laboratory research. In addition, he has been involved in interesting attempts to apply psychic abilities, or what he terms "extended perception," in an attempt to demystify what many practicing psychics would have us believe is a "special gift." He has written a number of popular and professional articles on parapsychology and psychology, and is co-author with Pamela Weintraub, of *Lucid Dreams in 30 Days: The Creative Sleep Program* and *Have an Out-of-Body Experience in 30 Days: The Free Flight Program*. He is also co-author (with Russell Targ) of the best-selling book *The Mind Race*, and is a frequent contributor to *Omni* magazine.

Part of our conversation, that which follows, had to do with the state and future of the field of parapsychology. The remainder, which you'll find elsewhere in this book, dealt more closely with dreams.

As mentioned earlier, the only people truly researching this area of human experience, even if we/they make a lot of assumptions that there is such a thing as psychic ability, are the ones who are going to find out that it doesn't exist if that's the case. Typically, these people are parapsychologists. **LA:** Keith, if we prove that psi doesn't exist or that there's another easy explanation for it, would you agree that such a finding would be a major addition to what we know about human psychology?

KH: A major addition. It would just be fantastically important, because it would tell you a great deal about human behavior. It would be crucial information about how we may fool ourselves. I would spend years studying that. You have to start out with believing that there's something going on, as I did. Now I've gotten to a very different place with it. I think the problem is—and I don't want to sound like I'm coming from on high when I say this—that most of the people working in the area are true believers. They're typically either true believers or true critics. Many of the critics also appear to be true believers in their own right. There are very few people in the middle taking a truly open-minded look at what's going on, and being able to look at whatever that may be in a whole, fresh way. I think we have to just throw out what many people put down as to what one must learn if you're going to do research in this field about how we should characterize *the* phenomena.

That's the worst thing that happens to people when they start studying this area, that they have to spend a lot of time learning all the mistakes that everyone else has made in the guise of learning how it's done and what's going on here. If the existing approaches are so successful, if all of that is so good and so right on, then we might have seen more reliable results already, wouldn't we? Maybe.

LA: If we were able to frame things appropriately so we could possibly understand what was going on, or if we could use what we know and apply it *properly*, we might be better off.

KH: I think there's going to have to be a massive upheaval in this field, a tremendous change in personnel, who's doing what, and in how things are being characterized. I think that a lot of the people who have been doing research in this field are just going to have to leave, because they have too much of an axe to grind, and their eagerness to loudly grind that axe is just drowning out the dissenting voices that desperately need to be heard. Too many people think that they're going to get the Nobel Prize for figuring it all out and proving that their limited point of view is the answer. I'm not sure that point of view is anything like valid.

LA: And there are real semantic problems here. Not just in the words we choose to use, but in the basic ideologies. We are almost approaching these abilities as super-powers, and while many parapsychologists say that everyone's psychic, that everyone has these abilities, they're also looking for the person who can do it repeatedly in experiments . . .

KH: And they're trying to define a special personality that does that, which I think is ludicrous.

LA: The likelihood that such a person would come forward to join in laboratory experiments is pretty low. I've been questioned by skeptic groups about such psychic people and why such a person doesn't come forward to take their ten thousand or so dollar awards. My answer is usually that if such people exist, they've learned to apply such abilities to real moneymaking, they've probably made a billion dollars and we probably know their names, though they'd never tell you they're psychic.

KH: Or they would never characterize themselves in that fashion. They would call it intuition or they would call it good analysis, being savvy.

Parapsychology is just a mess. it's holding on to its little island as the waves wash away at the shore. Parapsychologists define what they're doing in negative terms: "We study the stuff that has no explanation and then we decide that's a phenomenon onto itself." Oh, great. Well that really sets you up in a wonderful position scientifically.

LA: So that if what we discover does not fit the very limited definition of psi, it's not parapsychological and we may then be discarding the experience instead of transforming what we study and do and saying something on the order of "Here are the experiences, here are the explanations and we're the ones who can help you deal with them."

KH: Exactly. You can deal with it, first of all, on an experiential level. You can say "People have these experiences. We want to help them deal with these experiences. Here's what we don't know about this area, but we do know how to help people cope with unusual experiences or what they experience as unusual." That's a whole area of psychology that needs major attention; helping people deal with experiences that don't subjectively seem to fit in with their existing world-view.

And there's a whole other side of things as to what's going on. The idea that there's one explanation for what's going on is unlikely, pretty ridiculous.

I've been doing this work for nearly twenty years now, can you believe it?

LA: I believe it, I've been doing it for a little over ten.

KH: This is truly a fascinating area, but I don't think it's attracted great minds.

LA: Because it's too scary on one level, and too closed and narrow on another level.

KH: Instead of attracting great minds it has attracted a lot of misfits, people who seem to say "Well, I don't fit in so I'll study the stuff that doesn't fit in, or that I don't think fits in." That's a terrible place to start, because it gives you a vested interest in maintaining the role of the outsider and not solving the mystery.

Some people will probably get very mad at me for saying this kind of stuff. Too bad.

LA: I've said some of that also, though certainly not as strongly or as clearly. And others have said it, too. In thinking back on the Parapsychological Association Convention of 1989, after Michael Crichton's talk [about why parapsychology doesn't fit in mainstream science], I got the distinct impression that a few people were toasting to him being wrong. Here were people whose labs and funding were being shut down hoping that Michael Crichton was wrong about what it takes for acceptance, that the way it's going to work is if the general public accepts that these experiences are real.

KH: He also said that you have to show why the supposed phenomena are useful or relevant to everyday people.

You know, I also said that in a paper presented in Cambridge [England] at a conference years ago [1982 Parapsychological Association Convention]. It's always seemed obvious to me.

In the era of AIDS, and as we confront the possibility of global thermonuclear war, plus the fact that there are places in the world where people are literally starving to death, global ecological cataclysm hanging on the brink, and all kinds of other political violence all over the planet including terrorism, not to mention the abysmal poverty right here in America on the streets of the Mississippi delta and lots of other places; when people are dealing with major problems and major denial, if you want to say to them that this is an important thing to study, you'd better come up with a good reason.

The first thing they're going to ask is "Why? Why is that so important?" If you can't show them why this particular effort will make a meaningful difference in light of all of the above, then forget it.

LA: And the answer may be that whatever it is helps with some of that problem solving.

KH: Maybe that's the answer. Or maybe if we understand human behavior better we'll understand how we got ourselves into this mess, though I'm not sure that there is, in fact, a solution pending. In other words, one that we have enough time to figure out and then implement on a global scale, that will make a difference.

A lot of people have just given up. "It's too much for me to deal with. Let's see, we've got at least a generation before it all goes to hell, and maybe science will fix it, so in the meantime I'm going to drive my Maserati and get a fancy condominium."

I never could do that. I've given up some really high-paying offers for jobs to do something that I felt was worthwhile with the little bit of time I have. Some people may think that's crazy or too idealistic, but I thought it was more crazy when I was sitting behind a desk in a fat office overlooking San Francisco Bay in a very high-paying job wearing my standard issue power-suit and asking myself "What am I doing here?" At the end of it all the money will be spent, life will be over, and what difference will it make?

LA: In discussions with some of my students [at John F. Kennedy University] in a class on applied parapsychology, in which we were looking at ways to apply ostensible psychic abilities and also at other ways to apply what one learns in parapsychology, we concluded that what needs to be done is a repackaging of all of it. It may just be setting up a group of people who are better problem solvers, whether it's because of their supposed psychic abilities, intuition, or whatever, and marketing it as just another company that provides information as do other companies that digest and repackage information needed to solve all sorts of problems [in business, etc.].

KH: What you're doing is an interesting approach. I've been written up all over the place as supposedly being psychic. I don't buy any of that stuff, though it was an incredible trip to have had laid on me. It's not where I'm coming from. It's certainly not where I'm coming from today, and I wonder about what people mean when they say that, anyway. I think it's a bad idea to label people as being psychic.

But if you approach certain experiences as suggesting a kind of problem-solving ability and say "Look, we're not sure where the information is coming from or how, but we tend to get results," that's sort of where the business world is oriented anyway, even law enforcement. Many business people might say "What do I care? Call it a black box. If you give me the answer that I want, it's great." Scientifically that's got problems, but probably fewer problems than claiming that you've personally got *the* answer, or a direct connection to some cheap source of wisdom or easy answers.

Thus far, parapsychology as a field of human endeavor has been kept relatively small, and its job market with it. Will that open up, especially with the greater focus on the New Age and psychic experience? Perhaps, with a bit of ingenuity and the education of the general public and the media. What is really needed, however, is an infusion of new ideas of how to apply one's knowledge of parapsychology and psychic phenomena, as well as learning more and more how to actually apply psi abilities to everyday situations and other occupations.

Do you have ideas that might help us uncover the answers or show people, in the scientific community as well as the general public, "What good psi is?" Do you have ideas that might help the field of parapsychology get back on its feet to work on the new ideas and applications necessary to look for the answers we all would like to find?

If so, please feel free to write me, care of Warner Books or at The Office of Paranormal Investigations (P.O. Box 875, Orinda, CA 94563-0875).

Let's all brainstorm on the questions around psychic functioning.

APPENDIX C

What Can You Read?

A BIBLIOGRAPHY OF BOOKS ON DREAMS, PARAPSYCHOLOGY, AND PSYCHIC EXPERIENCE

DREAM READINGS

Bonime, Walter. *The Clinical Use of Dreams*. New York: Basic Books, 1988.

Bro, Harmon. *Edgar Cayce on Dreams*. New York: Warner Books, 1968.

Cartwright, Roseanne. *Night Life: Explorations in Dreaming*. New York: Prentice-Hall, 1980.

Coxhead, David, and Hiller, Susan. *Dreams: Visions of the Night*. New York: Thames and Hudson, 1976.

de Becker, Raymond. *The Understanding of Dreams and Their Influence on the History of Man*. New York: Hawthorn Books, 1978.

Delaney, Gayle. *Living Your Dreams*. San Franciso: Harper & Row, 1988.

————. *The Hidden Language of the Heart: Unlocking the Secrets of Your Dreams*. New York: Bantam Books, 1989*a*.

————. *The Dream Interview: A Refreshingly Practical Approach to Dreaming*. New York: Bantam Books, 1989*b*.

Domhoff, William. *The Mystique of Dreams: A Search for Utopia Through Senoi Dream Theory*. Berkeley, California: University of California Press, 1985.

Donahoe, James. *Dream Reality: The Conscious Creation of Dream and Paranormal Experience*. Oakland, California: Bench Press, 1974.

Evans, Christopher. *Landscapes of the Night*. New York: Pocket Books, 1983.

Faraday, Ann. *Dream Power*. New York: Berkley Books, 1980.

———. *The Dream Game*. New York: Harper Paperbacks, 1990.

Feinstein, David, and Krippner, Stanley. *Personal Mythology: The Psychology of Your Evolving Self*. Los Angeles: Jeremy P. Tarcher, 1988.

Freud, Sigmund. *The Interpretation of Dreams*. New York: Avon Books, 1966.

Gackenbach, Jayne, ed. *Sleep and Dreams: A Sourcebook*. New York: Garland Publishing, 1986.

Gackenbach, Jayne, and Bosveld, Jane. *Control Your Dreams*. New York: Harper & Row, 1989.

Gackenbach, Jayne, and LaBerge, Stephen. *Conscious Mind, Sleeping Brain: Perspectives on Lucid Dreaming*. New York: Plenum Press, 1988.

Garfield, Patricia. *Creative Dreaming*. New York: Ballantine Books, 1976.

———. *Your Child's Dreams*. New York: Ballantine Books, 1985.

———. *Women's Bodies, Women's Dreams*. New York: Ballantine Books, 1988.

Gendlin, Eugene T. *Let Your Body Interpret Your Dreams*. Wilmette, Illinois: Chiron Publications, 1986.

Grant, John. *Dreamers*. Bath, Avon, England: Ashgrove Press, 1984.

Green, Celia. *Lucid Dreams*. London: Hamilton, 1968.

Hall, Calvin. *The Meaning of Dreams*. New York: McGraw Hill, 1966.

Hall, Calvin, and Nordby, Vernon. *The Individual and His Dreams*. New York: Signet Books, 1972.

Hall, Calvin S., and Van de Castle, Robert. *The Content Analysis of Dreams*. New York: Appleton-Century-Crofts, 1966.

Harary, Keith, and Weintraub, Pamela. *Lucid Dreams in 30 Days: The Creative Sleep Program*. New York: St. Martin's Press, 1989.

Hartmann, Ernest. *The Nightmare: The Psychology and Biology of Terrifying Dreams*. New York: Basic Books, 1984.

Hobson, J. Allen. *The Dreaming Brain*. New York: Basic Books, 1988.

Johnson, Robert A. *Inner Work: Using Dreams and Active Imagination For Personal Growth*. San Francisco: Harper & Row, 1986.

Jones, Richard. *The New Psychology of Dreaming*. New York: Penguin Books, 1978.

Jung, Carl. G. *Dreams*. Princeton, New Jersey: Princeton University Press, 1974.

Krippner, Stanley, and Dillard, Joseph. *Dream Working: How to Use Your Dreams For Creative Problem Solving*. Buffalo, New York: Bearly, Ltd., 1988.

Krippner, Stanley, editor. *Dreamtime & Dreamwork*. Los Angeles: Jeremy P. Tarcher, Inc., 1990.

LaBerge, Stephen. *Lucid Dreaming*. New York: Ballantine Books, 1985.

LaBerge, Stephen, and Rheingold, Howard. *Exploring the World of Lucid Dreaming*. New York: Ballantine Books, 1990.

Mack, John E. *Nightmares and Human Conflict*. Boston: Houghton Mifflin Company, 1970.

Mindell, Arnold. *Working With The Dreaming Body*. Boston: Routledge & Kegan Paul, 1985.

Natterson, Joseph M., ed. *The Dream in Clinical Practice*. New York: Jason Aronson, 1980.

Palombo, Stanley R. *Dreaming and Memory: A New Information Processing Model*. New York: Basic Books, 1978.

Reed, Henry. *Getting Help From Your Dreams*. Virginia Beach, Virginia: Inner Vision Publishing, 1985.

Rossi, Ernest. *Dreams and the Growth of Personality*. Elmsford, NY: Pergamon Press, 1972.

Ryback, David, with Sweitzer, Letitia. *Dreams That Come

True: Their Psychic and Transforming Powers. New York: Ivy (Ballantine) Books, 1990.

Sabin, Katherine. *ESP and Dream Analysis*. Chicago: Henry Regnery Co., 1974.

Signell, Karen A. *Wisdom of the Heart: Working with Women's Dreams*. New York: Bantam New Age Books, 1990.

Sloane, Paul. *The Psychoanalytic Understanding of the Dream*. New York: Jason Aronson, 1979.

Thurston, Mark. *Dreams: Tonight's Answers for Tomorrow's Questions*. San Francisco: Harper & Row, 1988.

Ullman, Montague; Krippner, Stanley; and Vaughan, Alan. *Dream Telepathy*. 2d ed. Jefferson, North Carolina: McFarland & Company, 1989.

Ullman, Montague, and Limmer, Claire eds. *The Variety of Dream Experience: Expanding Our Ways of Working with Dreams*. New York: Continuum, 1987.

Ullman, Montague, and Zimmerman, Nan. *Working With Dreams*. Los Angeles: Jeremy P. Tarcher, 1979.

Van de Castle, Robert. *Our Dreaming Minds: The History and Psychology of Dreaming*. Virginia Beach, Virginia: Inner Vision Publishing, 1988.

Von Grunebaum, Gustave Edmund, and Caillois, Roger eds. *The Dream and Human Societies*. Berkeley California: University of California Press, 1966.

Wolman, Benjamin, ed. *Handbook of Dreams: Research, Theories, and Applications*. New York: Van Nostrand Reinhold, 1979.

Woods, T., and Greenhouse, H. eds. *The New World of Dreams*. New York: Macmillan, 1974.

"Psychic" Readings

GENERAL INTRODUCTIONS AND SURVEYS

Ashby, R.H. *The Ashby Guidebook for the Study of the Paranormal*. Revised edition edited by Frank C. Tribbe. New York: Weiser, 1987.

Auerbach, Loyd. *ESP, Hauntings and Poltergeists: A Parapsychologist's Handbook*. New York: Warner Books, 1986.

Bartlett, Laile E. *PSI Trek*. New York: McGraw-Hill, 1981.

Beloff, John, ed. *New Directions in Parapsychology*. London: Elek, 1974.

Beloff, John. *The Relentless Question: Reflections on the Paranormal*. Jefferson, North Carolina: McFarland, 1990.

Bowles, Norma, and Hynds, Fran, with Maxwell, Joan. *PSI Search*. San Francisco: Harper & Row, 1978.

Braud, William. *Psi Notes: Answers to Frequently Asked Questions About Parapsychology and Psychic Phenomena*. 2d ed. San Antonio, Texas: Mind Science Foundation, 1984.

Denning, Melita and Phillips, Osborne. *Psychic Self-Defense & Well-Being*. St. Paul, MN: Llewellyn Publications, 1988.

Douglas, Alfred. *Extra Sensory Powers: A Century of Psychical Research*. Woodstock, New York: The Overlook Press, 1977.

Ebon, Martin, ed. *True Experiences in Prophecy*. New York: New American Library, 1967a.

———. *True Experiences in Telepathy*. New York: New American Library, 1967b.

———. *The Satan Trap*. Garden City, New York: Doubleday, 1976.

———. *The Signet Handbook of Parapsychology*. New York: New American Library, 1978.

Edge, Hoyt L.; Morris, Robert L.; Rush, Joseph H.; and Palmer, John A. *Foundations of Parapsychology*. New York: Methuen, Inc., 1986.

Eisenberg, Dr. Howard. *Inner Spaces: Parapsychological*

Explorations of the Mind. Don Mills, Ontario: Musson Book Co., 1977.

Eisenbud, Jule. *Paranormal Foreknowledge: Problems and Perplexities.* New York: Human Sciences Press, 1982.

Ellison, Arthur. *The Paranormal: A Scientific Exploration of the Supernatural.* New York: Dodd, Mead, 1988.

Evans, Hilary. *Intrusions: Society and the Paranormal.* London: Routledge & Kegan Paul, 1982.

Eysenck, Hans J., and Sargent, Carl. *Know Your Own Psi-Q.* New York: World Almanac Publications, 1983.

————. *Explaining the Unexplained: Mysteries of the Paranormal.* London: Weidenfeld and Nicolson, 1982.

Fortune, Dion. *Psychic Self-Defense.* London: Aquarian Press, 1967 (1st printing 1930).

Gallup, George Jr., with Proctor, William. *Adventures in Immortality.* New York: McGraw-Hill Book Co., 1982.

Gauld, Alan. *The Founders of Psychical Research.* New York: Schocken, 1968.

Gittelson, Bernard. *Intangible Evidence.* New York: Fireside Books, 1987.

Grattan-Guinness, Ivor, ed. *Psychical Research: A Guide to Its History, Principles, & Practices.* Welingborough, Northamptonshire: The Aquarian Press, 1982.

Hammond, David. *The Search For Psychic Power.* New York: Bantam Books, 1975.

Hintze, Naomi and Pratt, J.G. *The Psychic Realm—What Can You Believe?* New York: Random House, 1975.

Inglis, Brian. *Natural and Supernatural.* London: Hodder and Stoughton, 1977.

————. *The Paranormal: An Encyclopedia of Psychic Phenomena.* London: Granada Publishing, 1985.

Irwin, Harvey J. *An Introduction to Parapsychology.* Jefferson, North Carolina: McFarland, 1989.

Jacobson, N.O. *Life Without Death? On Parapsychology, Mysticism, and the Question of Survival.* New York: Delacorte Press, 1974.

Jahn, Robert G., and Dunne, Brenda J. *Margins of Reality: The Role of Consciousness in the Physical World.* New York: Harcourt, Brace, Jovanovich, 1987.

Johnson, R.C. *Psychical Research*. New York: Funk and Wagnalls, 1968.

Koestler, Arthur. *The Roots of Coincidence*. New York: Random House, 1972.

Krippner, Stanley, ed. *Advances in Parapsychological Research. Volume 1: Psychokinesis,* New York: Plenum, 1978; *Volume 2: Extrasensory Perception,* New York: Plenum, 1978; *Volume 3,* New York: Plenum, 1983; *Volume 4,* Jefferson, North Carolina: McFarland, 1984; *Volume 5,* Jefferson, North Carolina: McFarland, 1987; *Volume 6,* 1990. Jefferson, North Carolina: McFarland, 1990.

Krippner, Stanley. *Song of the Siren: A Parapsychological Odyssey*. New York: Harper & Row, 1975.

————. *Human Possibilities: Mind Exploration in the USSR and Eastern Europe*. Garden City, New York: Anchor Press/Doubleday, 1980.

Krippner, Stanley, and Villodo, Alberto. *The Realms of Healing*. Millbrae, California: Celestial Arts, 1976.

LeShan, Lawrence. *The Medium, the Mystic, and the Physicist: Toward a General Theory of the Paranormal*. New York: Viking, 1974.

Levine, Frederick G. *The Psychic Sourcebook: How to Choose and Use A Psychic*. New York: Warner Books, 1988.

Mauskopf, Seymour H., and McVaugh, Michael R. *The Elusive Science: Origins of Experimental Psychical Research*. Baltimore: Johns Hopkins University Press, 1980.

McClenon, James. *Deviant Science: The Case of Parapsychology*. Philadelphia: University of Pennsylvania Press, 1984.

McConnell, R.A. *The ESP Curriculum Guide*. New York: Simon & Schuster, 1971.

————. *Encounters With Parapsychology*. Pittsburgh: Published by the author, 1981.

————. *An Introduction to Parapsychology in the Context of Science*. Pittsburgh: Published by the author, 1983*a*.

————. *Parapsychology and Self-Deception in Science*. Pittsburgh: Published by the author, 1983*b*.

McCreery, Charles. *Psychical Phenomena and the Physical World*. New York: Ballantine Books, 1973.

Mishlove, Jeffery. *PSI Development Systems*. New York: Ballantine Books, 1988.

Mitchell, Edgar D., et al. *Psychic Exploration: A Challenge for Science*. Edited by John White. New York: G.P. Putnam's Sons, 1974.

Mitchell, Janet Lee. *Conscious Evolution*. New York: Ballantine Books, 1989.

Moss, Thelma. *The Probability of the Impossible: Scientific Discoveries and Explorations in the Psychic World*. Los Angeles: Jeremy Tarcher, 1974.

Murphy, Gardner, and Dale, Laura A. *The Challenge of Psychical Research: A Primer of Parapsychology*. New York: Harper & Row, 1961.

Nash, Carroll B. *Science of PSI: ESP and PK*. Springfield, Illinois: Charles C. Thomas, 1978.

———. *Parapsychology: The Science of Psiology*. Springfield, Illinois: Charles C. Thomas, 1986.

Osborn, Arthur W. *The Future is Now: The Significance of Precognition*. New Hyde Park, New York: University Books, 1961.

Ostrander, Sheila, and Schroeder, Lynn. *Psychic Discoveries Behind the Iron Curtain*. New York: Bantam Books, 1970.

Pedler, Kit. *Mind Over Matter*. London: Thames/Methuen, 1980.

Pierce, Henry. *Science Looks at ESP*. New York: New American Library, 1970.

Pilkington, Rosemarie. *Men and Women of Parapsychology: Personal Reflections*. Jefferson, North Carolina: McFarland, 1987.

Pratt, J.G. *Parapsychology: An Insider's View of ESP*. New York: Dutton, 1966.

———. *ESP Research Today: A Study of the Development in Parapsychology Since 1960*. Metuchen, New Jersey: Scarecrow Press, 1973.

Randall, John. *Parapsychology and the Nature of Life*. New York: Harper & Row, 1975.

————. *Psychokinesis: A Study of Paranormal Forces Through the Ages.* London: Souvenir Press, 1982.

Rao, K. Ramakrishna, ed. *Basic Experiments in Parapsychology.* Jefferson, North Carolina: McFarland, 1984.

Reader's Digest Association. *Into the Unknown.* Edited by Will Bradbury. Pleasantville, New York: Reader's Digest Association, 1981.

Rhea, Kathlyn, with Rank, Cynthia. *The Psychic is You: How to Develop Your Intuitive Skills.* Berkeley, California: Celestial Arts, 1979.

Rhea, Kathlyn, with Quattro, Hoseph. *Mind Sense: Fine-Tuning Your Intellect and Intuition.* Berkeley, California: Celestial Arts, 1988.

Rhine, J.B. *The Reach of the Mind.* New York: Peter Smith, 1972 and New York: Morrow, 1971.

————. ed. *Progress in Parapsychology.* Durham, North Carolina: Parapsychology Press, 1973.

Rhine, J.B., and Brier, Robert, eds. *Parapsychology Today.* New York: Citadel Press, 1968.

Rhine, J.B., and Pratt, J.G. *Parapsychology: Frontier Science of the Mind.* Springfield, Illinois: Charles C. Thomas, 1962.

Rhine, Louisa E. *ESP in Life and Lab: Tracing Hidden Channels.* New York: Macmillan, 1967.

————. *Mind Over Matter.* New York: Macmillan, 1970.

————. *PSI, What is it?—The Story of ESP and PK.* New York: Harper & Row, 1975.

————. *Manual for Introductory Experiments in Parapsychology,* 2d ed. Durham, North Carolina: Parapsychology Press, 1977.

Robinson, Diana. *To Stretch a Plank: A Survey of Psychokinesis.* Chicago: Nelson-Hall, 1981.

Rogo, D. Scott. *In Search of the Unknown.* New York: Taplinger, 1976.

————. *Parapsychology: A Century of Inquiry.* New York: Dutton, 1977.

————. *Minds and Motion: The Riddle of Psychokinesis.* New York: Taplinger, 1978.

————. *Mind Over Matter: The Case For Psychokinesis*. Wellingborough, Northamptonshire, Great Britain: The Aquarian Press, 1986.

————. *Psychic Breakthroughs Today*. Wellingborough, Northamptonshire, Great Britain: The Aquarian Press, 1987.

Ryzl, Milan. *Parapsychology: A Scientific Approach*. New York: Hawthorn, 1970.

Sanders, Pete A. *You Are Psychic!* New York: Fawcett Columbine, 1989.

Schmeidler, Gertrude R., ed. *Extrasensory Perception*. New York: Lieber-Atherton, 1969.

Tanous, Alex, with Donnelly, Katherine Fair. *Understanding and Developing Your Child's Psychic Abilities*. New York: Simon and Schuster, 1988.

Targ, Russell, and Harary, Keith. *The Mind Race*. New York: Villard Books, 1984.

Targ, Russell, and Puthoff, Harold E. *Mind Reach: Scientists Look at Psychic Ability*. New York: Delacorte, Eleanor Friede, 1977.

Tart, Charles T. *Learning to Use Extrasensory Perception*. Chicago: University of Chicago Press, 1975.

————. *PSI: Scientific Studies of the Psychic Realm*. New York: Dutton, 1977.

————. *Waking Up: Overcoming the Obstacles to Human Porential*. Boston: Shambhalla, 1987.

————. *Open Mind, Discriminating Mind*. San Francisco: Harper & Row, 1989.

Tart, Charles T.; Puthoff, H.E., and Targ, Russell, eds. *Mind at Large*. New York: Praeger, 1979.

Thalbourne, Michael A. *Glossary of Terms Used in Parapsychology*. London: Heinemann, 1982.

Thouless, R.H. *From Anecdote to Experiment in Psychical Research*. London: Routledge and Kegan Paul, 1972.

Tyrrell, G.N.M. *Science and Psychical Phenomena*. New York: Arno Press, 1975.

Ullman, Montague; and Krippner, Stanley; with Vaughan, Alan. *Dream Telepathy*. New York: Macmillan, 1973.

Vasiliev, L.L. *Experiments in Distant Influence*. New York: Dutton, 1976.

Vaughan, Alan. *Patterns of Prophecy*. New York: Hawthorn, 1973.

White, John, and Krippner, Stanley, eds. *Future Science*. Garden City, New York: Anchor Books, 1977.

White, Rhea A. *Surveys in Parapsychology*. Metuchen, New Jersey: Scarecrow Books, 1976.

————. *Parapsychology: New Sources of Information, 1973–1989*. Metuchen, NJ: Scarecrow Press, 1990.

White, Rhea A. and Dale, Laura A. *Parapsychology: Sources of Information*. Metuchen, New Jersey: Scarecrow, 1973.

Wolman, Benjamin. *Handbook of Parapsychology*. New York: Van Nostrand Reinhold, 1977.

Zohar, Danah. *Through the Time Barrier*. London: Paladin Books, 1983.

Zollschan, Dr. George K.; Schumaker, Dr. John F.; and Walsh, Dr. Greg F., eds. *Exploring the Paranormal; Perspectives on Belief and Experience*. Bridpor, Dorset, Great Britain: Prism Press, 1989 (distributed in the United States by Avery Publishing Group, New York).

Time-Life Books has released a number of very nice volumes on the paranormal and related topics in their MYSTERIES OF THE UNKNOWN series, compiled by the editors of Time-Life Books. Relevant titles include:

Dreams and Dreaming
Hauntings
Mind Over Matter
Phantom Encounters
Powers of Healing
Psychic Powers
Psychic Voyages
Search for the Soul
Spirit Summonings
Visions and Prophesies

PSI IN EVERYDAY LIFE

MacKenzie, Andrew. *The Unexplained: Some Strange Cases of Psychical Research*. New York: Popular Library, 1970.

Rhine, Louisa E. *Hidden Channels of the Mind*. New York: William Morrow, 1961 (republished by Time-Life Books, 1990, as part of a new series "Collectors Library of the Unknown").

————*The Invisible Picture*. Jefferson, NC: McFarland & Company, 1981.

Schwarz, Berthold. *Parent-Child Telepathy*. New York: Garrett, 1971.

Stevenson, Ian. *Telepathic Impressions: A Review and Report of Thirty-five New Cases*. Charlottesville, Virginia: University Press of Virginia, 1970.

OUT-OF-BODY-EXPERIENCES

Blackmore, Susan J. *Beyond the Body: An Investigation of Out-of-the-Body Experiences*. London: Paladin, 1983.

Green, C. *Out-of-the-Body Experiences*. London: Hamish Hamilton, 1968.

Harary, Keith, and Weintraub, Pamela. *Have an Out-of-Body Experience in 30 Days: The Free Flight Program*. New York: St. Martin's Press, 1989.

Mitchell, Janet Lee. *Out-of-Body Experiences*. Jefferson, North Carolina: McFarland, 1981.

Monroe, Robert A. *Journeys Out of the Body*. Garden City, New York: Doubleday, 1971.

Rogo, D. Scott, ed. *Mind Beyond the Body*. New York: Penguin Books, 1978.

PSYCHICS AND CHANNELING

Eisenbud, Jule. *The World of Ted Serios: "Thoughtographic" Studies of an Extraordinary Mind*. rev. ed. Jefferson, North Carolina: McFarland, 1989.

Geller, Uri, and Playfair, Guy Lyon. *The Geller Effect*. New York: Henry Holt and Company, 1986.

Haraldsson, Erlendur. *Modern Miracles: An Investigative Report on Psychic Phenomena Associated With Sathya Sai Baba*. New York: Fawcett Columbine (Ballantine Books), 1987.

Heywood, Rosalind. *Beyond the Reach of Sense: An Inquiry into Extrasensory Perception*. New York: Dutton, 1974.

Kautz, William H., and Branon, Melanie, with Foreword and Forecast by Kevin Ryerson. *Channeling: The Intuitive Connection*. San Francisco: Harper & Row, 1987.

Klimo, Jon. *Channeling: Investigations on Receiving Information from Paranormal Sources*. Los Angeles: Jeremy P. Tarcher, 1987.

Manning, Matthew. *The Link*. New York: Holt, Rinehart, and Winston, 1975.

Swann, Ingo. *To Kiss Earth Good-Bye*. New York: Hawthorn Books, 1975.

Tanous, Alex, with Ardman Harvey. *Beyond Coincidence: One Man's Experiences with Psychic Phenomena*. Garden City, New York: Doubleday, 1976.

PARAPSYCHOLOGY AND PSYCHOLOGY/PSYCHIATRY

Ehrenwald, Jan. *The ESP Experience: A Psychiatric Validation*. New York: Basic Books, Inc., 1978.

Eisenbud, Jule. *Parapsychology and the Unconscious*. Berkeley, California: North Atlantic Books, 1984.

Fodor, Nandor. *The Haunted Mind*. New York: New American Library, 1959.

Mintz, Elizabeth E., with Schmeidler, Gertrude R. *The Psychic Thread: Paranormal and Transpersonal Aspects of Psychotherapy*. New York: Human Sciences Press, 1983.

Neppe, Vernon M. *The Psychology of Déjà Vu: Have I Been Here Before?* Johannesburg: Witwatersrand University Press, 1983.

Schmeidler, Gertrude R. *Parapsychology and Psychology: Matches and Mismatches*. Jefferson, North Carolina: McFarland, 1988.

Schmeidler, G.R. and McConnell, R.A. *ESP And Personality*

Patterns. Westport, Connecticut: Greenwood Press, 1974.

Schwartz, Berthold Eric. *Psychic Nexus: Psychic Phenomena in Psychiatry and Everyday Life*. New York: Van Nostrand Reinhold, 1980.

Van Over, Raymond, ed. *Psychology and Extrasensory Perception*. New York: New American Library, 1972.

PARAPSYCHOLOGY AND ANTHROPOLOGY

De Martino, Ernesto. *Primitive Magic: The Psychic Powers of Shamans and Sorcerers*. Bridport, Dorset, Great Britain: Prism Press (distributed in the United States by Avery Publishing, New York), 1988.

Ebon, Martin, ed. *True Experiences in Exotic ESP*. New York: New American Library, 1968.

Long, Joseph K., ed. *Extrasensory Ecology: Parapsychology and Anthropology*. Metuchen, New Jersey: Scarecrow Press, 1977.

Rose, Ronald. *Living Magic*. New York: Rand McNally & Co., 1956.

St. Clair, David. *Drum and Candle*. Garden City, New York: Doubleday, 1971.

PARAPSYCHOLOGY, PHILOSOPHY, AND RELATED SCIENCES

Braude, Stephen. *ESP and Psychokinesis: A Philosophical Examination*. Philadelphia: Temple University Press, 1980.

―――. *The Limits of Influence: Psychokinesis and the Philosophy of Science*. New York: Methuen, Inc., 1986.

Brier, Robert. *Precognition and the Philosophy of Science*. New York: Humanities Press, 1974.

Dubrov, A.P., and Pushkin, V.N. *Parapsychology and Contemporary Science*. New York: Consultants Bureau/Plenum, 1982.

Dunne, J. W. *An Experiment with Time*. London: Papermac, 1981.

————. *The Serial Universe*. London: Faber & Faber, Ltd., 1934.

Jahn, Robert, ed. *The Role of Consciousness in the Physical World*. Boulder, Colorado: Westview Press (for the American Association for the Advancement of Science, 1981.

Priestly, J. B. *Man and Time*. New York: Crescent Books, 1989.

Schmeidler, Gertrude R., ed. *Parapsychology: Its Relation to Physics, Biology, Psychology, and Psychiatry*. Metuchen, New Jersey: Scarecrow Press, 1976.

APPLIED PSI: APPLICATIONS OF PSYCHIC ABILITIES

Archer, Fred. *Crime and the Psychic World*. New York: William Morrow and Company, 1969.

Dean, Douglas; Mihilasky, John; Ostrander, Sheila; and Schroeder, Lynn. *Executive ESP*. New York: Prentice-Hall, 1974.

Ebon, Martin. *Psychic Warfare: Threat or Illusion?* New York: McGraw Hill, 1983.

Goodman, Jeffrey. *Psychic Archaeology: Time Machine to the Past*. New York: Berkeley Medallion, 1977.

Hibbard, Witney S., and Worring, Raymond W. *Psychic Criminology: An Operational Manual for Using Psychics in Criminal Investigations*. Springfield, Illinois: Charles C. Thomas, 1982.

Lyons, Arthur, and Truzzi, Marcello., *The Blue Sense: Psychic Detectives And Crime*. New York: Mysterious Press, 1991.

Murphy, Michael, and White, Rhea. *The Psychic Side of Sports*. Reading, Massachusettes: Addison-Wesley, 1978.

Schwartz, Stephen A. *The Secret Vaults of Time*. New York: Grossett and Dunlap, 1978.

————. *The Alexandria Project*. New York: Delacorte Press, 1983.

Tabori, Paul. *Crime and the Occult*. Newton Abbot, Devon, England: David & Charles, 1974.

White, John, ed. *Psychic Warfare: Fact or Fiction?* Wellingborough, Northamptonshire, Great Britain: The Aquarian Press, 1988.

Wilson, Colin. *The Psychic Detectives: The Story of Psychometry and Paranormal Crime Detection.* California: Mercury House, 1986.

NEAR-DEATH EXPERIENCES

Kubler-Ross, Elisabeth. *On Death and Dying.* New York: Macmillan, 1969.

Lundahl, Craig R., ed. *A Collection of Near-Death Research Readings.* Chicago: Nelson-Hall, 1982.

Moody, Raymond A., Jr. *Life After Life.* Atlanta: Mockingbird Books, 1975.

———. *Reflections on Life After Life.* Atlanta: Mockingbird Books, 1977.

Morse, Melvin, with Perry, Paul. *Closer to the Light: Learning from the Near-Death Experiences of Children.* New York: Villard Books, 1990.

Osis, Karlis, and Haraldsson, Erlandur. *At the Hour of Death.* New York: Hastings House, 1986.

Ring, Kenneth. *Life at Death: A Scientific Investigation of the Near-Death Experience.* New York: Coward, McCann & Geoghegan, 1980.

———. *Heading Toward Omega.* New York: Morrow, 1984.

Sabom, Michael. *Recollections of Death: A Medical Investigation.* New York: Harper & Row, 1982.

APPARITIONS, POLTERGEISTS, HAUNTINGS, SURVIVAL, AND CHANNELING

Barrett, Sir William. *Death Bed Visions: The Psychical Experiences of the Dying.* Wellingborough, Northamptonshire, Great Britain: The Aquarian Press, 1986.

Bayless, Raymond. *The Enigma of the Poltergeist.* West Nyack, New York: Parker Publishing Co., 1967.

———. *Apparitions and Survival of Death.* New Hyde Park, New York: University Books, 1973.

Berger, Arthur. *Aristocracy of the Dead: New Findings in*

Postmortem Survival. Jefferson, North Carolina: McFarland, 1987.

Crowe, Catherine. *The Night-side of Nature, or, Ghosts and Ghost-seers*. Wellingborough, Northamptonshire, Great Britain: The Aquarian Press, 1986.

Doore, Gary. *What Survives? Contemporary Explorations of Life After Death*. Los Angeles: Jeremy P. Tarcher, 1990.

Ebon, Martin. *Evidence for Life After Death*. New York: New American Library, 1977.

Finucane, R. C. *Appearances of the Dead: A Cultural History of Ghosts*. Buffalo, New York: Prometheus Books, 1984.

Fodor, Nandor. *On the Trail of the Poltergeist*. New York: Citadel Press, 1958.

————. *The Unaccountable*. New York: Award Books, 1968.

Gauld, Alan. *Mediumship and Survival*. London: Heinemann, 1982.

Gauld, Alan, and Cornell, A.D. *Poltergeists*. London: Routledge & Kegan Paul, 1979.

Gurney, Edmund; Myers; F.W.H.; and Podmore, Frank. *Phantasms of the Living*. Edited by Mrs. Henry Sidgwick. New York: E.P. Dutton & Co., 1918.

Klimo, Jon. *Channeling: Investigations on Receiving Information From Paranormal Sources*. Los Angeles: Jeremy P. Tarcher, 1987.

Lang, Andrew. *Dreams and Ghosts*. Hollywood, California: Newcastle Publishing Company, 1972.

MacKenzie, Andrew. *Hauntings and Apparitions*. London: Granada Publishing, 1982.

McAdams, Elizabeth, and Bayless, Raymond. *The Case For Life After Death: Parapsychologists Look at the Evidence*. Chicago: Nelson-Hall, 1981.

Myers, Frederic W.H. *Human Personality and its Survival of Bodily Death*. 2 vols. London: Longmans, Green, 1903.

Owen, A.R.G. *Can We Explain the Poltergeist?* New York: Garrett/Helix, 1964.

Owen, Iris M., with Sparrow, Margaret. *Conjuring Up*

Philip: An Adventure in Psychokinesis. New York: Harper & Row, 1976.

Rogo, D. Scott. *An Experience of Phantoms*. New York: Taplinger, 1974.

————. *The Poltergeist Experience*. New York: Penguin Books, 1979.

————. *The Infinite Boundary: A Psychic Look at Spirit Possession, Madness, and Multiple Personality*. New York: Dodd, Mead, 1987.

Rogo, D. Scott, and Bayless, Raymond. *Phone Calls From the Dead*. New York: Berkley Books, 1980.

Roll, William G. *The Poltergeist*. 2d ed. Metuchen, New Jersey: Scarecrow Press, 1976.

Tyrrell, G.N.M. *Apparitions*. New York: Collier Books, 1963.

Underwood, Peter. *The Ghost Hunter's Guide*. New York: Javelin Books, 1986.

Wilson, Colin. *Poltergeist!* New York: Putnam, 1981.

Wilson, Ian. *The After Death Experience*. New York: William Morrow, 1987.

REINCARNATION

Head, Joseph, and Cranston, S. L., eds. *Reincarnation: An East-West Anthology*. New York: The Julian Press, 1961.

Stevenson, Ian. *Twenty Cases Suggestive of Reincarnation*. 2d rev. ed. Charlottesville, Virginia: University Press of Virginia, 1974.

————. *Cases of the Reincarnation Type: Ten Cases in India*. Vol. 1. Charlottesville, Virginia: University Press of Virginia, 1975.

————. *Cases of the Reincarnation Type: Ten Cases in Sri Lanka*. Vol. 2. Charlottesville, Virginia: University Press of Virginia, 1977.

————. *Cases of the Reincarnation Type: Twelve Cases in Lebanon and Turkey*. Vol. 3. Charlottesville, Virginia: University Press of Virginia, 1980.

————. *Cases of the Reincarnation Type: Twelve Cases in Thailand and Burma*. Vol. 4. Charlottesville, Virginia: University Press of Virginia, 1983.

————. *Xenoglossy*. Charlottesville, Virginia: University Press of Virginia, 1984.

Wilson, I. *Mind Out of Time? Reincarnation Claims Investigated*. London: Victor Gollancz, 1981.

BOOKS DEALING WITH THE ART OF MAGIC, WITH PSYCHIC FRAUD, OR CRITICISMS OF PARAPSYCHOLOGY

Abell, George O., and Singer, Barry, eds. *Science and the Paranormal*. New York: Charles Scribner's Sons, 1983.

Alcock, James E. *Parapsychology—Science or Magic: A Psychological Perspective*. Elmsford, NY: Pergamon Press, 1981.

Blackstone, Harry, Jr.; with Reynolds, Charles; and Reynolds, Regina. *The Blackstone Book of Magic and Illusion*. New York: Newmarket Press, 1985.

Booth, John. *Psychic Paradoxes*. Los Alamitos, California: Ridgeway Press, 1984.

Christopher, Milbourne. *ESP, Seers and Psychics*. New York: Thomas Y. Crowell, 1970.

————. *Mediums, Mystics, and the Occult*. New York: Thomas Y. Crowell, 1975.

————. *Search For the Soul*. New York: Thomas Y. Crowell, 1979.

Corinda. *Thirteen Steps to Mentalism*. New York: Louis Tannen, 1968.

Frazier, Kendrick, ed. *Paranormal Borderlands of Science*. Buffalo, New York: Prometheus Books, 1981.

Gardner, Martin. *Science: Good, Bad, and Bogus*. Buffalo, New York: Prometheus Books, 1981.

Hansel, C.E.M. *ESP and Parapsychology: A Critical Re-Evaluation*. Buffalo, New York: Prometheus Books, 1980.

Hines, Terence. *Pseudoscience and the Paranormal: A Crit-*

ical Examination of the Evidence. Buffalo, New York: Prometheus Books, 1988.

Houdini, Harry. *Houdini: A Magician Among the Spirits*. New York: Arno Press, 1972.

Houdini, Harry, and Dunninger, Joseph. *Magic and Mystery: The Incredible Psychic Investigations of Houdini and Dunninger*. New York: Weathervane Books, 1967.

Kaye, Marvin. *The Handbook of Mental Magic*. New York: Stein and Day, 1975.

Keene, M. Lamar, as told to Allen Spraggett. *The Psychic Mafia*. New York: Dell, 1976.

Korem, Danny, and Meier, Paul. *The Fakers*. Grand Rapids, Missouri: Baker Book House, 1980.

Kurtz, Paul, ed. *A Skeptic's Handbook of Parapsychology*. Buffalo, New York: Prometheus Books, 1985.

Leahey, Thomas Hardy, and Leahey, Grace Evans. *Psychology's Occult Doubles: Psychology and the Problem of Pseudoscience*. Chicago: Nelson-Hall, 1983.

Leland, Charles Godfrey. *Gypsy Sorcery and Fortune-Telling*. New York: Dover Publications, 1971.

Marks, D., and Kammann, R. *The Psychology of the Psychic*. Buffalo, New York: Prometheus Books, 1980.

Nelms, Henning. *Magic and Showmanship*. New York: Dover, 1969.

Price, Harry. *Confessions of a Ghost Hunter*. New York: Causeway Books, 1974.

Randi, James. *The Truth About Uri Geller*. Buffalo, New York: Prometheus Books, 1982.

Rawcliffe, D.H. *Occult and Supernatural Phenomena*. New York: Dover Publications.

Steiner, Robert A. *Don't Get Taken!* El Cerrito, California: Wide-Awake Books, 1989.

JOURNALS AND ANNUAL PUBLICATIONS:

Anabiosis, published by the International Association for Near-Death Studies, Box U-20, University of Connecticut, Storrs, CT 06268. Semi-annual. Deals with near-death experiences, as does "Vital Signs," a newsletter.

European Journal of Parapsychology, c/o Koestler Chair of Parapsychology, University of Edinburgh, 7 George Square, Edinburgh, EH8 9J2, Scotland. Annual. Published in English. A scientific journal dealing with parapsychological research reports, case studies, and theoretical discussions.

Fate magazine, published by Llewellyn Publications, P.O. Box 64383, St. Paul, MN 55164-0383. Digest magazine for the general public on the paranormal, anomalous phenomena, and supernatural/occult beliefs and experiences. Often includes articles written by parapsychologists.

The Journal of the American Society of Psychical Research, published by the American Society for Psychical Research, 5 West 73rd Street, New York, NY 10023. Membership in the ASPR (write for current cost) entitles one to the quarterly journal, as well as the ASPR quarterly newsletter. The journal is mainly oriented toward the scientific community, presenting experimental reports, case studies, historical articles, theoretical discussions, and book reviews. The newsletter is oriented toward the lay public, and includes articles on many areas in parapsychology, as well as news of the ASPR.

The Journal of Parapsychology, published by Parapsychology Press, P.O. Box 6847, College Station, Durham, NC 27708. Quarterly, $20. Scholarly journal presenting research, case reports, theoretical articles, and book reviews.

The Journal of the Society for Psychical Research, published by the Society for Psychical Research, 1 Adam & Eve Mews, Kensington, London W8 6UG, England. Quarterly. A variety of articles on research, investigation, theory, and history, as well as reviews of books and news of the Society for Psychical Research.

"Iridis," published by the California Society for Psychical Study, P.O. Box 844, Berkeley, CA 94701. Newsletter published ten times a year (September through June). Write for cost and further information on the CSPS.

Parapsychological Journal of South Africa, published by the South African Society for Psychical Research, P.O. Box 23154, Joubert Park 2044, Republic of South Africa. Twice a year. Primarily research and theoretical articles.

Exceptional Human Experience, published by the PSI CENTER, 2 Plane Tree Lane, Dix Hills, NY 11746. Twice a year, write for cost. This publication presents abstracts of articles from parapsychological journals, general interest publications and books, and disertations and these dealing with parapsychological topics, as well as UFO encounters, peak experiences and exceptional human performance.

Research in Parapsychology, published by the Scarecrow Press, 52 Liberty Street, P.O. Box 656, Metuchen, NJ 08840. The annual proceedings of the Parapsychological Association.

The Skeptical Inquirer, published by the Committee for the Scientific Investigation of Claims of the Paranormal, Box 229, Buffalo, NY 14215-0299. A quarterly journal dealing with criticisms and debunking of ostensible paranormal, anomalistic, occult, and supernatural phenomena, study, and beliefs.

The Zetetic Scholar. Available from Zetetic Scholar, Department of Sociology, Eastern Michigan University, Ypsilanti, MI 48197. This journal deals with explorations (both pro and con) of anomalous phenomena from UFOs to ESP, and with occult and pseudo-scientific beliefs, such as astrology and vampires.

The Parapsychology Foundation also publishes annual collections of papers presented at their annual conferences. Write to the Parapsychology Foundation 228 East 71st Street, New York, NY 10021, for details and prices.

The American Society for Psychical Research has other publications available, such as its course list, compilations of articles from the ASPR newsletter, and special bibliographies. Write to the ASPR, 5 West 73rd Street, New York, NY 10023.

The PSI CENTER, 2 Plane Tree Lane, Dix Hills, NY 11746, recently published a number of specialized, in-depth bibliographies. Write for list.

The Office of Paranormal Investigations will begin publishing information pamphlets as well as a newsletter in 1991. Write to the Office of Paranormal Investigations, P.O. Box 875, Orinda, CA 94563-0875. Please include a self-addressed stamped envelope.

APPENDIX D

Surveys

As I mentioned early on in this book, the surveys included in my first book, *ESP, Hauntings, and Poltergeists*, were very interesting and very helpful. Not only is there a rich amount of data in those surveys already received, some of them related very interesting psychic experiences with dreams, as you've already read in this book.

Unfortunately, I have yet to really analyze the data from those surveys, mainly due to a (vast) lack of time (there's a lot of info there). The information has, however, been helpful to me and others in the field of parapsychology. I thank you if you returned the surveys.

As the first book is still available, the surveys are still coming in. If you decide to seek out that book and send in those surveys, I ask just one favor. Please send all surveys, from this book or the first one, to:

The Office of Paranormal Investigations
PSI Surveys
P.O. Box 875
Orinda, CA 94563-0875

I'd appreciate the inclusion of your name and address on the survey, though the anonymity of all concerned will be preserved. We may want to contact you directly in the future with another questionnaire (so please answer the last question which pertains to this). If you do not wish to put down that information, that's all right, too (though it would still be a help if you could put down your city and state).

As you answer these surveys, if you have experiences to report, please feel free to write (legibly, please) or type them. If you do require some sort of reply, please include a self-addressed stamped envelope. Answer "yes," "no," "not sure," or "n/a" (not applicable) to the questions, and, if possible (with the "yes" answers, of course), provide an example. Some of the questions do require answers other than those provided above.

PART ONE: PSYCHIC DREAMING

This survey is a follow-up to the information presented in this book, dealing with psychic connections in your dreams.
1. Do you remember your dreams?
2. How often do you remember your dreams (every day, a few a week, etc.)?
3. Do you keep a dream log or dream journal?
4. Have you ever tried to increase memory/recall of your dreams?
5. Have you ever tried to control your dreams (content, issues, etc.)?
6. Do you have lucid dreams?
7. Have you had dreams where you were flying to other locations?
8. Have you ever felt that you were "out of body" while in a dream?
9. Have you ever had an out-of-body experience while awake?
10. Have you had dreams that relate to historical events?
11. Have you had dreams you relate to a possible past life?
12. Have you had dreams of events occurring at other locations, those events taking place during the time you were asleep?
13. Did you try checking to see if those events were real?
14. Have you had dreams of future events?

15. Did those events come true (did they match your dream of the events)?

16. Were you aware that the dream was of a future event at the time you remembered the dream?

17. If the dream matched an event, how and when did you learn this?

18. Have you ever had the same dream (the same night) as another person?

19. Have you ever felt that you were really visiting someone while dreaming?

20. Have you ever dreamed of what another person was thinking, doing, or dreaming?

21. Did you check the dreamed information with that person?

22. Have you ever dreamed of encountering a person you knew was dead?

23. If so, did you feel that the person really visited your dream?

24. Do you believe dreams are one avenue for us to connect with people and or the environment (psychically)?

25. Will you try the exercises in Appendix A of this book?

PART 2: PSYCHIC EXPERIENCES WHILE AWAKE

1. Have you ever had a psychic experience while awake?

2. Have you ever felt you knew about a future event before it happened?

3. Did the event check out as you predicted?

4. Have you ever realized as a situation was occurring that you had foreseen the situation or dreamed about it in advance?

5. Have you ever felt you received information psychically about an event (or person or location) in the "present" that was out of reach of your senses or logical inference?

6. Did you check the information against the real situation?

7. Have you ever felt you "picked up" information from the mind of another person?

8. Have you ever felt a "psychic" connection to another person?

9. Have you ever witnessed object movements or sounds which had no "normal" physical explanation that you could discover (psychokinesis)?

10. Do clocks, appliances, computers, office machines, or other machines tend to function differently for you than for others (better or worse)?

11. Have you witnessed occasions where appliances, clocks, technical devices, or machines have functioned in an unusual/non-normal way which had no discernible physical/"normal" explanation?

12. Have you ever felt you were responsible for an unusual physical effect (as described in questions 9, 10, or 11)?

13. Have you ever had, while awake, a vivid impression of seeing, hearing, "sensing," or being touched by someone or something which you could not explain by normal means?

14. Have you ever "seen" (or "heard" or "smelled") a person or persons you would consider to be apparitions?

15. If you've had contact with an apparition, did you feel the apparition was aware or conscious of you (was there some sort of interaction between you and the apparition)?

16. Have you ever been in a location you would consider "haunted?"

17. Have you ever had, awake or asleep, the feeling that you were *located outside of or away from* your physical body?

18. Have you ever had a near-death experience . . . that is, one in which you were thought to be physically dead, then came back to life?
    a. Do you have any memories from the time you were thought dead?
    b. Did you experience seeing a light?
    c. Did you experience hearing a voice?
    d. Did you feel the presence of other beings?
    e. Were you aware of things going on in the location where your physical body lay?

19. Have you ever been to a professional "psychic" reader or healer?
    If yes, how often, and what kind of "psychic"?

20. Has anyone ever told you about their (first-hand) experiences like those above?
    If yes, what was this person's relationship to you?
    What experiences were related to you?
21. Have you ever felt the need to talk to someone about these types of experiences?
    If yes, did you actually talk to someone about them?
    With whom did you talk (relationship to you)?
    What kinds of experiences did you talk about?
    What was the person's response to your experience(s)?
22. For each of the categories on the list below, please indicate ("Y" for "Yes" or "N" for "no") whether you would *consider* going to such a person if you ever felt the need to talk to someone about experiences like those in this questionnaire or in the book:

_____friend   _____parapsychologist

_____relative   _____psychologist

_____minister/priest/rabbi   _____psychiatrist

_____doctor (MD)   _____professional psychic

23. Would you be interested in participating in future surveys or studies?
24. Would you like to see more books in this series?
    If yes, please check the topics below you would like to see as main topics of future books:

_____a. Out of body experiences
_____b. Reincarnation
_____c. Channeling and mediumship
_____d. Practical applications of psychic abilities
_____e. "Real" psychics vs. "phoney" psychics
_____f. Current research in parapsychology
_____g. Psychokinesis
_____h. The occult and supernatural from a parapsychologist's point of view

_____i. Telepathy
_____j. Clairvoyance/remote perception
_____k. Precognition and retrocognition
_____l. Parapsychology and the media
_____m. True cases of parapsychological investigators
        (apparitions, poltergeists, and hauntings)
_____n. Mind, spirit, and the survival of bodily death

24. a. What is your name?_____
    b. Address?_____
    c. Age?_____
    d. Sex?_____
    e. Married?_____
    f. Occupation?_____
    g. Religion?_____

Send the above survey to:

The Office of Paranormal Investigations
PSI Surveys
P.O. Box 875
Orinda, CA 94563-0875

Thank you very much for your kind cooperation. Your responses will be totally anonymous, but you may see your experience (the names and other personal facts changed to insure your anonymity) in future books. I hope you enjoyed this one.
—Loyd Auerbach